A senior economist with the Federal Government of Canada, **Maurice F. Estabrooks** has held positions as a systems analyst, engineer, planner, and manager. He studied at Mount Allison University, the University of Alberta, Carleton University, and holds degrees in physics, applied mathematics, and economics.

# PROGRAMMED CAPITALISM

# PROGRAMMED CAPITALISM

## A Computer-Mediated Global Society

**Maurice Estabrooks**

**M. E. Sharpe, Inc.**
ARMONK, NEW YORK
LONDON, ENGLAND

**Library of Congress Cataloging-in-Publication Data**

Estabrooks, Maurice, 1943–
    Programmed capitalism.

    Bibliography: p.
    Includes index.
    1. Computers and civilization. 2. Technological innovations—Social aspects. 3. Capitalism. I. Title.
QA76.9.C66E88      1988        303.4′834        88-4476
ISBN 0-87332-480-3

Printed in the United States of America

To Lisa, Lorie, and Ahren

# Contents

*Preface*                                                                     xi

**1.** Introduction: Metamorphosis in the Making                               3

**2.** The Rise of the Computer-Based Information Infrastructure               38

**3.** Computerizing the Money and Payments System:
The New Public Landscape of a Computer-Mediated Society                       58

**4.** The Evolution of an Electronic Trading Infrastructure                   77

**5.** Transformation of the World Stock Exchanges                            92

**6.** Strategically Managing Computer Systems Synergies
and Integrated Service Financial Supermarkets                                113

**7.** And the Walls Came Tumbling Down:
The Erosion and Obsolescence of the Four Pillars of the
Financial Community                                                          133

**8.** The Making of a Computer-Mediated Global Economic System               150

**9.** Toward a Computer-Mediated Global Society                              175

*Bibliography*                                                               197
*Index*                                                                      201
*About the Author*                                                           207

# List of Figures

Figure 1.1   Conceptual Model of a Computer-Initiated
             Societal Metamorphosis                              17

Figure 1.2   The Computer Transforms and Mediates
             the Eight Basic Functions Performed
             by the Market Economy                               24

Figure 1.3   Evolution of Money as Market Exchange
             Medium and Its Relationship to the Organization
             of the Economic System                              32

Figure 1.4   Relationship Between the Real Economic
             System and the Intelligence and Psychological
             Economic Systems                                    34

Figure 1.5   The Four Pillars of the Financial Community
             and the Industrial and Institutional Boundaries
             of Industrial Society Before the Computer           37

Figure 2.1   Industries Involved in the Development of the
             New Computer-Based Information Industry             50

Figure 3.1   Industries Involved in the Development of the
             Computer-Based Money and Payments System           64

Figure 4.1   Industries Influencing the Evolution of
             Computer-Based Trading                              80

Figure 6.1   Stakeholders in the Financial
             Supermarkets Game                                   116

Figure 8.1   Hierarchical Power Structures and the Economic
             Order in Traditional Society and a Computer-
             Mediated Society                                    169

# Preface

The nature of socioeconomic change is a subject of special concern to everyone at this time, when scientific and technological advances and breakthroughs are being made each day, and economic and political changes are taking place at an unprecedented rate. Even the definition of work is changing. This book is about all these changes. It is about the impact of computers on our economic system and on our society in general, and it develops the theme of a metamorphosis or transformation of society that has been initiated and is being propelled by the computer and by every person and organization using it.

The book posits that American society, like all Western societies, is evolving into a global society that is entirely mediated by computers. The book should leave no doubt in the reader's mind that the basic rules, laws, and institutions under which industrial society has operated for several centuries are in a period of profound change and that a new society operating under new rules, new dynamics, and new institutions is in the making. This book describes not only how this transformation is taking place but also why it is taking place. Finally, it looks into the future to ponder how computers will affect our society.

Chapter 1 views current events from the perspective of the twenty-first century. It briefly describes how every sector of the economy is being transformed by the computer and how the profound technological and economic metamorphosis already well underway is causing a fundamentally new social, economic, and political order. It also briefly examines history, particularly the Industrial Revolution, and the dynamic nature of capitalist change as described by economist Joseph

Schumpeter. It proceeds to develop and describe a model of society's transformation by the computer.

The model consists of both hierarchical and horizontal dimensions, beginning with microlevel changes that affect the nature of work, management, and the corporate organization. These changes ultimately transform the relationships among various sectors of the economy and affect the ways they are administered at the political level. In turn, they affect the political and economic institutions and the operation and organization of society.

Fundamental to the metamorphosis and the model is the view of the economic system as an information-processing and intelligence system, with the information, banking, and financial services sectors at its core. The effect of computerization on this core segment of economic activity is to mutate the nature of capitalism.

This view suggests that the information, banking, and financial services sectors of the economy constitute the leading edge of the transformation of the market and the capitalist system. The emerging computerized global infrastructure has begun to mediate all the uses of money, capital, and wealth, and has changed the way economic and political power are wielded at both national and global levels.

Chapters 2, 3, and 4 describe the computerization of special segments of the economic intelligence system, beginning with the information segment, proceeding to the money and payments segment, and on to the electronic trading segment. The underlying technology of each component of the new infrastructure is described, together with the ways in which corporate players apply it strategically. This technology changes the corporate organization in profound ways, and the resultant corporations in turn change the marketplace in which they operate. The strategies of several major corporate players in the information, banking, retailing, and other industries are detailed.

Chapter 5 traces the stages in the evolution and transformation of global stock exchanges, culminating in the formation of computer-based global linkages between the exchanges in the major centers of the world. It also examines the events of October 19, 1987, the day stock markets around the world took their biggest beating in history.

Computer-based infrastructures are sources of enormous synergies and economies of scale that, combined with programmable features and multifunctional capabilities, made it possible for companies such as Merrill Lynch, Citicorp, American Express, and Sears, Roebuck, to create financial supermarkets. This is the subject of Chapter 6.

Chapter 7 traces the steps leading to the erosion of the four pillars of the financial community. It examines how computer-based infrastructures helped smash the legal and regulatory barriers and boundaries that separated the commercial banks, the thrift institutions, and the securities and insurance industries. It also looks at how this infrastructure made obsolete the regulatory institutions and jurisdictional boundaries that separated not only state and federal levels of government but also the national and global economic systems.

Chapter 8 covers how computer-based infrastructures were also critical to the creation of an integrated global financial and economic system. They integrated national markets on a scale never before possible, but in the process eroded not only the effectiveness of monetary and fiscal control and power of nation-states but also the economic and political sovereignty of the nation-state. Ultimately, they are creating a new global economic order. This chapter also describes how nation-states are coping with this new order and suggests some options on how to resolve the enormous problems that are arising.

Chapter 9 provides a social, cultural, and humanistic perspective on the new computer-mediated global society. It exposes some of the risks and challenges associated with accelerated technological and economic change because, it is argued, many people and organizations are finding the change difficult or impossible to cope with and manage because they are not able to understand its significance. The chapter proposes that new societal institutions at the national and the global levels are necessary to cope with and harness the benefits of the evolving computer-mediated society. This chapter also creates a vision for administering and harnessing global financial markets in order to realize the benefits of a computer-mediated global economy and to create a programmed democratic society at the global level.

I would like to acknowledge the assistance of those people who helped to bring this book to publication. I am indebted, in particular, to Harry Trebing of Michigan State University, and the late Alfred Eichner, former Consulting Editor at M. E. Sharpe, Inc. and Professor of Economics at Rutgers University, for their comments on early drafts of the manuscript and their recommendations of ways of improving it. I am also grateful to Richard Bartel, Economics Editor, and David Biesel, former Editorial Director of M. E. Sharpe, Inc., for their encouragement, assistance, and patience through all of the publication stages. Special thanks are also extended to Kathleen Silloway and Joan Matthews for their editorial comments. Finally, I appreciated the opportunity to present the ideas contained in this book to the members of the International Business Forum, sponsored by the Business School of Indiana University, and I thank them for their comments. It was a pleasure working with all of these people.

# PROGRAMMED CAPITALISM

# 1

# Introduction:
# Metamorphosis in the Making

When the history of the twentieth century is written, it will be seen as an age of revolution and transformation that, in terms of its speed, pervasiveness, and technological complexity, was greater than any in the history of civilization. That future history will record how computers transformed the banking, brokerage, and insurance industries and how they revolutionized the currency, commodity, and stock exchanges. It will describe how computerization transformed offices and factories, how it made possible the development of the ''Star Wars'' antiballistic missile defense system, and how it furthered the initial exploration and commercialization of outer space.

Historians will explain the dramatic effects of the new intelligent machinery on the telecommunications, retailing, and publishing industries. They will reveal how computerization changed the nature of work and management, and how it subsequently revolutionized the organization and operation of corporations, the economy, and society.

Events such as these will be seen as a metamorphosis on the grandest of scales that gave rise to a new social and economic order in which intelligent machines emerged to mediate all the essential activities of the new society. This revolution will have produced a new global society, integrated financially, economically, and politically, and historians will call this the age of *programmed capitalism*.

## The Nature of Computerized Hyperstructures

A revolution is indeed under way but it cannot be understood without comprehending the nature of the computer. It is a machine in some respects, but it has no cogs, rotors, or moving parts. Rather, it is one incorporating considerable artificial intelligence capabilities that facilitate the management and execution of intelligence activities and enable the computer to control the physical world around it. In other respects, it is a new form of societal infrastructure, unlike those of the past that were dedicated to the production and movement of physical goods. Instead, the new computerized infrastructure collects, processes, moves, and distributes intelligence. Charles Babbage, one of its early pioneers, called it an Analytical Engine.

The new machine or infrastructure is like none other before it. It controls, coordinates, and makes decisions. It is also invisible to the eye to the extent that the instructions, programs, and flows of commands, money, and information it mediates constitute forms of artificial intelligence. If we view all the computer systems and networks as a single entity, whether they are interconnected and integrated together or not, we could call this computerized infrastructure a *hyperstructure* because its capabilities are so far above and beyond those of any other machine, infrastructure, or technology that has preceded it. It is able to undertake intelligence activity, to communicate, and to control activity and make decisions on its own according to programmed instructions.

The new world of intelligence must be regarded as distinctly different from the physical world and the physical economy. The physical economy comprises physical resources and products and the transportation systems needed to distribute them. Imposed on the physical world and the physical economy are a world of intelligence and an intelligent economy that order, structure, and mediate the physical world. In a seemingly mystical manner, they facilitate production processes, coordinate the interaction of units, and give the physical world purpose and meaning.

It is no accident that computers have become ubiquitous and essential to modern society and our economic system. It is no accident that they have become vital to the efficient operation of our offices, factories, and stock exchanges. It will be no accident when they quietly invade the home in large numbers, as they appear to be doing. It is all part of the transformation process that is taking place around us, and it will not stop until it is complete sometime in the next century.

At that time, literally nothing will be the same—not our work, language, culture, economic system, or society. Evidence of this transformation and metamorphosis is all around us. As the decade of the eighties draws to a close, it is becoming easier to discern the effects of computerization on our social economy at the present time, the potential effects in the future, and how the transformation might be described from the perspective of the twenty-first century.

## The New Industrial Revolution

It is in the office environment, the most ubiquitous place of work activity, where computers are having their greatest impact. They have been transforming offices for several decades, and have been improving the quality of management and decision making while increasing productivity and efficiency. No matter what kind of activity one examines in the office environment, in whatever size the corporation, computers are involved one way or another. In many there will be more computers than there are people, although computers will not be as visible.

In one way or another, computers are rapidly becoming the common new medium for the management of all office activity. They are used in corporate planning, in financial planning and control, and in project management, marketing, sales, and distribution. Computers have become strategic to the control of inventory and the management of human resources and capital assets. Payroll systems and cash management systems are based on them.

Computers are also known in offices as word processors, electronic mail and message systems, and desktop publishing systems. Even the new generation of telephone systems in the office is dependent on the computer. This plethora of intelligent machinery is being used strategically in business and government and in factories and laboratories. It is governing activity in organizations from customs, excise, immigration, and air traffic control centers, to defense establishments and hospitals. It is slowly and quietly invading the home environment, disguised as television and telephone sets and home banking systems.

## Computers Transform the Factory

Computers are being used throughout production and manufacturing processes in factories in the design and simulation of parts and components, as well as in manufacturing, milling, and assembly, where they constitute robots. CAD (computer-aided design), CAM (computer-aided manufacturing), CIM (computer-integrated manufacturing), and FMS (flexible manufacturing systems) are changing the language, organization, and operation of factories around the world. They have become so pervasive in some industries that few people can be seen any longer in the highly automated plants that are becoming increasingly common in the United States, Japan, and Europe, as well as in so-called developing countries.

In these most advanced plants, all the operations of the factory are under the control of an enormous computer system that monitors, schedules, and guides its entire operation. Researchers are working on future plants so automated that an engineer will only have to create a crude model of a component or device and the computer will be able to optimally design all its parts, produce all the components, and assemble them together automatically. These may be common in the next century.

## Computerized Military Weaponry

It is in the defense and aerospace industries that some of the most advanced applications of computer technology have occurred. Computers were one of the critical technologies that put Americans on the moon before the Soviet Union. They have become strategic to the exploration of space and the operation of laboratories and factories in space, and could be critical to the colonization of outer space in the next century.

Computers have made it possible to monitor global military activity from anywhere in the world, to control sophisticated weapons systems, and to conduct hypothetical war games on land, in the oceans, in the skies, and in space in a completely integrated fashion.

Computers are the brains of the new generation of "smart missiles," including the Cruise, the Silkworm, and the Exocet missiles, that have become familiar to the public around the world. To a considerable degree, the latest generation of computerized military weaponry has made existing weapons systems obsolete. Intelligent weapons are far superior to the typical weapons systems deployed today, and the next generation already under development will accelerate this trend. As it is conceived, the Strategic Defense Initiative (SDI), or Star Wars, is a sophisticated computer-, laser- and space-based antiballistic missile defense system that would make all other planned weapons systems obsolete. Its supporters claim that SDI could monitor the entire world for military activity, and take offensive and defensive maneuvers in response to enemy actions. It could also identify and destroy enemy weapons in space and on the ground using its particle beam guns.

Theoretically, computers could herald the day when a global war would take place entirely in "computer space." The strategies would be conceived of and coded in the programs of the computer systems in space and on the ground, and the battles fought between these programs. Computers would simulate the various strategies and automatically order and initiate strike action. Such a war, however, would not affect the physical world as we know it, and it would make warfare as we know it obsolete technically, operationally, and economically.

## The Transformation of Telecommunications

Computers are having a revolutionary impact on telecommunications as well. They are transforming telephone systems through their effects on switching and transmission, and have given the telephone sophisticated processing and intelligence capabilities such as voice store-and-forward, directory service, and call management. They are responsible for the enormous improvements in the quality and economics of telephone services, and are the source of the new integrated digital telecommunications services that combine voice, data, graphics, and image communications. It is these capabilities that make it possible to provide information retrieval, electronic mail, and television pictures over the telephone.

Computer technology has also revolutionized radio, satellite, and mobile telecommunications, and it is effectively turning the telephone system into a gigantic global information-processing and communications system.

## Transportation

Computers are becoming indispensable to air traffic control and landing systems, and to air, sea, and land navigation and collision avoidance systems. Some of this technology has already made its way into the automobile, where it is used to control engine emissions and operations and to monitor and diagnose mechanical and electrical problems. Eventually, the navigation and collision avoidance systems will be available on the family automobile.

Computers have also found strategic applications in the airlines, railway, and shipping industries for managing reservations and scheduling, for the transportation and tracking of freight, and for customs administration and clearance.

## And Communications Sectors

In the communications industries, computers are transforming publishing, film, broadcasting, and advertising. They have revolutionized publishing, for example, through the introduction of on-line databases and computerized newswire services, and have revolutionized the operations of publishing companies through computer graphics, layout, and composition. Now this sophisticated technology is being brought to the desk of every office worker and homeowner in the form of desktop publishing so everyone can become a publisher to one degree or another.

In film and television broadcasting, computers are used in areas such as animation and camera control and for the creation of special visual effects and color enhancements through video processing. Who would have believed only a few years ago that a computer-based artificial personality embodied in Max Headroom would become a television star?

Computers have also become the new medium for artists, in turn affecting advertising and the graphic arts and stimulating the growth of desktop video, which brings color graphics and sound creation tools to the office worker, the homeowner, and the individual.

## Education

Computers have not left any field untouched, not even education and training. Computer-aided learning (CAL) and computer-aided instruction (CAI) have been under development for several decades but their utility and productivity are steadily improving. The newest multimedia environment uses special sound effects, simulated motion pictures, and computerized imagery and control. These new computer-based education and training systems have become as important as books to universities and engineering and medical schools. They are also becoming common in flight training centers and throughout business and some day will make their way into the home, changing the way we learn and educate ourselves and our children at home and on the job.

In an advanced computer-mediated society, our machines, our buildings, and our learning systems will enable us to interact with many media. They will be programmed to respond to most contingencies, prepared to answer just about any question, capable of providing us with information and instructions on just about any subject, and able to recommend decisions for us. Humans will be occupied with learning and keeping up with the rapid pace of events and the enormous amounts of information and knowledge produced, with being creative in the interaction and mediation of social and economic activity, and with making the ultimate decisions.

## Medicine and Health Care

In medicine and health care, computers are making an enormous difference in quality, comfort, and economics. They help manage hospital admissions and patient records, as well as scheduling, drug use, and food distribution. Patient well-being can be monitored by them, and they assist in the diagnosis of patient ailments. They are the basis of new life-monitoring and -support systems, artificial organs, and wonder machines such as the CAT (computer axial tomography) scanner and the PET (positron emission tomography) scanner. Computers are also used in the design and production of new devices, limbs, and organs, and they serve as aids to the deaf, the blind, and the disabled.

## The Sciences

Computers have also initiated a scientific revolution. They constitute the new microscope and the new telescope of science, and they enable man to penetrate the innermost depths of matter and life itself, to examine them under a microscope, to simulate them, manipulate them, and eventually synthesize them. They are behind the scenes in the materials revolution, the superconductor revolution, and the biotechnology revolution, and they are enabling man to design new materials atom by atom, and new life forms gene by gene.

Computers provide yet another means of human control over nature. They are altering all the physical and the social sciences.

## The Transformation of the
## Natural Resource Industries

The resource industries of agriculture, mining, oil and gas, forestry, and fishing have not been left untouched by the computer. Robots are making their way into the mining industry; farmers are using computers to improve the efficiency of routine farm operations, and are finding them on traditional farm machinery. In technologically intensive fields, such as remote sensing of the environment, computers are indirectly affecting many resource-based and other industries.

Computers are used in the processing of satellite photographs to produce electronic maps and charts. These can be scanned by computer or by eye to identify information that helps farmers to spot crop diseases before they cause too much damage. Exploration companies can decide on the best place to search for mineral deposits or oil and gas reserves. Forestry officials can spot forest fires and diseases. Environmental officers can monitor the movement of wildlife and schools of fish, as well as identify sources of pollution, monitor and study changes in weather conditions, and keep track of the movement of icebergs that pose hazards to navigation. Since computers are also improving record keeping and administrative activities as well as research and development in the resource industries, they are essentially changing and improving the way our environment is managed.

## The Financial Services Sector

The entire public landscape of twentieth-century society has been radically transformed by the computer in little more than a decade. Automated teller machines (ATMs) can be seen in shopping centers, on street corners, in convenience stores, and in remote locations where no bank would have conceived of having a branch. They are open 24 hours a day and you can do just about anything you can do at a branch that used to be staffed by people. Point-of-sale systems are proliferating in retail outlets, where they are used in monitoring sales, performing security checks, assisting with customer identification and payment, and tracking inventory. Completely automated retail machines are dispensing a wide variety of merchandise, from fruits and vegetables to theater tickets and videocassettes.

Debit cards and smart cards are slowly replacing the magnetic strip card and are gradually displacing paper money as an exchange medium. They are also being used as universal security and identification cards for military establishments, customs and immigration centers, and health care systems. Networks of computerized teller machines, retail systems, and databanks interconnect shopping centers, gasoline outlets, and convenience stores with banks and brokerage companies (as well as travel agents), and will eventually link to computers in the home, maybe by the turn of the century.

In the decade of the eighties, the effect of computerization has been nowhere more revolutionary than in the securities, banking, and other financial service industries. High capacity computer-processing and transmission networks connect the computers on the stock exchanges in New York, London, and Tokyo with one another and with other leading financial centers of the world. Securities dealers, professional traders, and multinational corporations now play on completely electronic markets through these networks, as do insurance companies and mutual and pension fund managers.

Twenty-four-hour global trading in securities, commodities, and currencies is an established fact, and it has enormous economic and political implications for all mankind. The stock exchange floors of some leading world exchanges are being abandoned altogether in favor of computer-mediated trading. Traders, arbitragers, and speculators make optimum use of new instruments of the computer age, including options, futures, index futures, and options on futures, and they can be had on securities as well as currencies and commodities. They use new computer-based strategies such as program trading, portfolio insurance, and arbitrage to protect themselves from computer-generated volatility and to increase their profits.

**Black Monday**

There is at least one date in history in which all these forces came together and changed the way most people view the economic world around them: October 19, 1987, the date of the greatest stock market crash in history. After that, it was clear that the fundamentals of the economic system had changed, that we have now become part of a computer-mediated global economy, in which all securities, currencies, and commodities are manipulated, traded, and exchanged electronically, independent of space and time. Ours is truly a programmed global capitalist society.

## The Future: Coping with a Computer-Mediated Society

The computer revolution poses many challenges for society and for all mankind. Whether we call it automation, cybernetics, or computerization, the emergence of intelligent machines and infrastructures in the office, factory, and marketplace has enormous impact on our way of life. What we regard today as science fiction is rapidly becoming a reality. We have barely begun to identify the symptoms and problems arising from this metamorphosis even though it has already enveloped our society. The solutions, now remote, are going to have to be found very quickly.

Technology is sweeping away all the old problems and creating new ones. Most people cannot keep abreast of the rapid pace of events in this new society. Intelligent machines, infrastructures, and organizations challenge our definitions of work, value, and culture, and ultimately our concepts of man, the machine, and God.

The significance of the computer to the evolution of society and the transformation that is taking place can best be appreciated by way of an analogy with biological evolution. There is a distinct trend in the evolution of living animals from lesser to greater intelligence, from lesser to greater efficiency, and to some degree, from relatively greater to relatively lesser mass, bulk and physical strength. The dinosaurs roaming the world millions of years ago were massive creatures that dominated the world because of their physical strength. They were succeeded by smaller, more agile, more intelligent animals and eventually by human beings, who now dominate the biological world because of their superior intelligence, not their size. A similar trend is taking place in the economic world.

The machines of the old industrial age were bulky and of lower intelligence, like the dinosaurs. The new industrial age employs smaller, less bulky, and more flexible and intelligent machines, which are emerging to dominate economic activity. The ultimate economic and social impact of the computer on the organization and evolution of human society is of as great a significance as the long process of transformation from the dinosaur age to the age of man—but on a scale of decades.

*     *     *

## Societal Revolutions in Perspective

The way societies evolve and change is a very complex matter, but one that can be explained using relatively simple logical paradigms or models which represent the essential factors and their interaction and dynamics. A sufficiently broad, open, and dynamic view of history tells us a great deal about the causes and the significance of the computer revolution that is taking place around us, as well as its effects on our society in the future.

This involves going back 500 years to the Copernican Revolution, which began about the fifteenth century. At that time, the prevailing belief was that the earth was the center of the universe and that the sun revolved about it. The earth was also believed to be flat. This was the divine order of things and it was fixed and immutable. These beliefs, in turn, influenced the way society was organized, and the way it operated extended right down to the day-to-day life of the peasants.

It was Copernicus and his successor Galileo who were able to observe the movement of celestial bodies with the aid of a telescope; their observations and deductions caused a revolution. They created a new model of man and the role he played in the universe, thereby changing the perceptions of man, nature, and God and the relationship between them. This model ultimately resulted in the overthrow of the political, economic, and religious order of the day.

Coincident with the Copernican Revolution was a communications revolution brought about by the invention of the Gutenberg press in about 1450. Print provided an inexpensive medium whereby ideas, knowledge, wisdom, and experience could be recorded and communicated through space and across generations. In turn, it initiated a knowledge and intelligence revolution and gave ordinary people the freedom to think and act, individually and together, according to what they thought was in their individual and collective interest.

The Copernican and Gutenberg Revolutions culminated in the scientific revolution of the seventeenth and eighteenth centuries, propelled by the work of great scientists like Isaac Newton, the founder of physics, Johannes Kepler, the astronomer, and René Descartes, the mathematician. The foundations of physics, chemistry and biology were laid. Ordinary people applied scientific principles and together with engineers created a technological revolution. Political forces were also at work creating new institutions that reflected these ideas, culminating in what we know as the Industrial Revolution of the eighteenth and nineteenth centuries.

The Industrial Revolution was synonymous with an economic and political revolution that changed the cultural and religious fabric of society. It resulted in a revolution in education, finance, transportation, and management. It also resulted in what we recognize as capitalism, socialism, and democracy.

## The Smithian, Marxian, and Schumpeterian Visions of Societal Evolution

A number of economic visionaries tried to explain the significance of the Industrial Revolution. Adam Smith, who lived in its midst, viewed it as being driven by fundamental capitalist forces which he thought were operating to the benefit of the entire society. He said it would result in greater wealth for everyone. Karl Marx, because he lived about a century later, viewed the Industrial Revolution from a different perspective. He saw industrialized capitalism as an intermediate step in an evolutionary process that would lead to the creation of a utopian communist state without the need for private corporations or even a government. He thought that capitalism contained the seeds of its own destruction and that it would soon be overthrown by the proletariat.

Joseph Schumpeter, an economist who lived during the early part of the twentieth century, had the advantage of hindsight over Marx and Smith. Schumpeter was better able to understand the roles of science, technology, and capitalism, and the way they interacted to change society. According to him, capitalism was essentially a form of political and economic organization for managing change. Moreover, it was a necessary means of creating change in order that economic progress take place. Capitalism was the most dynamic form of society because it was designed to harness change. Two sets of forces are at work under Schumpeter's view of capitalism, one creating new ideas, new inventions, and new products and services, and the other destroying them. These dynamics he called "Creative Destruction" and he saw them as working for the good of mankind, although he was not very clear what kind of society capitalism would evolve into. He wrote:

> Capitalism . . . is by nature a form or method of economic change and not only never is but never can be stationary. And this evolutionary character of the capitalist process is not merely due to the fact that economic life goes on in a social and natural environment, which changes and by its change alters the data of economic action; this fact is important and these changes (wars, revolutions, and so on) often condition industrial change, but are not its prime movers. . . . The fundamental impulse that sets and keeps the capitalist engine in motion comes from the new consumer goods, the new methods of production or transportation, the new markets, the new forms of industrial organization that capitalist enterprise creates. . . . The opening up of markets . . . and the organizational development from the craft shop and factory to such concerns as U.S. Steel illustrates the same process of industrial mutation—if I may use that biological term—that incessantly revolutionizes the economic structure from within, incessantly destroying the old one, incessantly creating a new one. This process of Creative Destruction is the essential fact about capitalism. It is what capitalism consists in and what every capitalist concern has got to live in.[1]

## The Computer, Capitalism, and the Evolution of Society

To be sure, one of the lessons from this brief review of history is that science, technology, and knowledge play fundamental roles in the evolution of capitalist society. They affect the way society is organized both economically and politically and, in turn, affect the ways science, technology, and knowledge are developed and how they are used and applied throughout society. Second, all these forces influence the cultural and religious foundations of society, which in turn influence the political and economic organization of society and the way it operates—in some respects, even influencing the role of science, technology, and knowledge. Each segment plays a role in explaining the computer revolution that is currently underway. Like the revolutions of the past, the computer revolution involves powerful scientific, technological, economic, political, and cultural forces. How can all of these be made to fit together?

## Toward a Paradigm of a Computer-Initiated Metamorphosis of Society

A model of the computer society metamorphosis must involve all these factors and forces. It must involve factors such as technology, corporations, and the economic system, as well as political and institutional factors. Each impacts the others in complex ways. The socioeconomic and political systems shape the nature and the kind of technology, systems, and infrastructures that are developed from scientific, engineering, and managerial efforts operating hand in hand with nature. Their efforts are rewarded and they eventually become the very foundation of a new order and a new society, changing and transforming the old society in the process.

Over sufficiently long periods of time—of the order of centuries, but sometimes of the order of decades—certain technologies can create, destroy, and transform the organization and operation of an economic order, a political system, and an entire society. In the case of the computer, the time scale of the transformation is of decades rather than centuries, and the transformation is well under way.

The computer-society transformation process comprises both a horizontal and hierarchical dimension. The hierarchical dimension consists of five sequential and complementary stages, beginning with microlevel changes and transformations, and progressing through intermediate level changes to the macrolevel. These are illustrated in Figure 1.1. The horizontal dimension is complementary to the hierarchical dimension. Whereas the hierarchical dimension emphasizes the sequence of changes and transformation from a microlevel to a macrolevel, the horizontal dimension emphasizes the nature and sequence of changes among industrial sectors and economic activities that are essential for the entire society to be transformed. The dynamics of the hierarchical transformation process are described in considerably greater detail in this section. The horizontal dynamics will be described in the next section.

### Level 1: The Workplace

The first stage of the process is the working level where most people in

17

Figure 1.1. **Conceptual Model of a Computer-Initiated Societal Metamorphosis.**

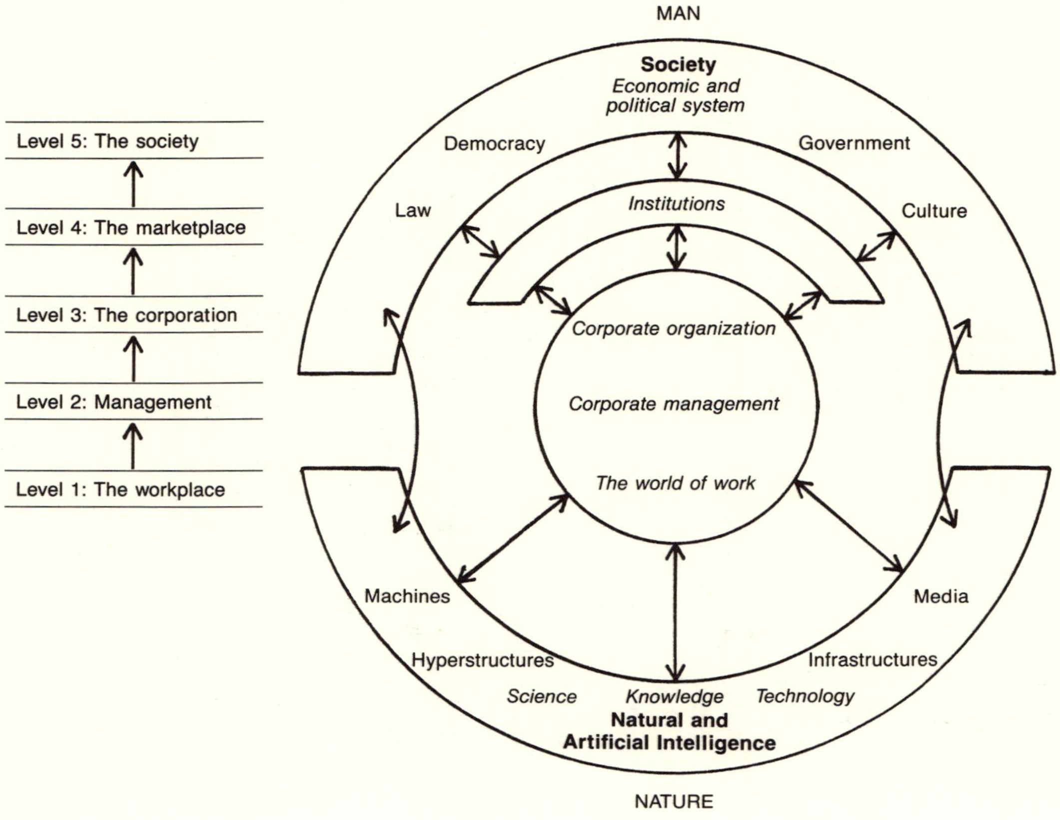

MAN

NATURE

**Society**
*Economic and
political system*

Culture

Government

Democracy

Law

Institutions

Corporate organization

Corporate management

The world of work

Media

Infrastructures

*Knowledge*

*Technology*

**Natural and
Artificial Intelligence**

*Science*

Hyperstructures

Machines

Level 5: The society

Level 4: The marketplace

Level 3: The corporation

Level 2: Management

Level 1: The workplace

the corporation and in society are employed. The second stage is management. Both are fundamental to the computer revolution, for it is here that computer technology is applied in ways that are conducive to a new kind of work. Under capitalism, all corporate players are forced continually to search for ways to improve their performance, to seek profitable opportunities in the marketplace, and to dominate the market and their competitors as best they can. Although there are many avenues open to them, one of the most important is through the strategic use of technology, for technology can be developed, applied, and managed in ways that lead to advantages over competitors in the marketplace.

Every corporation therefore seeks to use technology in a more effective and superior manner than its competitors. Technology is most visible at the working level, where it is developed and applied in practical ways, but it ultimately affects the position of the corporation in the marketplace.

One of the unique characteristics of the computer, and one that is essential to enable it to transform an entire society, is its multifunctional and intelligent nature, described briefly above and detailed in subsequent sections. This flexibility and adaptability, stemming from its programmability, makes it possible to shape it to meet an endless variety of applications and needs. Applying computer technology in its most intensive ways changes the nature of work performed by people, eliminating older ways of doing things, transforming others, and creating entirely new kinds of work. In the process, the nature of skills changes as well. In this case, the nature of the new work is one of computer mediation.

Computer mediation is the symbiotic relationship among human intellectual effort, computer-augmented control and communication, and physical activity. It simply means that the computer becomes a necessary and essential means of creativity and design, of exercising effort, and performing economic activity.

## Level 2: Management

In the real world, work and management interact in very subtle and intimate ways, and distinctions between them often become blurred. Changes in the nature of work cannot take place without an innovative, cooperative, and flexible management style. It takes one style of management to initiate and manage the necessary changes, and it takes another to operate in the new computer-mediated environment. When capitalism is operating at its best, it breeds these styles of manager naturally.

Computer mediation integrates previously separate work and management activities and creates enormous interdependencies to the point of blurring distinctions among them. It significantly expands the responsibilities of managers and their scope of control. Computers make up the infrastructure that permits the corporation more effectively to manage, coordinate, and control its resources.

However, competitive pressures make it essential to manage and control the human and intelligent resources together with the financial and capital resources of the corporation in a more integrated fashion. The computer provides the means to make this possible. The result is that computer systems and resources become essential to the effective management and control over production, quality control, and marketing. They are integral to the management of innovation, finance, and the overall decision-making process.

### Level 3: The Corporation

The third stage in the hierarchy of change and transformation involves interaction between technology, work, and management, and the organization and operation of the corporation, with the result that transformations in the former induce related transformations in the latter. It can often happen that the inherent nature of the technology will dictate certain organizational forms or structures. For example, it can require greater centralization or decentralization from the point of view of decision making or of geographical operations. The new technology and the new management alter the nature of the organization by forcing it to redefine, reposition, and restructure itself in ways that make more effective and strategic use of computer systems and infrastructures.

The product of the computerization of the corporate organization is an organization mediated by computer systems and computer networks, representing a new form of corporate infrastructure capable of running the entire intelligence operations of the enterprise. In the new environment, the embodiment of systems, networks, software, and their applications in computer-based infrastructures becomes a weapon for repositioning the corporation in a manner that leads not only to its survival but also to competitive advantages that are necessary for the corporation to grow and profit.

These systems restructure the nature of the corporate organization and the marketplace it serves, and significantly increase the geographical scope and coverage of its operation. Computer-based infrastructures redefine and transform the nature and composition of the products and services produced by the corporation. They create a new kind of organization enjoying much greater economies in its scale of operation, particularly in its processing and communication of information, and in the delivery of multiple computer-based products and services over large geographical markets. This new organization, in turn, induces a related transformation in the organization of the industrial sector and the market it serves, and in the institutions which are set up in every society to control and administer economic and political power.

### Level 4: The Marketplace

The fourth stage of the hierarchical transformation process focuses on the nature of the relationships among corporations, markets, and the institutions created to organize, regulate, and administer them, and with the remainder of the economic system and the society as a whole. Computer technology profoundly affects the organization of the industry and the marketplace that it serves. It can create great economies and synergies that enable a single corporation to grow and monopolize the market it once shared with other corporations. It can provide the means for those companies most successful in the strategic application of the technology to diversify their activities and extend their power over multiple industries and sectors of the national and global economy and by so doing to dominate them.

This, in turn, has the effect of integrating and redefining major sectors of the economy and creating great antagonisms between regulatory institutions set up to administer, regulate, and control industrial power at the national and the global levels. This consequently encourages greater political conflicts among jurisdictions that administer economic activity and control economic power locally, regionally, and nationally. Computerized corporate systems, therefore, influence the nature of competition and the concentration of economic power within the national and global economies in terms of the productivity, efficiency, and geographical nature and scale of operation of the organization. These, in turn, bear on the ways particular industrial sectors are organized, controlled, or regulated, and the rules under which they are operated and administered from both a legal and political perspective at the national and global levels.

## Level 5: The Society

The fifth stage of the societal transformation process is one in which the influences of computer technology and infrastructures, both directly as well as indirectly, extend far beyond the confines of a particular industrial sector to affect the basic social, cultural, economic, and political foundations of society.

The emergence of a computer-mediated society modifies the nature of employment, skills, income and wealth, and the educational requirements of the entire society. It reforms economic activity at the national level, the manner and effectiveness by which nation-states exercise sovereignty and political power, and how they control and stimulate economic activity within their geographic economies.

In this way, the technological transformation imposes on the nature of politics and the way power and control are exercised throughout the world. Ultimately, it affects our views of the world, of ourselves, our beliefs, our religion, and our language, identity, and culture. At this level, everything about our global economic system and global society is transformed, and new political, economic, and cultural institutions evolve as foundations for the new computer-mediated society. This is what the computer revolution is all about.

*    *    *

## The Capitalist System and Economic
## Power and Democracy

Every sector of the economy is undergoing a metamorphosis in its own way and at its own pace, but the transformation of individual sectors is not sufficient to alter the nature and operation of capitalism in its entirety—except for the information, banking, and financial service sectors. Their role in the organization and operation of the market illustrates the horizontal transformation process.

For a variety of reasons, these sectors are foundations of capitalism's organization and operations, and what we have come to accept as economic democracy. In many respects, they are among the most important and fundamental pillars of modern capitalism. Once we understand the critical nature and role of information, banking, and financial services to the capitalist system, and once we understand the correspondence between the activities and functions carried out in these sectors and those performed by the computer, it will become obvious why they represent the leading edge in the metamorphosis of capitalism.

Capitalism is a unique form of social and economic organization that is different from all others in a number of key respects. First, most capital and other productive assets, by far, is owned not by the state but rather by private individuals and corporations, giving them enormous control over the economic system, which they exercise through decisions relating to the management of their money and wealth.

Second, capitalism harnesses one of the most basic human emotions and motivations—that of capital accumulation (although some people know it by names such as greed). Individuals and corporations are free, and they have the incentive to strive to increase and to maximize the growth of their capital and wealth by engaging in legitimate activities such as investment, production, and exchange.

Third, the focal point of capitalism is the corporation, which organizes factors such as land, labor, capital, materials, and technology to produce goods and services for the marketplace. The corporation is a privately owned organization dedicated to the creation and maximization of wealth, and defined in this way, it is a key construct of capitalism.

Fourth, embodied in capitalism is the marketplace, which represents the mechanism or facility whereby individuals and corporations interact on their own behalf and in their own interests, and make decisions about the purchase and sale of factors of production and the goods and services they produce. Buyers and sellers compete in the marketplace through the price system for the right to own and control factors of production, goods, and services. Revenues from the sale of goods and services finance production and investment and contribute to profit. In this way, resources are allocated to competing demands in a manner that reinforces economic efficiency.

Under capitalism, economic power and control are therefore exercised through the abilities of individuals and corporations to determine the allocation and use of their wealth. For as long as markets are competitive, power and control will be decentralized throughout the economic system. Economic activity, therefore, takes place more or less among autonomous decision makers. Their actions consist of trading and exchange, and investment and decision making; in this way, they determine what is produced and how it is produced.

## Computerization in the Marketplace

The computer's most significant impact is through its effects on the organization and operation of the market. There are two basic ways in which the computer transforms the market. First, it transforms the role of information—how it is produced, collected, distributed, and processed—and the role it plays in the decision-making process. Since information and decision-making are prerequisites to wielding economic power and wealth, the effect of computerization is to change the way these are exercised in the marketplace. Second, the computer redefines how the rights to power, wealth, and control over goods and services are traded, transacted, and made to grow in the market. These rights are incorporated in or mediated by money and capital.

The role of information in the market economy and the creation of a computer-based information infrastructure is the subject of Chapter 2. The significance of money and capital to the capitalist system is discussed briefly in the following section and is the subject of Chapters 3, 4, and 5. Chapters 6, 7, and 8 illustrate the effects of computerization on the information, banking, and financial industries individually, and on the relationship between them and the other industries and sectors of the economy.

The simplest way to understand the effects of computerization on the market is by examining its effects on the eight basic functions that all markets perform. These are illustrated in Figure 1.2.

Eight information-based activities or functions are essential to the operation of every market. First, all markets require a mechanism dedicated to the collection or production of information. Second, they need a mechanism for accessing, distributing, and communicating this information and making it available throughout the economy. Third, they need a system for processing information, leading to the fourth function—decision making.

These four functions and activities are prerequisites to the ultimate purpose and function of every market, that of trading and exchange, which constitutes the fifth activity carried out in the market economy and the fifth function facilitated by the computer.

Figure 1.2. **The Computer Transforms and Mediates the Eight Basic Functions Performed by the Market Economy.**

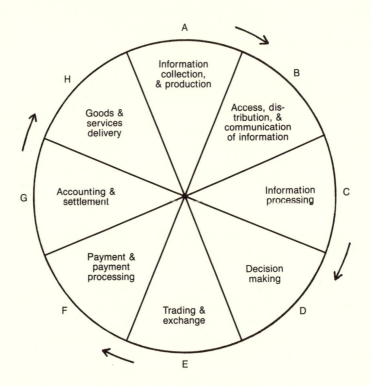

Three other functions are necessary for markets to operate, and each is transformed and mediated by the computer as well. The sixth is the payment and payment-processing system. The seventh is the accounting and settlement processing system, and the eighth is the delivery system, which facilitates the movement, transmission, or distribution and consumption of physical or invisible goods and services being exchanged. All eight functions and activities are interrelated, and all can be mediated by computers.

From this perspective, the entire economic system can be seen as one gigantic information processing and intelligence system, which is why computers are evolving to mediate it in its entirety.

The principle of the economic and societal transformation process by the computer is based on its centrality to all economic activity and to the essence of capitalism. Computers are revolutionizing all information, communications, and decision-making activities. They serve as the medium for trading and exchange activity, and facilitate the operation of the payment- and account-processing of all markets. But the information, banking, and financial services sectors are unique because they have a wide influence on the manner in which markets operate and are organized. They are part of all market activities because information, money, and capital facilitate the operation of the market economy. They are also the backbone of wealth creation and capital accumulation, which are basic to capitalism.

It is these sectors that administer and control money and capital and, therefore, the nature of capitalism itself.

## The Effect of Computerization on Information, Decision-Making, Power, and Wealth

One of the primary impacts of computerization as explained above is through its effects on information. In a paper-based society, information was costly to collect, produce, distribute, process, and access, and there were tremendous physical, economic, and psychological barriers and problems in managing it. Consequently, decision making was severely confined, restricted, and inefficient in comparison to a computer-based system, which can collect, produce, distribute, and process enormous volumes of information from all over the world about all manner of events at significantly lower cost.

The emergent computerized infrastructures have made global information instantly available through databanks, satellites, personal computers, and telephone systems. Weather, news reports, stock market quotations, economic forecasts, and so on can be accessed and analyzed by computers, and their effects made evident in the marketplace within minutes. The information gathering, intelligence, and surveillance system even extends into outerspace, where satellites photograph the surface of the earth and send the signals back to computers on earth, which process the raw information to supply valuable information on crop disease, growth, and probable yield.

This surveillance and intelligence system is constantly in operation, forecasting consumer demands, economic growth, predicting wants, and distributing technical information to improve business. It is always listening to everything of relevance to the economic system. This preponderance of information is essential to guiding expenditures, investment, and the operation of the marketplace. It is ultimately translated into revenue, profit, wealth, and control.

Information is distributed and accessed through reports, databanks, newswire services, radio and television, and newspapers. Ultimately, it makes its way into the stock exchanges of the world where it affects the prices of commodities, goods and services, returns on investment, and the profits of farmers, producers, institutions, companies, and individuals throughout the world. Enormous volumes of information now can be easily accessed and processed inexpensively where it was impossible to do so in a paper-based economic system. The combined effects of computerization on information and decision making are to expand the means by which economic wealth and political power and control are exercised over global proportions.

### Money, Capital, and the Computer in a Capitalist Economy

Money and capital represent the pillars of capitalism. In one sense, they are commodities that are traded in the marketplace. In another sense, they are factors of production, and in still another sense, they have attributes that make them constitute a medium. But they have such a fundamental value and purpose to capitalism that their management and control determine the nature of the capitalist system. They mediate its operation; they can make it more or less efficient and successful, or they can make it fail. Both touch on all sectors and all segments of society, and represent levers that exercise power and control in markets and the economic system by individuals, corporations, and the government.

One of the most important roles that money serves is as a medium in the exchange of goods and services. Before money was invented, ancient societies used a barter system. It was clumsy, cumbersome, inefficient, and very limited in its convenience and value. The invention of money changed all that. Money made the market economy a more efficient and desirable place to do business. In a money economy, for example, a person who wanted to exchange beef for sugar no longer had to make an extensive search for someone who had sugar and wanted to trade it for beef. Instead, each individual would exchange his or her produce for a common unit of value, which could be used to purchase other commodities. As long as everyone had confidence in the acceptability and purchasing power of a common currency, it was a safe and reliale medium for exchange. Eventually, money became a universal medium for the exchange of goods and services.

But before this universal confidence developed, institutions had to be set up to administer money. The government had to guarantee its value, and it had to make sure there was a sufficient amount in circulation to support the volume of exchange trading and transactions demanded of it. Money is special for all these reasons. It is the only universally acceptable legal tender, but its value and use must be backed up by the government through legislation.

Money also represents a measure and a store of value. It should not deteriorate with time—otherwise people will lose confidence in it, and the entire system will deteriorate to one based on barter or precious metals. In an inflationless economy, the value of money is represented by its purchasing power—its control over goods and services. Inflation can degrade the value of money, resulting in a loss of confidence in its value, thereby diminishing its utility and productivity. Consequently, a necessary responsibility of governments is to ensure that inflation is always kept under control; this is done in the United States, for example, through the power delegated to the Federal Reserve Board (Fed), which controls the amount of money in circulation.

Money also serves as the basis for the system of accounting for the economy as a whole. It is used, for example, to measure the value of goods and services produced in the economy during any period of time. It is also used as a measure of the return on investment in production. Finally, money acts as a measure of wealth and the stock of capital owned by individuals, corporations and the economy as a whole. For all these reasons, money acts as a fundamental measure of economic activity and is central to the operation of a market economy. In some respects it constitutes an information system in itself. If computers transform the nature of money, as will be demonstrated, they transform the economic system as well.

Capital is as important as money in a market economy. Like money, capital is an artificial and abstract economic concept and commodity, but this does not diminish its utility and value in the economy as a whole. It is synonymous with money and wealth, and with property, machinery, plants, and equipment. It is also a basic factor in the production process, and it can be invested in such a way that it earns a return like any other factor. The productivity of capital, measured by its return on investment, is important to economic growth and wealth creation. The greater its productivity, the greater the overall growth and wealth of the economic system.

Capital assets denote the productive capacity of a plant, a corporation, or an economic system. Capital assets, represented by paper-based instruments, can also be traded in the marketplace, exchanged for money, and invested in specially designed capital markets.

Capital and capital markets, like their money counterparts, have been mediated by paper for over two hundred years. Now however, we see taking place before us the substitution and replacement of paper by the computer as the new medium for money and capital and all that they represent. It is this transformation that is wreaking so much havoc in money and capital markets throughout the world.

## Central Economic Intelligence, Processing, and Control

The banking and financial services sector is to the central economic processing and control system of a national economy as the brain is to the operation of the human body. It is through its effects on this economic and financial control system that the computer transforms society.

Several central economic institutions, in particular, play a pivotal role in making the market economy operate more or less smoothly and efficiently. One of these is the Securities and Exchange Commission (SEC), which regulates the securities industry in the U.S. and sets the rules by which securities are traded and exchanged.

Perhaps the most important, however, is the Federal Reserve Board, which wields enormous control over all economic activity through the powers it exercises over the U.S. banking system. The Fed is able to maintain public confidence in money by controlling the quantity of money in circulation and the rate it charges commercial banks for loans. By means of various mechanisms, the Fed is able to regulate, control, and stabilize economic activity, thereby preserving the essential features of money and capital and making the entire economy work.

In all these ways, the federal government through the Federal Reserve Board exercises considerable control over the quantity, quality, and value of money and credit, the pace of economic activity, and the inflation rate.

Keynesians and monetarists have been divided for decades on the most effective ways for governments to intervene in and thereby control economic activity. Fiscal and monetary policies and the effectiveness of specific policy instruments advocated by Keynesians and monetarists have been the only formats governments have been able to use to control investment, economic growth, inflation, and unemployment. Although Keynesianism and monetarism may have been effective and practical in a paper-based economic system, they are no longer as relevant or potent in a computer-mediated economic system.

By manipulating interest rates in the past, for example, the Fed has been able to influence the rate of domestic capital investment. In so doing, it was able to encourage savings and investment to take place or create incentives to spend money. The indirect effects of such macroeconomic policies have led to an increase in the rate of economic growth and employment creation.

Governments have also controlled and regulated the exchange rate. By intervening in the market for foreign exchange or by regulating the exchange rate, governments could often influence the import and export of goods and services, and the flows of international investment capital. These policies, in turn, have affected national employment creation, economic growth, and capital investment.

The effect of the computer on this control system is significant, and, as I will argue throughout this book, its ultimate result is to erode the controls governments have been accustomed to exercising over their national economies in the past. Electronic money, capital, and information do not obey the old laws of money, banking, and economics which have been liberated from the controls governments and geography have traditionally exercised.

Computerization transforms the way money and capital, as financial instruments, are mediated, and how they are traded, invested, distributed, and controlled. It results, for example, in a commoditization of money, making it capable of being traded and exchanged like any commodity or security. The computer creates an infrastructure capable of channeling money and capital into global markets independent of national borders and time. It increases the spatial dimensions of the marketplace from purely national to global proportions.

It erodes the power of the Fed and the sovereignty of the nation-state, and in the end transforms the nature and the distribution of economic power under capitalism.

## Synchronization of Economic Activity

The ultimate effect of the development of computer-based infrastructures is to telescope space and distance, and to process information and facilitate decision making in ways that were impossible in a paper-based economic system. They collapse the barriers to time, information processing, coordination, and synchronization of economic activity at the global level. For all intents and purposes, information, money, and capital can be made instantly available and accessible anywhere in the world. They can be collected, processed, and communicated instantly in the same way.

Consequently, the time required to make decisions and invest money, trade, and transact business is continually diminishing. Furthermore, the synchronization takes place over spatial environments increasingly global in scope and is accompanied by information, decision making, and intelligence activity that is increasingly complex in nature.

## The Four Great Economic Transformations

The analysis presented in this chapter clearly demonstrates that a correspondence exists between the nature of the economic system and the nature of the medium that is used to record, communicate, and process information, money, and capital, the technological underpinnings of the medium. Based on this correspondence, it is possible to place the interrelationships of paper, the computer, and capitalism in an historical perspective.

We can make a technological and spatial interpretation of the entire history of money, capital, and economic societies, and their centuries of history and future, all based on the technology of mediation.

This perspective is concerned with market mediation and the technology and intelligence associated with trading and exchange, which are the building blocks of economic society. It requires an examination of the principles of trading and exchange, the technology and infrastructure underlying them, the nature of intelligence, the distribution of power, and the political institutions associated with them in each stage of evolution—all of which are interdependent.

Ultimately, this perspective means that the foundations of our social and economic systems and their institutions are a function of, and dependent on, the technology of information, money, and capital mediation. That is, they depend on the nature of the medium by which economic activity is facilitated and carried out and the related rules. Four stages can be identified, and they are illustrated in Figure 1.3.

As previously described, one of the first great economic transformations in history occurred when mankind began to trade and barter goods and services. Barter made people better off, increasing their wealth, and giving them time to pursue other activities, since individuals no longer had to produce everything themselves or in their own tribe or clan.

A second transformation occurred when people began using precious metals such as gold or silver as a medium for exchange. Again, it provided greater convenience, and was more efficient than barter. Gold, for example, was easier to carry around and transport than beef, bread, or clothing, and for centuries was a primary medium for exchange between people and between nations. It is still with us, waiting in reserve in case we need it—in case we lose confidence in our governments and our institutions.

A third great economic transformation, which was simultaneous with the Industrial Revolution, occurred when paper money replaced its predecessor as a more efficient medium for exchange. As long as governments managed it properly, it was ideal when used as it was intended, i.e., as a medium of exchange and a store of value. It synchronized and mediated economic activities in such a way that it raised productivity and brought increasing wealth.

A fourth great economic transformation is occurring right now, and it has to do with a further shift in the nature, use, and functionality of money and capital.

In a sense, the computer is becoming the medium for exchange and replacing paper money (although we may never be able to completely dispense with paper money or coins). Money, in turn, is becoming a commodity. Money has lost its relationship with paper, and it can be traded freely, inexpensively, and instantaneously anywhere in the world when it is mediated by computers.

It may have been no accident that the nations of the world severed the links between paper money and gold in the 1971–73 period, when they agreed to abandon the now-famous Bretton Woods Agreement of 1944. For several decades, we have been witnessing the partial abolition of the use of paper as a medium for exchange, communications, trading, and the recording of transactions, since money and capital are difficult and expensive to manage and control in their paper form. Electronic mediation offers superior economic efficiencies and other advantages as a means of controlling information, wealth, and power in markets and economic systems generally, but it comes at a price for the nation-state. It makes it much more difficult, if not impossible, to maintain sovereignty and control over an economic system, which has been defined since its beginning as a continuous segment of geographic space.

Figure 1.3. **Evolution of Money as Market Exchange Medium and Its Relationship to the Organization of the Economic System.**

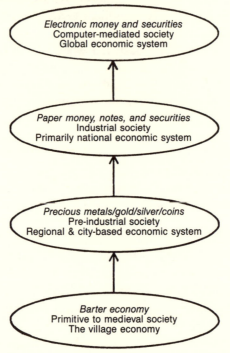

These four economic revolutions provide us with a perspective on how our economic system and society are developing and evolving, and they may provide us with some insight into what lies ahead. Figure 1.3 illustrates these four stages or economic revolutions and their significance to money and money media. There is, for example, a clear trend in economic evolution and human history, beginning with the exchange or barter of physical goods, leading to the use first of material substitutes such as gold as the medium for the exchange of physical goods, and later to the use of paper money as the principal medium for exchange. Paper was more efficient and convenient than gold and it contained more information. It was also country denominated whereas gold was not.

Now the computer is evolving as an instrument for exchange and trading, and is effectively replacing paper money and national currencies. It mediates the trading and exchange of all goods and services, and is transforming paper capitalism into computer capitalism.

In the same way that the introduction of paper money necessitated the creation of new institutions unique to the age of the Industrial

Revolution, the conversion to a computer-mediated economic system requires new institutions unique to the new age. Computer infrastructures, computer money, and computer capitalism are creating a more abstract, intelligent, invisible, and global-centered society, where everything in it can be traded and exchanged for anything and everything else.

## The Psychological Dimension of the Economic Intelligence System

Human psychology plays as important a role in economic society as the artificial intelligence system. In this respect, the economic system can be seen to consist of three components, as illustrated in Figure 1.4. The first is the real economy that we see around us: physical goods, materials, and equipment, and the activities associated with their production and distribution. The second component is the intelligence economy: it covers information, money, mathematical calculations, surveillance, and analytical activities. It is this system that is being mediated by computers, and that drives the real economy to a considerable degree. Next is the psychological economy: people's expectations, their beliefs and perceptions, and the confidence they have in the economic system and the world around them. This third component drives the other two components, yet the three are complementary to one another.

The entire economic system is much more complex than the traditional body of accepted knowledge that is taught in economic courses and business schools. These intelligence and psychological components are not well recognized, although they are addressed implicitly. Most of the economic statistics generated on economic performance, such as trade flows, productivity, output, and growth, for example, focus on the material economy even though an ever smaller portion of economic resources is being devoted to it, and even though the intelligence economy and the psychological economy are of equal importance.

It is desirable, of course, to have a perfect intelligence system, one that reflects the exact state of affairs in the real economy and the psychological economy. Corporations, for example, spend considerable time and money and invest large amounts of capital in equipment and activities that are designed to monitor the state of the economy, the wants of their customers, and the strategies and performance of their competitors. The intelligence system, even though it does not always

Figure 1.4. **Relationship Between the Real Economic System and the Intelligence and Psychological Economic Systems.**

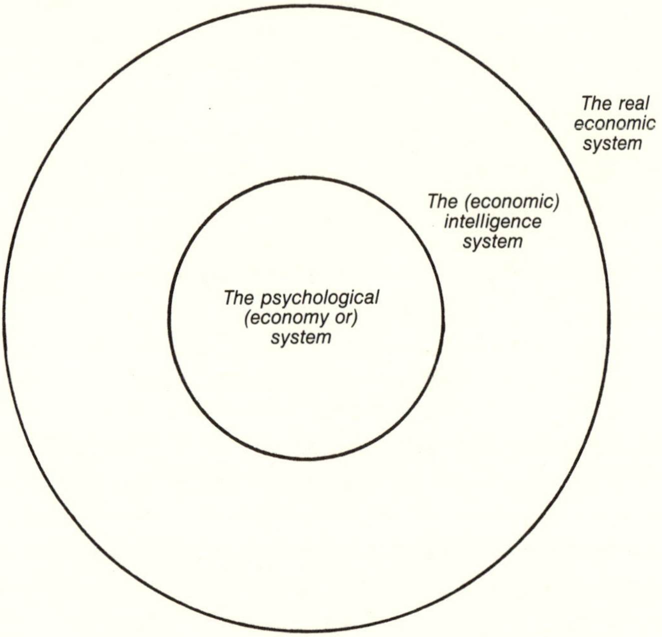

provide a true representation or picture of the real economy, it is what we have to depend on in making economic decisions.

The intelligence and the psychological systems often mask or hide the real economy, and can be out of synchronization with it for a while. At times, the intelligence and psychological systems can make the real economy obsolete. A change in the information and the messages economic actors obtain, for example, changes their perceptions, and alters the decisions based on these, which, in turn, revise the way the physical or real world is organized and operated.

In this respect, the psychological and intelligence economies dominate the real economy, and order and command it to perform in the ways they dictate. At other times, the real economy dominates the other two. After all, it often takes considerably longer to reorganize and restructure the real economy than it does the intelligence and psychological economies. It is the interaction among these three forces that is upsetting the global economy. Capital investment, production, and material flows between nations cannot keep pace with changing exchange rates or psychological factors.

It was primarily the psychological economy (the psychology of panic) that caused the Great Crash of 1929. The Crash of 1987, on the other hand, was caused by anomalies in both the psychological economy as well as in the intelligence economy. The intelligence infrastructure had changed the way stock markets around the world operated and the role that psychology played in them. Computers had linked all the markets in the world together to form a global instantaneous intelligence system, so that a global psychology was at work. The intelligence system magnified perceptions and their interaction by orders of magnitude. It was only a matter of time until a spark ignited the psychological fears that had been building up with the bull market that, at the time, was in its fifth year.

It is in ways such as these that the psychological economy controls the real economy. It can initiate signals that almost instantaneously propel the real economy into a recession or depression, as almost took place in October 1987.

In such fashion do the real economy, the intelligence system, and human psychology interact. The intelligence system is like a prism, a microscope, by which every economic actor perceives the real world around him or her, as Copernicus did with his telescope. But in addition to perceiving the real world, economic actors have to use this same prism to perceive the psychology of the world around them, and the psychology of the market and everyone who plays it, something that Copernicus in some respects did not have to contend with. In other respects, however, he did, because he knew that his views and perceptions violently contradicted those of the people around him, particularly those of the Church, so he was careful to ensure that his views and reports on what he saw through his telescope were not published until after his death.

In an abstract way, the telescope has been replaced by the computer. Everyone—businessmen, governments, scientists, and individuals—is using it to conduct intelligence activity.

This does not mean that there are inherent weaknesses in the psychological economy or that there is anything unnatural about it. To the extent that it is dependent on the intelligence system for messages, analyses, and information about what is going on in the market and in the real world, the nature of the intelligence system does have very important and profound effects on both the psychological and the physical economies.

The computerized infrastructures, which now constitute the medium

Figure 1.5. **The Four Pillars of the Financial Community and the Industrial and Institutional Boundaries of Industrial Society Before the Computer.**

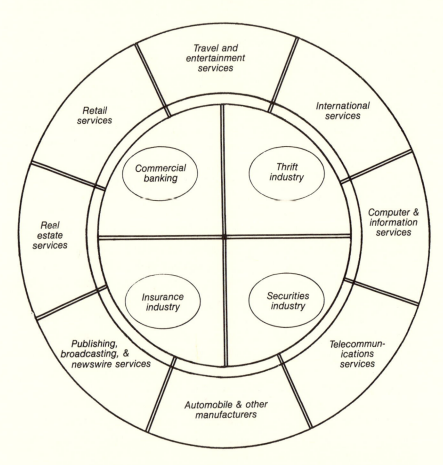

for the operation of the intelligence economy, have fundamentally altered the roles that both the intelligence system and the psychological system play in the real economy. They have collapsed all the constraints of the real world, including space, geography, time, information, and intelligence. As a result, the real world will never be perceived in quite the same way.

## Transformation of the Industrial Organization of Society

The rise of computer-based infrastructures has also modulated the organization of industrial societies throughout the world, although the process is far from complete. This multifunctional computer-based intrastructure has integrated and fused together previously separate and distinct industries and sectors of the economy, and it has eroded and made obsolete the geographical institutional and jurisdictional boundaries between political states and the functions they performed.

It is possible to provide a simplified view of how the United States economic system was organized before and after the computer. In this respect, Figure 1.5 illustrates the functional divisions and boundaries between industries. In the center of the figure are the four pillars of the financial community—the commercial banking industry, the thrift institutions, the securities industry, and the insurance industry. Information activities are distributed throughout these and other industries.

In the outer ring are further industries and activities. These include retail services, travel and entertainment, telecommunications, information and computer services, communications, and so forth.

Before the computer, all these were separated by technological, geographical, and economic factors, as well as political, legal, and regulatory barriers. By the end of the eighties, all these walls lay in ruins. Computers provided companies with enormous economic efficiencies, synergies, and economies of scale, which the companies used to expand their power and control over the entire economic system.

Armed with sophisticated computer-based infrastructures and related computer-based services, the biggest corporations in the United States broke out of their industrial cells, and embarked on a mission to dominate as great a segment of the economic system as they could possibly manage. They went national and global. They internalized banking, securities, real estate, travel, and entertainment services, and any others they could dominate.

In the process, they transformed the industrial landscape of the United States economy and economies around the world.

## Note

1. Schumpeter, *Capitalism, Socialism and Democracy*, 3d ed., pp. 82–83.

# 2

# The Rise of the Computer-Based
# Information Infrastructure

### Information: The Raw Material of Corporate, Economic, and Political Decision Making

Information is the raw material of the decision-making process in the corporation and the marketplace, and it is an essential prerequisite for political democracy. This raw material must be collected, mined, and processed. Value must be added to it at the processing stage. It must also be marketed and distributed and eventually transformed into decisions. But here the analogy with natural raw materials stops.

Unlike natural raw materials, information comes in an infinite variety of forms from an infinite variety of sources. Its economic value is highly variable. It can be everlasting or it can depreciate and become worthless instantly. It can be worth millions to one person and nothing to the next.

Information influences peoples' purchasing habits, votes, investment decisions, and wealth. It is the instrument of control in the corporation, the economic system, and political democracy. Information is the signaling system of all organizations. It is the lubricant and key component of all organizational intelligence.

Information is an important source of social, political, and corporate power and wealth. Those who own it, control its circulation, or regulate its access can exercise enormous power. It was information and knowledge, mediated by print, that led to the overthrow of the old medieval order and precipitated the Reformation and the Industrial Revolution. In more recent times, information has been transmitted by television, one of the most powerful purveyors of instant ideas and messages that the world has ever known. Like information, television synchronizes social and economic activity and influences our thoughts, votes, language, and culture.

Indeed, television has required leading contenders for national political positions to submit to television debates before they can be considered serious candidates. This trial by fire often determines whether they are elected. The Nixon-Kennedy and Reagan-Carter television debates were instrumental in determining who would succeed as President of the United States.

Advertising, another facet of information, exerts such pervasive influences over our lives that it controls our tastes and purchasing habits. The Dennis Levine and Ivan Boesky affairs and the other insider trader scandals that rocked Wall Street in 1986 are additional examples of how information can be used to control wealth and power. Ours is truly an information society.

Computerized databanks have become the brains and the memory systems of the modern corporation, the modern economy, and the modern society. Computer networks have become the nervous system of this emerging corporate and societal environment, channeling information to all decision-making centers and coordinating all activity. Modern societies and economies have become so dependent on these computer systems, networks, and databases that anarchy would surely reign if but a fraction of them were to fail simultaneously for just a few minutes.

The networks have introduced a degree of complexity into organizations that was unimaginable a few decades ago. They are so important that they determine the efficiency, survivability, and performance of corporations and governments. Databanks and electronic information infrastructures have changed all aspects of the modern organization, from their management and operation to the way they make decisions.

More than by any other means, power in modern society is exercised through the decision-making process. Since information is the most important ingredient in decision making, power and wealth can be wielded through the control individuals and corporations exercise over information and the networks by which it is collected, distributed, or processed. Every organization can be seen to be an intelligence system that collects and processes information and channels it to the decision-making centers of power, and any person or any organization able to gain access to this intelligence system or to dominate it can hold considerable influence.

The power exercised over and wealth generated from information, decision making, and the information and communications infrastructures of a corporation or an economic or political system are dependent on the value of the information, its reliability, its accuracy, and its timeliness. Computer-based infrastructures affect these factors at their cores, and through them modify the power structures in the corporation and in society.

The nineteenth-century financier Nathan Meyer Rothschild recognized the importance of the information and intelligence system to wealth and power. In 1815, he used carrier pigeons to relay the message of Napoleon's defeat at the Battle of Waterloo to London; he was able to use this information to make a fortune in the stock market by taking advantage of all the others in the market, none of whom had it. In the same way, computer-based infrastructures have become instruments for the control of corporate, economic, and political power and wealth. They have become weapons for attaining dominance in the corporation, the marketplace, and the global economy.

## A Brief History of Databank Developments

The application of computer systems to the management and communication of information is a natural one growing out of computers' inherent use and applications as universal database machines. Literally all information can be coded in digital form so it can be stored, processed, and retrieved according to the instructions contained in a computer program or by a user's interacting and communicating with it through a terminal. This capability gave birth to the databank industry in the late fifties and early sixties, but before it could grow and mature into a financially viable industry in its own right, many advances in computer technology were necessary. These included very large memory and storage media, efficient, high-speed processors, and sophisticated information management software systems.

Such technological improvements made it economical for the databank supply industry to maintain truly large volumes of information online so they could be accessed by remote computer terminals that were connected to national and international telecommunications networks. Users could search these volumes of information, selectively retrieve the information required, and then process and communicate it as necessary.

Gradually, a viable databank industry emerged specializing in the search and retrieval, processing, and distribution of an increasingly wider variety of information. Some suppliers provided access to bibliographic information, newspaper articles, and financial, economic, and demographic statistics and information. Some specialized in science, engineering, and technology. Others went into computer-based economic analysis and forecasting, financial analysis, and business planning.

A growing number of suppliers began to provide access to corporate reports, marketing information, and news and weather information. Some offered services to big business and governments; others developed the market for small businesses and professionals; while still others catered to computer hobbyists, serious home computer users, and those interested in shopping on-line. One of the highest growth segments turned out to be the delivery of instant up-to-date information on stock market quotations, futures prices, commodity prices, options, trading volume, and currency rates. This new computer-based information-processing and communications medium, in fact, created all these new markets.

## The Personal Computer, the Telephone, and the Databank Industry

More efficient, higher-capacity computer systems reduced the cost of databank services, making them economically attractive, but it was yet another technological innovation that stimulated an explosion in demand. That occurred in the latter part of the seventies, when the microprocessor revolution was gaining momentum. Up until then, the databank industry was highly specialized, very expensive, and not easily accessible by users. For the most part, databank services had been the preserve of researchers, librarians, scientists, engineers, scholars, and academics in large corporations, universities, and governments. Considerable technical expertise, experience, and specialization were necessary to use these services. Costs of telecommunications, processing, and storage were prohibitive for all but the largest organizations.

The microprocessor, and subsequently the personal computer, changed all this. These, together with the development of efficient, low-cost telecommunications services that connected users to the large computers where the databanks were located, stimulated the rapid growth and maturity of the databank industry. Both developments made it much simpler, less expensive, and more efficient and productive to market, access, and use information in a greater variety of ways.

In 1981, IBM announced its new PC line of personal computers in response to the success of competitors such as Apple and Commodore. In 1982, *Time* voted the personal computer the "person"ality of the year.

At the same time, computer literacy was increasing in the general population as personal computers were becoming more common. Databanks became larger, more sophisticated, and more tailored to market needs, and their economics continued to improve. Further improvements in telecommunications facilities and services made it even more efficient and cost-effective to access databanks from national and international locations, to collect, distribute, and retrieve information, and to process it remotely or locally. Developments in satellite communications, lower long-distance telephone rates, and the emergence of efficient, lower-cost digital data communications networks and services all contributed to improved the economics of communications and on-line access.

By the mid-eighties, personal computers were becoming as powerful as the mainframe computers of a decade earlier. Businesses and home owners were buying them in great numbers. The ability of the personal computers to process enormous amounts of information locally further stimulated the demand for databank services by professionals, hobbyists, and homeowners. Brokerage houses, banks, and insurance companies bought the new personal computers in large numbers to access and share information resources, to develop new business, and to improve their competitiveness. New and more efficient operating systems, integrated software packages, and less expensive equipment were complemented by the development of specialized communications network interfaces and built-in smart modems with automatic dial features.

Innovations such as these effectively eliminated the last barriers to the emergence of a convenient, productive, and cost-effective medium for accessing virtually universal information services. Inexpensive, high-quality telecommunications systems together with efficient databank operations and powerful personal computers represented the last links in the evolution of a global information infrastructure.

## Electronic Information in Its Own Right

By the end of 1984, approximately 2400 on-line databases were in existence, and scores of new ones were being created every month. They had begun to transform the way executives and professionals obtained vital information and made decisions. Databases contained financial, economic, and political information reported at the local, regional, national, and international levels. They also contained the full texts of major scientific, economic, and technical journals, newspapers, magazines, and research reports. News, weather reports, and public announcements could also be obtained on-line.

Specialized databases with up-to-date information on the decisions of government bodies and regulatory commissions were supplied by the Environmental Protection Agency, the Securities and Exchange Commission, the Federal Energy Agency, and the Federal Trade Commission, among others. They contained information on recent legislation passed by Congress and the Senate, judgments handed down by federal and state courts, and regulations and decisions of various federal and state commissions. Other kinds of information that could be accessed included corporate reports, competitive analyses and strategies, acquisition and diversification strategies, industry and economic statistics and reports, market forecasting and development, research and development, patents, and technology trends.

In the mid-eighties, the U.S. government was developing its own policy on databases. It embarked on a program of farming out its enormous files of information to the private sector to be exploited for their commercial value. The Securities and Exchange Commission also undertook to put all its documents and corporate reports into a database, and it began to accept corporate reports on floppy disks.

The largest databank suppliers are very large and successfully manage highly sophisticated and specialized volumes, all accessible by computer. Mead Corporation's LEXIS database, for example, is the largest legal citations database in the United States, providing information on up-to-date regulations and judicial opinions in all major law libraries in the United States. By 1986, its NEXIS database was the largest of the media databases, providing full text search and retrieval from the major wire services, ten newspapers including *The New York Times* and the *Washington Post*, forty-eight magazines, the financial statements of 4000 public corporations, and the contents of the *Congressional Quarterly*, the *Federal Registry*, and specialized trade publications.

The Dialogue Information Service, a subsidiary of Lockheed, offers access to over 200 databases containing over 100 million records and citations to articles in 10,000 journals. It also contains abstracts of just about every book or article on issues in philosophy published in the United States as well as on-line citations for every book in the Library of Congress.

Financial information services, particularly stock quotations, have been one of the fastest-growing segments of the electronic information industry. Everyone, it seems, is interested in stock quotations, including newspapers, investors, brokerage agents, traders, individuals, and large corporations. They want to know the prices of securities, commodities, and foreign currencies, as well as options and futures contracts on them, their yields, volumes, spreads, and many other kinds of detailed statistics. Weather information, crop reports, breakthroughs in technology, government policies and regulations, the lowering of a corporation's credit rating, and changes in the money supply, the budget, or trade deficits, are all relevant to financial markets, and traders and speculators will pay a price for such information as long as it helps them keep ahead of the market.

Text and statistical information can be supplemented by graphical information, and more sophisticated methods of presentation are being developed each year. For example, it is already possible with the new technology to convey database information in the form of multicolored charts, maps, graphs, and images. The databank industry is creating a new world that is rich and wealthy in information resources. It represents the new social, economic, and corporate capital assets of a computer-mediated society, and, together with the associated telecommunications facilities and personal computers, it constitutes the new information infrastructure of society.

## High-Capacity Storage, Processing, and Delivery

Computer-based media complement, broaden, and enrich, as well as displace, traditional information media in many ways. But in general, the impact of the computer has been to increase the scope and diversity of means by which information is accessed, communicated, and distributed. Today, the variety of information media and their economics have never been greater nor more attractive. Delivery mechanisms for the distribution and retrieval of information can take a number of forms depending on the cost, volume, and urgency of the information. If the information is not retrieved directly on-line by computer, it can be sent via the mail. It also can be stored and distributed on magnetic tape or on a floppy disk. It is becoming increasingly attractive, for example, to distribute an entire databank in this manner to companies and individuals so it can be processed locally on a personal computer.

In the meantime, the costs of using telephone services, special digital communications services, and satellite networks have been continually decreasing. With the advent of very-high-capacity optical fiber transmission systems and continued improvements in other telecommunications transmission facilities, the costs associated with accessing databank services will continue to decline in the foreseeable future.

Electronic delivery systems such as radio and television, and paper-based systems such as newspapers, are also changing the procedures for accessing databanks and the pathways through which information is packaged and sold. Computers have made it possible to broadcast information over radio or television channels and by satellite to banks, brokerage houses, and other financial institutions; cable companies carry information services into homes and business over special television channels. For most of the eighties, cable television and broadcasting companies have been attempting to develop new home and business information services to complement their traditional audio and video services. Knight-Ridder and Times Mirror have tried developing the home market for information and retrieval services, and Sears, IBM, Citicorp, and AT&T have combined on two fronts for an assault on the home market. In recent times, the financial services sector has attracted companies supplying fully dedicated, live broadcast television programming.

In the eighties, a new, very-high-capacity storage medium began to receive a great deal of attention from publishers, databank suppliers, software suppliers, computer companies, and others. The new medium, called the compact disk (CD), was a hybrid technology making optimal use of the laser to access and read information stored on the disk, and of the computer to encode and decode the information in digital form, store and retrieve it, and process it as text, graphs, images, voice, and even moving pictures. The CDs' attraction was their very high capacity, high quality, and low cost as a storage and retrieval medium, and their multimedia capabilities. Compact disks were a derivative of optical disks (so-called because of their use of optical lasers), which companies like N.V. Philips of the Netherlands used to store motion pictures for marketing to homes and businesses in the early eighties. (However, the videocassette recorder, based on magnetic recording technology, turned out to be more attractive to the consumer.)

The latest marketing push of optical disk technology has been in personal computer applications. CDs and the personal computer were perfect matches for individuals in the office, in the library, and in the home who needed to tap into vast stores of information. The only weakness CD technology possessed was the high expense of writing and updating the disk, but as a retrieval medium it was a natural evolution of digital computer technology.

By 1985, CDs had made their way into the business market for specialized information. Lotus Development Corporation, for example, marketed a database of stock market information for financial analysts and investors. In the same year, Grolier Inc. announced that it would market a compact disk that stored the twenty-one volumes of its *Encyclopedia Americana* for use in CD drives and personal computers. And the British Broadcasting Corporation announced, in the same year, an ambitious project to produce a second edition of the 900-year-old Domesday Book on video disks for personal computers. Over 1 million volunteers including many professional people began producing 20,000 maps, 120,000 photographs, and 2 million pages of textual information for storage on two video disks, covering topics such as people, demographics, resources, architecture, and social life.

In 1987, IBM, Eastman Kodak, Microsoft, Philips, and a number of other suppliers announced new CD-based products. Microsoft introduced Bookshelf, a single CD containing a dictionary, a thesaurus, a national ZIP code directory, Bartlett's *Familiar Quotations*, the *World Almanac*, and other reference works. Kodak introduced a jukebox-type system that held 150 disks that could be retrieved by a computer in a matter of seconds. The 14-inch disk could hold 6.8 gigabytes (6.8 billion bytes) of memory. Philips was preparing to introduce optical disks that could combine text, video, and sound in an interactive fashion.

As the end of the decade approached, personal computer manufacturers, software suppliers, databank suppliers, publishers, broadcasters, and others were all gearing up for the new age of the interactive optical disk. They were targeting libraries, educational institutions, scientific laboratories, and the business and home markets with learning materials, statistical information, and bibliographical and encyclopedic information in the form of text, graphics, audio, and moving pictures.

**Newspaper and Book Publishers**

Computers offered significant opportunities for publishers in other ways. Some got into the software business in a big way while others began to develop products for the education, personal computer, and home computer markets. In some cases, they were able to create new computer-based products tied to their traditional ones. For example, Houghton Mifflin began to use its *American Heritage Dictionary* and *Roget's Thesaurus* as the foundation for a series of personal computer programs that automatically checked spelling and came up with synonyms. McGraw-Hill's College Division found that a floppy disk produced to assist students using its sociology textbooks was so popular that it increased the demand for the textbook by over 30 percent. McGraw-Hill put into effect a plan making available 200 software titles for sale by the end of 1984.

Newspaper and publishing companies were fully exploiting computer-based media in a number of other ways, and some were diversifying into the entire field of electronic information services. Major newspaper publishers today use the computer to collect, process, compose, and typeset their pages, to send the final product to print, and to actually print the product. They also transmit the information to databank publishers, who sell it to the public through their on-line services.

Since rapid distribution is essential in the age of the computer, more and more publishers are beaming their newspapers via satellite in electronic form to computer systems in distant cities, where they are printed and distributed, often at the same time as they are available in the home market. Computers and communications systems, therefore, enable publishers to market their newspapers almost instantaneously all over the world.

In 1981, the British publication, the *Economist*, began printing in the United States, and its circulation doubled within four years. On July 1, 1985, the *Financial Times* of London also started feeding its international edition via satellite to a printing plant outside Philadelphia, guaranteeing same-day service to twenty-two North American cities. *The Wall Street Journal* had also began to publish and distribute a European edition in the same way in 1983, and since then, *Business Week*, *USA Today*, *Newsweek* and *US News and World Report* have gone the same electronic route.

Obviously the lines between databank suppliers, publishers, and even communications companies are beginning to blur as they are in other sectors of the economy, all owing to the pervasive influence of the computer.

## The New Electronic Financial Information Services Game

The development of a computer-based information infrastructure in the United States in the seventies and eighties created an implosion in an economy already being torn apart by the application of computer technology in other sectors. Without any warning, companies large and small found themselves swept away from their traditional moorings by a tide of technological and industrial forces and into a vast sea of change that threatened their survival and their profitability. In one way or another, they had become part of the new computerized information services business.

Formerly separate and noncompeting industries found themselves playing in a new poker game with high stakes. They included publishers, brokerage houses, broadcasters, newswire companies, and even computer and telecommunications service suppliers. The payoff was a stake in the rapidly developing integrated financial information services business. Each company and each industry brought certain strengths and weaknesses to this game. Each had one or more pieces of the complex puzzle, although none had all the pieces needed to complete it.

When an industrial sector is transformed or when a new industry, such as the electronic financial industry, is born, many companies converge on it looking for opportunities, and anything can happen. A bloody battle can ensue, with consequent casualties. Every company comes away bruised in one way or another, and sometimes a number of companies disappear. The rules are never clear, especially when each company has only one weapon, but there are rules nevertheless.

One strategy is for two companies to form an alliance and pool their strengths and resources. They can simply cooperate and combine their market power, or they can merge completely and integrate their corporate organizations and infrastructures to gain strategic advantages. They can also seek acquisitions to strengthen their competitive position, and they can begin to develop new markets.

This is what happened in the formation of the electronic information industry, particularly in the eighties. The most important industries are illustrated in Figure 2.1. System suppliers, computer service companies, and telecommunications carriers looked for suitors with complementary assets and advantages in information services. They sought to join forces with an information service supplier, a brokerage company, a bank, or a financial service company with marketable information resources.

Banks and finance companies looked for companies with assets and strengths in the information and publishing businesses as well as in the computer services business. Publishers, familiar with the information business, were interested in companies with strengths in telecommunications or computer services. Some brokerage companies were enticed into the information business as well. In one way or another, there were advantages for a company with strengths in one of these market segments to join forces with one in another. Once a supplier had accumulated all the necessary components to provide an electronic information service on a national basis, it could diversify into other segments, developing a full range of services by taking advantage of computer system synergies and economies of scale in the business.

Evidently this diversification, acquisitions, and joint venture activity is an instrinsic part of the transformation of a sector of economic activity and the birth of a new one. It is part of the dynamic mutation and selection process that is characteristic of the competitive capitalist economy that was described by Schumpeter.

The publishers and newswire services were among the most strategically positioned of any of the industries in the formation of the new business. McGraw-Hill, one of the largest book publishers in the United States and the owner of *Business Week*, was one of these. The company began to diversify throughout the range of electronic and electronic-related financial information and databank services. Reader's Digest, another major publisher, entered the business when it purchased *The Source*, an electronic information and bulletin board service supplied in conjunction with an electronic home shopping service.

Dow Jones, the owner of two major financial publications, the *Wall Street Journal* and *Barron's*, also diversified aggressively into the whole field of electronic financial information services through the Dow Jones News/Retrieval Service, which supplied a wide range of news services, stock quotations, and other information services including airline flight information. Knight-Ridder, a major publisher and the owner of several cable television franchises, became very active in the

Figure 2.1. **Industries Involved in the Development of the New Computer-Based Information Industry.**

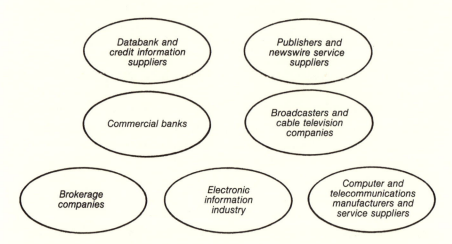

business in the late seventies. Finally, Reuters PLC of London chose to diversify out of the newswire services business and went on to become one of the strongest players in the electronic financial information business.

A second group of players in this new electronic information industry was the brokerage industry. For example, Merrill Lynch entered into a joint agreement with IBM to develop a fully integrated financial information network (IMNET), supplying financial news, quotations, and data. Other brokerage houses, such as E. F. Hutton, followed this lead either by developing their own services and infrastructures or by relying on those of others.

The third group comprised companies already in the financial information business—for example, Dun & Bradstreet and TRW—which were primarily involved in supplying credit information, but that had to diversify in order to develop computer-based services as well.

A fourth group of players in the electronic information business was those companies that developed as suppliers of stock quotation services and those originally in the computer services business but who diversified into the financial quotations business. These included Quotron, Automatic Data Processing (ADP), Telerate, I. P. Sharp, and Bunker Ramo. Quotron, a dominant player in the quotations business, tried a joint venture with AT&T, and was eventually purchased by Citicorp in 1986. Telerate, another major player in the quotations business, was purchased by Dow Jones in 1985 to prevent the company from being bought by Reuters, its most formidable competitor. I. P. Sharp, an international supplier of computer processing and databank services operating out of Canada, was purchased by Reuters in 1987.

ADP, also a major supplier of computer services, had made a name for itself in the quotations business when it created the automated quotations network for the National Association of Securities Dealers (NASD). Subsequently, in 1983, ADP enlarged its share in the stock quotations and front office service business when it acquired GTE's Telenet Information Services, a value-added network (VAN) telecommunications carrier supplying packet-switched digital data services.

Reuters was the largest supplier of on-line services in 1985, with revenues of $505 million, which it received from selling its commodities and securities quotations and news services. These accounted for 80 percent of the total revenues of the company. Following Reuters was Dun & Bradstreet with $325 million in revenues, obtained from its credit and miscellaneous business information services. This constituted only 12 percent of D&B's total revenues but was a growing rapidly segment. Quotron was in third place with revenues of $187 million. Its securities quotation business provided about 91 percent of its total revenues. TRW was in fourth place with revenues of $160 million from credit checks, which represented 3 percent of its total revenues. Mead was in fifth place with revenues of $154 million, which it received from its legal and general business information. This constituted about 6 percent of Mead's revenues in 1985. Telerate's commodities and securities quotations business had revenues of $149 million, for 100 percent of its business. McGraw-Hill received $120 million in revenues from its financial information business, representing 8 percent of its total revenues. Finally, Dow Jones had revenues of $100 million from its securities and general business information, which amounted to 10 percent of its total business revenues. With this brief statistical picture of the new industry, let's look at some of the players and their strategies.

## Reuters Diversifies

Reuters PLC has become a heavyweight in the electronic information business, having been in the business of supplying financial information by one means or another since 1850. The company was well known for its use of carrier pigeons to communicate financial and banking information throughout Europe in the mid-nineteenth century until the development of the telegraph and the telephone. It was in managing applications such as these that the company demonstrated its skills and understanding of the strategic use of information, communications, and money.

Reuters subsequently entered the newswire business and developed an international network of correspondents that collected news and information from around the world, distributing and marketing it everywhere. Throughout the sixties and seventies, the company built an electronic financial services business which grew to dominate the entire electronic information industry.

In the sixties, Reuters began offering financial data services by teletype. In 1971, the company developed a terminal that could display complete sets of stock quotation prices on a single screen, and began to supply currency prices to banks. When currencies were allowed to float in December 1971, the business took off. All major banks, currency traders, multinational corporations, and even governments needed this information almost instantly.

An automated interactive network-based system, capable of storing and retrieving information as soon as a quote or a transaction was made, was superior to one based on paper, or to on any other communications or information medium for that matter. Organizations had to go to Reuters for this service, and the company quickly jumped into an early lead in this emerging business. Subsequently, the company added Eurobonds, commodity prices, and business news to its quotations services. Its network of correspondents around the world proved to be an asset as well, for they could be used to supply news for quotations buyers.

Between 1977 and 1982, Reuters' revenues grew tenfold and its services to financial institutions accounted for 85 percent of its total business, overshadowing its news to media, which constituted 5 percent. Through its now-famous Monitor Service, it was providing a relatively complete range of financial information comprising financial news and data and including quotations on commodities, currencies, and securities. The Monitor Service was one of Reuters' most successful products and it was a prerequisite to fully electronic trading worldwide in foreign currencies, which the company began in 1981.

Reuters proceeded to further expand its services, tailoring its financial news and information for specific market segments. It started bundling services together for the oil industry, for example. It also implemented a plan to provide information profiles on about fifty nations, supplying news, statistics, and political information to large multinational corporations, credit analysts, risk specialists, and banks.

Another service under development was the provision of historical information from Reuters' files of data, in table and graphical formats, so that trends could be spotted more easily and quickly. Reuters also produced a sophisticated communications strategy to get more mileage out of its networks. It designed the software so that it would allow its customers to manipulate as well as retrieve information from its database. One software program was created to help arbitragers collect data so they could spot opportunities more quickly, and another to allow subscribers to conduct financial transactions in currencies, bonds, and bullion.

Reuters chose to expand its operations through acquisitions as well. In February 1985, the company purchased Rich Company, a Chicago supplier of communications systems for financial trading rooms. In March of the same year, it signed a deal with Instinet, which supplied automated trading in equities and options in the United States. Reuters wanted to market this stock trading service outside the United States as well as to put stocks of non-U.S. exchanges on the service for marketing in the United States. These moves were designed to ensure greater coverage of U.S. news and stock quotations.

To further strengthen its position, the company set out to acquire other businesses, especially those that let subscribers perform transactions via the Reuters network. In March 1987, Reuters announced its intention of purchasing 100 percent of I. P. Sharp, one of the most successful international computer time-sharing companies, based in Canada. The acquisition made Reuters an instant owner of an international computer and communications network connecting over twenty-two countries, and put it in the computer-processing and databank services industry as well as in the communications and electronic mail industries. With each acquisition, Reuters was becoming an ever more dominant player in the evolving global information industry.

**Dun & Bradstreet Evolves**

Dun & Bradstreet is a major player in the electronic financial information services business. In 1986, the company had some 3000 products and services. From its origins in 1841 as a supplier of credit information, D&B proceeded to diversify in the 1960s and 1970s into an information services conglomerate through the acquisition of companies supplying yellow pages and classified telephone directories, financial ratings (such as Moody's Investor Services Inc.), and even broadcasting. In the late seventies, it began making several big moves to take advantage of the opportunities confronting it, which proved to be key to its long-term growth and profitability.

To complement its vast databases of credit information, corporate information, and household demographic information, D&B acquired National CSS in 1979, a leader in computer time-sharing services and software development. National CSS gave D&B an enormous technological capability to develop and diversify into many new financial information markets, to market its database services nationally and thereby penetrate new markets, to tailor its database resources by packaging information for specialized market segments, and to provide a broad base for major forays throughout the financial services sector. D&B's databanks contained credit information on over 80,000 companies, financial information on over 15,000 corporations, and demographic and purchasing information on over 65 million households. All these could be marketed through National CSS's extensive telecommunications network facilities. D&B's new processing, information, and network resources also provided the infrastructure necessary to enter segments of the brokerage and banking service business.

In 1984, D&B acquired A.C. Nielsen, the largest market and media research company in the United States. In the same year, it acquired Datastream PLC, a major British supplier of electronic financial data offered by computers. By 1985, D&B's domestic credit information service was bringing in $425 million, more than half from electronic delivery, and its aftertax margin was about 30 percent. In March 1988, D&B paid $140 million cash for Interactive Data Corporation, which supplied securities information, corporate performance data, and prices on equity and fixed income securities. As the decade of the nineties approached, Dun and Bradstreet was becoming a powerhouse of intelligent capital.

## McGraw-Hill Expands

McGraw-Hill, a pure information company, has a major stake in the electronic and paper publishing business. The company was founded in 1899, and in 1929 started *Business Week*. It bought F. W. Dodge in

1961 and Standard & Poor's in 1966, both suppliers of information to business about business. In 1979, it fought off a bitter takeover attempt by American Express, which had begun to recognize the opportunities in the information services business. In the same year, McGraw-Hill paid $103 million for Data Resources, which was in the business of economic and econometric information and forecasting.

The company was already in a number of other traditional information-related businesses, but competitors were beating it in the new electronic segments of McGraw-Hill's existing markets. Companies such as Dun and Bradstreet were already dominating electronic publishing, causing McGraw-Hill to lose considerable ground overall. Electronic information markets were growing anywhere from 22 to 25 percent per year compared to 11 percent for the traditional publishing business.

In the early part of the eighties, under its new president, Joe Dionne, McGraw-Hill started on a new course to gain what it believed was its share of the new electronic markets. In 1984, it undertook a complete reorganization, abandoning its old organization along media lines in favor of one along nineteen market focus groups. With this reorganization, McGraw-Hill hoped to become a more market-oriented company. It hoped to use and to profit from its tremendous wealth of information by tailoring it to particular markets rather than by simply selling it in bulk in a general marketplace.

Dionne believed that in the nineties, most large corporations would be big purchasers of electronic information to feed their information centers, and he wanted his company to begin immediately to develop the products and to position itself for this market. He started by concentrating the efforts of each of the nineteen market focus groups on the many new products, by purchasing other companies outright, and by entering into joint ventures with other strong companies having complementary assets in the information business.

One of McGraw-Hill's first acquisitions was Monchik-Weber, which delivered stock and commodity information. The new company complemented McGraw-Hill's other big electronic information concerns, specifically Standard & Poor's and Data Resources. In 1985, McGraw-Hill entered into a joint venture with Citibank to set up a twenty-four-hour worldwide trading, information, and financial services company for commodity markets. The company also started joint ventures with two cable companies to deliver news and financial information to cable subscribers who had their own computers.

Like other major concerns in the information business, McGraw-Hill depends on telecommunications and computers for its competitive strength, so in 1986 the company embarked on a strategy to begin developing its own computer networks as a way of reaching its target customers who were otherwise inaccessible using the networks of other vendors such as computer, telephone, and cable companies. It went on to acquire a number of companies to help reach its goals, including a systems company, a microcomputer market research company, and several smaller companies specializing in new markets.

By 1986, McGraw-Hill was publishing 30 specialty magazines, the biggest and best known being *Business Week*. Standard & Poor's Compustat database contained basic information on 6500 companies ranging from their earnings to descriptions of their businesses. Standard & Poor's also ranked $170 billion worth of corporate and municipal debt. The S&P 500 stock index was another product that was a stock market barometer as well as a widely followed economic indicator.

Many of McGraw-Hill's very aggressive moves have been part of an overall strategy to build an information empire. Its goal has been to build a financial and economic information company that furnishes a complete range of financial information services to complement its traditional information business.

### The Evolving Computer-Mediated
### Global Information Infrastructure

Throughout the eighties, a new information-intensive economic system was evolving, with the computer as the driving force. The computer also constituted the essential infrastructure for the operation and organization of an emerging global economic and political system. Every company was becoming dependent on this computer-mediated information infrastructure for its survival and profitability.

Newspapers and book publishers were collecting, processing, and distributing their products throughout the world using computer-based infrastructures. They were beaming their computer-edited, computer-composed, and computer-assembled editions by satellite to major cities of the nation and around the globe for reception by computers for computer typesetting and printing.

Newswire companies were collecting their material over telephone lines from correspondents all over the world who were using small, easy-to-use personal computers, word processors, and portable computers. This information was being distributed by telephone and other telecommunications systems to their subscribers, who also were equipped with computers, both big and small, and who assembled it for publishing or public broadcasting. Some book publishers were shipping their manuscripts to Asia or Africa for keyboarding, where labor was cheaper, and having their ready-made manuscripts sent back on magnetic disks or beamed back by satellite, where, once again, the computers took charge. Computers were taking over all stages of the information production and distribution process, from the collection and processing to the editing, typesetting, and printing.

Computer-based media, which included magnetic disks, optical disks, and computer networks, were distributing information throughout the world, where it was printed or accessed on-line at an ever-increasing speed.

The new computer-mediated global information infrastructure is a universal information- and decision-making medium for the operation of a new global social, political, and economic order. It mediates the essential activities of brokerage companies, banks, and retailers. It facilitates the operation of stock markets, currency markets, and commodity markets. Insurance companies, real estate companies, and advertising agencies use it in strategic ways, and it is fundamental to the publishing, broadcasting, and travel and entertainment businesses.

In all of these ways the new information hyperstructure is rapidly becoming essential to the existence and survival of every corporation, every market, and every national economy.

# 3

# Computerizing the Money and Payments Systems: The New Public Landscape of a Computer-Mediated Economy

### The Money Economy Goes Electronic

Money is to the economic system what blood is to the human body. It facilitates the operations of the entire economic system, and without it the economy would fail to function. Computerization was changing the meaning, significance, and behavior of money in the sixties and seventies; by the end of the eighties it had also changed the way the economic system was organized and how it operated. The computer had transformed the public landscape of American society, as it had all industrialized societies throughout the world.

A new breed of manager emerged to take over many leading banking, financial, and other institutions. Computer technology was designed and applied both to improve the quality, efficiency, and cost-effectiveness of services, and to provide many innovative kinds of services. The new breed of executive used computers and computer networks as weapons in the fight for a greater share of local, regional, and national markets. For the first time in their history, computers were determining who the winners and losers were in entire industries and sectors of the economy.

Before computers came along, banking was a highly profitable and highly regulated business in America with many thousands of small banks enjoying a geographical monopoly, protected as they were from competition by state and federal regulators. After the computer, the industry was substantially deregulated; thousands of small banks and many large banks were threatened with insolvency, competing head to head against huge national and international financial conglomerates and giant retailers.

Before the computer age, banking and financial services companies and retailers operated in a low-tech environment; they were paper-based organizations employing large numbers of people engaged in processing transactions and accounting. In the computer age, they became very technologically-intensive organizations in which people and paper played an increasingly smaller role in their processing operations.

Most service-based organizations, to one degree or another, had also become intensely network-based, capital-intensive organizations dominated by automated teller machines, retail computer terminals, computerized bank cards, and intelligent plastic. By the end of the eighties, the money and payments systems in the United States and around the world were well on their way to becoming fully electronic. A new computer-based environment was emerging.

## ATMs, POS Systems, and Bank Cards

By the mid-seventies, computers had restructured many back offices of banking and financial institutions, where the truly big processing tasks associated with accounting and record keeping were located; the next frontier was the front office. More efficient, high-capacity computer systems that could support distributed processing and were complemented by new network-based systems made it increasingly cost-effective to extend service right out to the front office, where bank tellers and customers were located. Computers became the means by which customer services could be improved and transformed.

When bank tellers went on-line, they were able to access customer accounts in the computer files, record cash deposits, withdrawals, and check payments, transfer funds between accounts, and provide information to customers about their accounts. But the work was still labor intensive; lineups were getting longer; service was slow; and overall operations remained inefficient.

The human teller had, in effect, become a serious bottleneck in the operation of the more efficient and competitive banking system of the late seventies, and managers began to look to automation for a solution. If computers were so superior in capturing, processing, storing, and retrieving information, mediating banking transactions, performing accounting functions, and communicating information among people, why not bypass the human teller altogether and put the customer instantaneonsly on-line with the computer?

Why not let customers access the bank's computer systems directly so that they could make deposits, obtain cash, transfer funds between accounts, and pay bills?

The technology was developing to do all of this, but several major obstacles had to be overcome. The human tellers displaced from the business would have to be retrained and relocated to other parts of the business. Security was a great concern, because it was dangerous and irresponsible to let customers access the company computers without safeguards. Illegal use, tampering with the accounts of other customers, and theft had to be prohibited, and the technology had to be developed to ensure that this did not occur. A final hurdle was customer acceptance. Would the majority of customers give up personal service for the added convenience and perhaps better quality and variety of services if they were provided by a machine?

The technology came in the form of the automated teller machine (ATM) and the magnetic strip card. The ATM consisted of a computer that the customer accessed from a keyboard and display panel to withdraw cash, make deposits, and pay bills. The machines were made secure by coding a magnetic strip on the back of the card with recorded information that the computer could read to identify the user and his or her accounting information. The systems were made more secure by requiring the account holder to type in an access code which the computer could verify; only once verification was successfully completed would the computer permit the customer to proceed with the transaction.

The public gradually accepted the new automated teller machines as a convenient way of doing much of the traditional business with the bank. ATMs could be located in many convenient locations—on street corners, in shopping centers, as well as at the various branches of the bank. They could be operated 24 hours a day unattended and give customers immediate access to their accounts for up-to-date information and better management of their funds. Bank balances and transaction records could be displayed and printed for the convenience of the customer. Customers could easily switch temporary surplus cash into daily interest savings accounts or invest in money market funds, thereby enjoying a better rate of return. Lineups were shorter. None of this was conceivable before the automated teller machine made its debut.

The magnetic strip card could also serve as a means of identification as well as a universal payments instrument for the public and for retailers; because of this it became a convenient and safe substitute for checks and cash. The same computer technology that made the ATM possible was also utilized in what has become known as the retail point-of-sale (POS) system. Here the card could be used for customer identification and account verification, and the POS terminal could record transaction information and communicate it to a central computer.

As computer networks evolved, it became possible for retailers to connect directly to banks and financial institutions so that customer accounts could be debited and credited automatically. The proliferation of ATMs, POS systems, and computer cards made retailers and the public less dependent on the commercial banks because they could take their business to other financial institutions, for example savings and loan companies and credit card companies such as American Express. Banks, retailers, thrifts, and credit card companies could also connect their ATM and POS terminals into regional and national networks to obtain greater efficiency. These evolutions allowed retailers, financial services companies, and credit card companies to offer services over which commercial banks originally had a monopoly. The commercial banks were in effect bypassed—in other words, losing ground to the competition.

One of the major reasons for the big push into ATMs was economic. The *Economist* described the new economics of computerized banking in the mid-eighties in the following way:

> In a system built on paper transactions, unit costs are roughly stable once a bank has reached a certain moderate size. So big banks have no cost advantage per se over their medium-sized competitors. By contrast . . . electronic banking involves high initial capital costs but low marginal cost on each individual transaction. For example, the cost of an automatic teller machine (ATM) runs to between $25,000 and $50,000—depending on its sophistication and location. But the cost of each individual transaction once the machine is up and running may be as little as half that of a conventional deposit or withdrawal processed by a human teller. And this type of cost equation holds for many other processing functions in banks, whether they are directly with the customer (the so-called "front office") or internally (the "back office").[1]

The new economics meant that significant economies of scale were possible for standard transactions such as deposits and withdrawals. As the *Economist* noted:

Bigger is better. And because it is becoming more difficult for banks to differentiate their standardized products—such as cheque accounts—from those offered by their rivals, the profits will be made by those banks which can become the lowest cost, highest volume producers. That is a startling change from the old concept of customer service for all with which many branch managers are still embued.[2]

The *Nilson Report*, a newsletter that tracks ATM developments in the U.S., corroborated these costing estimates. It determined that the average cost of completing one ATM transaction was 66 cents compared with the average teller cost of between 90 cents and $1.20. About 41 billion checks were used in the United States each year in 1985. The cost of printing, processing, and returning them was about $1 each for a total of $41 billion, or 20 percent of the annual revenues of the 5,800 member banks of the Federal Reserve System. ATMs were adopted to cut these costs.

Chemical Bank is reported to have installed the first automated teller machine in the United States in 1969. In 1970, Banc One in Columbus, Ohio, began installing ATMs as cash dispensers in its various branches around the state. Between 1973 and 1985, U.S. banks acquired 71,000 ATMs, at a cost of $2.1 billion plus a six-year payback. It was an expensive but necessary proposition for banks to adopt ATMs in a big way, but the enormous economies of scale they introduced into the business resulted in considerable reductions in the cost of processing transactions, making banks more competitive.

ATMs also performed many other services, thereby lowering transaction costs even further. These advantages, together with the possibilities of sharing and configuring ATMs into networks, added to their cost savings and contributed to their strategic significance.

For many banks, it became technologically feasible and economically attractive to put a terminal in a particular location where it had been previously unfeasible. In some cases, fully automated bank branches could be serviced from a central site using telephone lines to communicate between customers and bank staff for information and assistance when required. In other localities, ATMs complemented the work of banking personnel, who could provide assistance unavailable through the automated machines. For most banks, who were feeling the heat of growing competitive pressures from retailers, ATMs also provided a way of decreasing the size of their branches. In 1984, for example, some banks began to test no-cash mini-branches, branches that did not deal in cash but that offered services that the ATMs did not, such as opening an account and applying for an ATM card.

Automated teller machines proved to be popular and convenient with the public, the banking industry, and retailers. They soon became a permanent fixture on the public landscape of the new computer-mediated economy.

## The Growth of Magnetic Strip Cards

By the late seventies, computer systems, ATMs, POS systems, and computerized bank cards had emerged as strategic weapons in the arsenals of companies in a growing number of industries, as Figure 3.1 illustrates. Banking and finance companies as well as retailers, in particular, were in a pitched battle for new markets, new customers, and new services made possible and economically attractive by computerization. Computer capital had become a valuable asset in concentrating and controlling enormous industrial power in the new banking and financial services marketplace.

The economic advantages associated with the scale of ATM networking and network operations resulted in a new set of competitive equations in which strength and success were measured in network and processing capacity and efficiency, and in national market presence. These improved economics dictated that as the number of ATMs an institution had in the marketplace increased, as they became more strategically located, and as the number and variety of services they offered grew, the more potential customers the institution could serve, the better position it was in competitively, and the more valuable the network of machines.

In these ways, ATMs became the means to consolidate old markets, to penetrate new markets, and to develop services on a national and an international scale.

Similar economics were operating in the magnetic card market. The card had become an extremely valuable asset and a source of strategic advantage. The consuming public loved the convenience of computer cards and the many purposes they served. The more uses these cards had, the more valuable they became to the public. But they became even more valuable to the company issuing them, especially if they were widely used and distributed nationally and internationally.

Companies having the deepest card penetration also benefited from their higher frequency of use, the greater demand by the general public and by companies wanting to accept them as means of payment, and by

Figure 3.1. **Industries Involved in the Development of the Computer-Based Money and Payments System.**

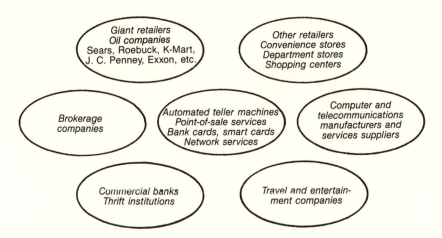

their interconnection with ATM networks. Since the company owning the card could charge a transaction fee for usage, the more the cards were in the market and the more that companies accepted them, the higher the revenue the company issuing it could receive. In the extreme case, the company issuing the card could enjoy considerable monopoly power over the use of these cards. For these reasons, the cards became very valuable assets.

For many years, banks were prohibited from issuing credit cards, but these restrictions were lifted in the late seventies when banks were allowed to compete directly with other purveyors of credit cards and magnetic strip cards. From then on, banks and nonbanks began to strive fiercely for a share of what looked like a gold mine in new services and new sources of revenue, profit, and growth. The banks immediately lined up behind Visa and MasterCard against competitors such as American Express, which dominated the credit card business. Some banks such as Citibank saw their proprietary cards as integral to their future. Those companies involved in the travel and entertainment business—including airlines, restaurants, and those issuing traveler's checks—also had an upper hand when it came to cards.

Major retailers such as Sears, Roebuck, which enjoyed large national retailing operations and distribution outlets and operated in many diverse markets, had an obvious advantage in issuing their own cards. The big oil companies, of course, were already in an ideal position financially and nationally to capitalize on their broad customer base with their own credit cards. Every major company operating regional or national networks of automated teller machines could also benefit from issuing its own card.

What attracted many of these companies was the profitability of cards. In the mid-eighties, for example, banks were charging anywhere from 13 to 22 percent on unpaid balances on their Visa and MasterCard accounts, compared with less than half that for traditional loans at the prime rate. In addition, they received an annual fee for each card in circulation. Major banks were also doing a profitable business in processing credit card transactions for merchants, taking 2 to 3.5 percent off the total charges and passing 1.5 percent on to the bank that issued the card.

American Express was getting most of its card revenues by processing all its own transactions and charging merchants 3 to 5 percent of their billings. Its annual card fees in 1984 were $35 for the green card, $65 for the gold card, and $250 for the platinum card. Its total card fees exceeded $650 million in 1984. Estimates were that the company netted $252 million for its card business in 1984, amounting to 42 percent of its total corporate profits.

By 1984, the biggest players in the U.S. credit card market were Visa, MasterCard, American Express, Sears, and Citicorp. Visa had 77.2 million credit cards in circulation with billings of $60 billion, while MasterCard had 60 million cards and billings of $49 billion. American Express in the travel and entertainment business had 15 million cards in circulation with billings of $36.6 billion. Sears, Roebuck was the largest retailer issuing cards with 60 million in circulation and billings of $13.6 billion. Citicorp had 6 million MasterCard and Visa cards in circulation, 2.2 million Diners Club cards, 300,000 Carte Blanche cards, and 1 million Choice cards.

## The Age of ATM Networks

If ATMs by themselves were competitive weapons, then networks of ATMs were soon to become an even more important development, especially when operated over a regional and nationwide basis. Besides being a source of tremendous economies of scale, ATMs became a form of high value-added real estate, as well as a valuable medium for marketing a wide range of financial services, especially when in a network environment covering very large geographical areas and when located in convenient, high-traffic public areas. For these reasons, networking became a key element to banks, finance, and retail service companies that previously had concentrated their efforts on developing proprietary networks that were not interconnected or shared in any way.

But as competitive pressures became more intense, especially in the latter part of the eighties, it became evident that the first organization to construct a truly national network could enjoy enormous advantages over its competitors. A national network required a national presence together with huge outlays of capital and new technological and managerial strengths at a time when competition was demanding more productive use of all resources. This meant that only the largest organizations could afford to build national proprietary networks. Those that could not do so by themselves, however, were able to compete by sharing and interconnecting their networks. Major institutions enjoying market penetration and competitive advantages in complementary geographical markets obviously had an incentive to offer reciprocal access to their networks for their respective clients and customers.

This cooperation meant new opportunities including regional, national, or international coverage, increased customer convenience and perceived value, as well as the chance to develop new business. It also made it more difficult for competitors to penetrate network markets and enabled cooperators to share the enormous capital investments and to shorten significantly the time horizon required to develop completely national markets.

Shared ATM networks opened up windows of opportunity to network owners. The networks' high fixed costs meant that the owners could more rapidly write off their investment by charging increased fees to the customers of other networks. For every customer transaction, for example, network owners were able to levy fees for access, communications, processing, and managing the transaction. Reciprocal agreements of this nature eventually enabled companies to expand their services from regional into national markets and from national into global markets.

This kind of cooperation was not restricted to large companies. Small companies could obtain similar advantages by cooperating to form national networks or by buying a franchise. Network operators evolved to fill a gap for these smaller companies by supplying the computer network and processing facilities on a fee-for-service basis. In some cases, these operators offered a complete package of services, from site leasing, terminal leasing, and network and processing to maintenance and operation. These functions went a long way to giving even the smallest companies many of the competitive advantages enjoyed by the much larger companies.

### Shared ATM Networks for Banks and Retailers

Sharing had strategic advantages for every banking and financial concern as well as for retailers. It gave banks the means to circumvent restrictions on branching across state or county lines. For example, Pulse and Mpact gave Texas bankers an opportunity to offer statewide services to their customers in spite of intrastate branch banking restrictions. For small banks, networking ATMs was a way of competing with large banks, which themselves were beginning to realize that there were limits to the speed and the number of terminals they could afford to deploy in building national networks.

But the pressure on the major banks to seriously consider sharing was prompted by other factors as well, particularly the actions of the nonbanks. One threat came from the securities broker PaineWebber, which gained access to MasterCard's MasterTeller network for its Resource Management Account (RMA) customers. This access came through State Street Bank & Trust Company of Boston, which issued a MasterCard gold card to PaineWebber's RMA customers.

Other threats were coming from supermarkets that wanted to offer their customers improved check cashing services. Supermarkets began to consider buying ATMs and POS terminals for their customers' use and charging the banks for access instead of the other way around. It was this menace to their payment business that prompted banks in Florida and California to form statewide shared networks. In Florida, they formed a network called Honor and laid the infrastructure for a more sophisticated network offering a greater variety of services than the supermarkets had envisioned.

Some thrift institutions were also busy building ATM networks. First Texas Savings Association, one of the leaders in the ATM business, did so not only to defend but also to make money. First Texas chose to approach the market through the use of a shared network to interconnect 1000 ATMs in 7-Eleven stores throughout the state.

To make its network profitable, the company needed access to the state's major shared networks, Mpact and Pulse. It obtained permission to interconnect with these networks only after it had launched and subsequently won an antitrust suit against their owners. First Texas then contracted with the owner of 7-Eleven to undertake the venture, agreeing to pay 7-Eleven rent for the terminal's floor space together with a transaction fee. First Texas itself would collect fees from other banks connected to the network. The company could never have justified the enormous investment in its ATM network without ensuring that all its statewide customers could gain access to the terminals and without the fees the banks paid.

There are, however, sacrifices to be made in joining a shared network. Each company in a shared network suffers a loss of corporate identity to some degree, and this was perceived to be very important to companies such as Citicorp, which decided to forgo the opportunity and to concentrate on building a proprietary network. Each company involved in a shared arrangement also suffers from a lack of control over the network, its operations, its standards, and its efficiencies, as well as the kinds of services it offers.

By 1986, ATMs had reached the point where consolidation in the industry was taking place rapidly and sharing was gaining momentum. By then, according to Raymond Farrell, AVP of ATM operations at Chemical Bank, "ATMs [had] passed the stage where banks [used] them as marketing vehicles because virtually all banks [had] proprietary networks. Having one [was] not a competitive advantage anymore. The question [was], if all your customers [wanted] ATM access, how [did] you deliver the service relative to where they [lived] and [worked] without going to the poorhouse."[3]

## A Wired Up America

In 1983, there were seven national shared ATM networks in the United States. These included American Express Company's Express Cash, a network of traveler's check dispensers that also interchanged with bank-owned ATMs and linked 1000 terminals in 16 states; Master-Teller, owned by MasterCard, which linked 1000 ATMs in 24 states; Visa's ATM network linking 3500 terminals in 30 states; Nationet, based in Dallas, Texas, linking 13 regional networks consisting of 6000 terminals in 26 states; Automatic Data Processing Inc.'s The Exchange, connecting 1000 terminals in 33 states; and Cirrus, a national network started in 1982 by 13 banks, with 3500 terminals in 41 states. Plus, another bank-owned network, embarked on a plan to put 3000 terminals on-line by the end of 1985.

The number of ATMs in the United States had expanded to 64,000 by the end of 1986, with 46,000 belonging to regional shared networks. Predictions were that by 1990, all ATMs would belong to shared networks of one kind or another. The Cirrus ATM network had expanded to 13,416 on-line terminals while Plus had 10,500. There were 100 regional networks in existence, of which the largest was the Texas-based Pulse network with 4,434 ATMs. NYCE was another regional shared network, formed in 1985 by 8 banks in 19 counties in New York, New Jersey, and Connecticut. The largest nonshared network was that of Citibank with 19,500 terminals.

## Competition Heats Up in the Credit Card Business

The credit card business was a strategic target among retailers and other financial service companies in the eighties, especially as the momentum toward financial supermarkets gained strength. Competition increased among banks such as Citicorp, retailers such as Sears, Roebuck, and other companies such as American Express, all of which were developing financial supermarkets.

The business became an important target for Citicorp in the early eighties in its effort to compete in and dominate the entire range of financial services. Under its leader, John Reed, Citicorp purchased Diners Club and Carte Blanche, which were targeted at the market dominated by American Express. A third card company purchased by Citicorp was renamed Choice and marketed throughout the United States as an all-purpose card. Citicorp promoted it aggressively with a line of credit, no annual fees, rebates on certain purchases, and the choice of several interest-bearing accounts with attractive rates. These multiple features were built into the marketing strategy to enable Choice to gain as wide and rapid an acceptance across the United States as possible.

American Express, which dominated the travel and entertainment business, used its position in this market to launch forays into every segment of the financial services sector, with the American Express Card one of its most effective weapons. It began to develop new markets—including the small business market, the women's market, and the retail market—with its Optima card launched in March 1987.

By the mid-eighties, Sears Corporation was well established as a financial services supermarket and it was making a number of tactical moves in the credit card business. With its enormous financial and retail strength, it could compete with the biggest competitors in the financial services business. It launched an all-purpose card called Discover, which enabled its customers to access its network of ATMs as well as use the card for services offered by Sears's securities subsidiary, Dean Witter, and its banking subsidiary, Sears Savings Bank. It was also working with Phillips Petroleum to market its sophisticated electronic network to check customer credit and process credit purchases.

Other retailers besides Sears were very active in the credit card and electronic financial transactions business in the early part of the eighties. In 1983, J. C. Penney set up a new subsidiary called J. C. Penney Systems Services to market its electronic network services. Shell Oil and Gulf Oil were two of its customers. They paid J. C. Penney 10 to 13 cents per transaction to check customer credit and to put through credit transactions. The company also signed up a bank in Utah, which used the network to transmit data for its own bank card operations.

By the mid-eighties, banks were being forced to pay for credit card–processing services by retailers. Publix, a $3-billion supermarket chain in Florida, installed a network of ATMs in its outlets and began installing POS terminals as a means of achieving what it estimated were cost savings of $750,000 in check processing alone. It began charging banks 40 cents for ATM withdrawals and 15 cents for POS transactions. Mobil also built a POS debit system and provided its customers with an incentive to use it by giving them a 4-cent discount on each gallon of gas they purchased. By the end of 1985, Mobil had about 1000 terminals in high-volume gas stations across the United States and planned to double that number within the next year.

In Phoenix, Exxon began issuing its own debit card to customers who were willing to sign a form authorizing the company to debit their accounts through the automated clearinghouse (ACH) system. Exxon gave its customers an incentive to use the new system in the form of a 5 percent discount on their gasoline purchases. By taking the ACH route and initiating debits through Chase Manhattan Bank, Exxon was in a position to issue a nationwide debit card without waiting for the banking industry to come up with one.

Banks prefer the debit card to checks because the costs associated with processing checks are significantly greater than the costs of doing the equivalent task using the debit card. But as the decade progressed, it began to look as if the commercial banks were not the leaders they envisioned themselves to be in the debit card business. Instead, it appeared that retailers were taking the lead. However, it might be impossible for a debit card system to develop without the cooperation of and major participation by the banking community.

## Universal, Multipurpose Retail Machines

The nature of ATMs goes far beyond their original design and intent. They have become strategic because of their universal processing, communications, and multifunctional capabilities. They can be used to dispense insurance, stocks, and bonds, to provide access to credit, and to obtain loans. Merrill Lynch uses them for accessing cash management services and money market funds, for buying and selling brokerage services, and for managing investments. American Express uses them for dispensing everything from cash and credit cards to travelers checks. Sears uses them for furnishing cash and credit and selling other services.

The new machines coming onto the market in the late eighties were equipped with capabilities that enabled them to talk to their users, and with video disks that let them display photographs, graphics, and moving images in full color. The versatility of the ATMs explains why so many financial and nonfinancial companies, including retailers, developed an obsession about them.

ATMs also incorporate the basic technology for more sophisticated financial and many nonfinancial services. They are being used to automatically sell theater, airline, and lottery tickets, and even to take bets at the horse races. In the early eighties, Avis began to use ATMs in its automated return system, which allows clients to return rented cars, key in the relevant information, and obtain a receipt automatically. American Airlines began testing ATMs to allow their customers to make flight reservations, pay their purchase fees, and receive their tickets automatically.

The same technology is being deployed in the retail services industry for the automatic dispensing of food, videocassettes, automobile accessories, and other goods. In these ways, the automated teller machine technology can be augmented and applied to automate entire retail outlets. Combined with robot vehicles, ATMs can deploy the robots to retrieve, assemble, package, and deliver a complete package of commodities and services without human attendance. The significance of the ATM was captured by *Datamation* when it observed, ". . . the ATM is leading the way toward the self-service society and all the convenience that the American consumer is widely believed to prize so highly."[4]

By the end of the decade, there were many competing solutions to the way electronic funds transfer services and the computer-based financial services landscape of the United States should evolve, and many questions were being raised about the roles of ATMs, POS, ACHs, and the banks, retailers, and other players who owned them. According to D. Dale Browning, president of Plus System Inc., one of the national shared ATM networks:

> . . . [the potential of shared networks runs far beyond point-of-sale and home banking.] . . . there is even more potential on the wholesale or corporate side. The networks could be used as an alternative to the Federal Reserve System to clear checks electronically. . . for such corporate cash management products as cash concentration, funds transfer to disbursement accounts and vendor payments. In many ways, they could provide an alternative to the bank-operated automated clearinghouses (ACH), another electronic funds transfer network. . . . [Others . . . take the opposite view. Instead of creating new ATM networks, the industry should adapt the existing automated clearinghouse system to support point-of-sale and ATM interchange.][5]

### Intelligent Plastic

Computerized cards have become the passports to the electronic computer age, and they, too, are proliferating far beyond the universal payment and identification instruments that we take for granted today. The potential is particularly great with the so-called smart card, a device or a card about the size of an ordinary credit card but that can either contain large amounts of information in a magnetic strip or can incorporate the major components of a basic computer. A product of the latest developments in computer and semiconductor technology, the latter version of the smart card has sufficient memory to store large amounts of information, keys to input and manipulate the contents of memory, a small display to communicate to the user, and a microprocessor to process all this information. The recent introduction of computerized personal diaries is a widespread example of this innovation. This card, or computer, is capable of functioning as a debit card or a payment card as well as of capturing accounting and transaction information, which can be stored in its memory for access, processing, and printing at a later time. It is also possible to attach the smart card to a small printer.

In France, when you want to purchase certain items at retail outlets or to use a telephone, for example, users first have to buy a smart card from a bank. This card acts as a substitute for cash, giving the users the right to purchase goods and services up to the amount stored in the card's memory, which is coded when users purchase the card. Each time users make a transaction, the cost of the transaction is deducted from the card's memory until the purchase limit is reached. Then users have to go back to the bank and pay to have the card replenished. This is only one form in which the emerging computerized payment society could function. There are many other ways depending on which solution and which organization or institution we choose to administer them.

Other enhancements and uses of the smart cards are on the horizon. Some could have a holographic image of the user or owner on the front, enabling the card to be used for security and identification. NASA and medical and health care companies are experimenting with their use for storing personal medical records, and commercial uses of them are planned in the United States for the year 1989. The cards could be used by individuals to carry around their personal medical history in their pockets. They are also being used in applications such as building, military, and home security. For all these reasons, computer cards can more properly be called the personal electronic passports to the computer age.

## The Computer Creates a National and Global Financial Village

ATMs have become as common as public telephone booths in shopping malls, supermarkets, retail stores, and convenience stores. They can be seen in airports, restaurants, gas stations, and the lobbies of hotels and private companies. Point-of-sale systems are proliferating throughout these same organizations and locations and are becoming common at all major retail outlets, gasoline stations, airline ticketing offices, vending machines, and fully automated retail outlets. Credit cards, debit cards, smart cards, and variants of them are already more common than driver's licenses; some people have special wallets just to accommodate the many cards they feel they need to conduct their daily business.

It is rapidly becoming a world in which computer systems and networks form the essential infrastructure of a new financial economy and indeed the entire society. Local banking and financial networks are merging into regional ones, which are in turn merging into national networks. National computer and communications networks are merging into global ones. National ATM networks are interconnecting banks, financial service companies, and retailers. National POS networks are connecting retailers with banks and financial institutions. Banks are testing ways of penetrating the home market, and soon retailers, banks, insurance companies, and brokerage houses will be connected to the home, perhaps to be joined by databank producers, publishers, and stock exchanges. Every home and every individual will be interconnected to this global money network.

Computer networks constitute the infrastructure for the operation of the automated clearinghouses, which interconnect member banks and serve in the daily exchange of checks, drafts, and notes among their members. A computer network called Fedwire connects the member banks of the Federal Reserve System with the Federal Reserve Board, the Treasury, and other government agencies. It enables the Treasury Department to transfer government securities to its member banks and helps the Fed to fulfill its policy, supervisory, and administrative responsibilities. It also permits banks to transfer reserve account balances and to exchange funds for transaction purposes with one another.

CHIPS (Clearinghouse Interbank Payments System) is a computer network that makes possible the electronic transfer of large amounts of funds between member banks, thus eliminating the need for checks. The network connects user terminals of its members by telephone lines and routes messages among the various banks to facilitate transfers. Balances among the various banks are settled through the Federal Reserve System. Bankwire, which is similar to Fedwire, is another computer communications network used by an association of banks to transfer messages and funds among its members.

(In 1985, the volume of electronic money transmitted around the United States over Fedwire and CHIPS had mushroomed to more than $1.3 trillion daily, about a quarter of the annual GNP, and was growing at an annual rate of 25 percent. The balances held in the Federal Reserve Bank by individual banks were turning over 100 times per day while the value of negative balances accumulated by all banks had reached a staggering $100 billion by noon on a typical day. A single bank's overdraft could reach many times its capital base, and concern was increasing in U.S. financial circles that one bank's inability to pay could result in a domino effect and trigger a series of bank failures throughout the nation.)

Computerized banking networks are going global, as are national banking, payments, and transactions services. For years, the international banking community has been communicating, clearing, and settling accounts among its members through SWIFT (Society for Worldwide Interbank Financial Telecommunications). In 1984, Hudson's Bay and Simpsons in Canada announced an agreement to give their credit card holders access to the 5000 terminals of Nationet, the Dallas-based network. In 1985, the Bank of Montreal announced the interconnection of its network of 500 terminals in Canada and the 7500 terminals of the Cirrus network in the United States. In 1987, Citicorp announced an agreement to access a national ATM network in Japan. Banks in Asia, South America, Australia, and other countries were also progressing toward global interconnection of their ATM and computer processing networks.

By 1987, MasterCard had 8,000 Master Teller machines worldwide, with services available in multiple languages and cash in more than one currency. Visa cards could be used to access machines in 18,000 locations in 21 countries, including 8,000 in the United States and 6,200 in Europe, the Middle East, and Africa. American Express covered 20 countries with 20,000 machines, providing local currency, dollars, and traveler's checks.

In the Fall of 1987, Mastercard purchased Cirrus Systems, the largest network of shared ATMs in the United States, for $38 million, and Visa obtained an option to purchase Plus. Both companies were showing some interest in joining forces to sponsor Entree, a point-of-sale service that would let customers use their ATM cards to make retail purchases as well as to conduct transactions at their ATM terminals. These moves are part of the unrelenting trend taking place in all financial markets toward greater consolidation, and ultimately the creation of several nationally and globally integrated POS-ATM networks.

## The Invisible World of
## Artificially Intelligent Money

Money has gone electronic with this transformation to a computer-based economic system, and you can open the "door" to almost any market in any nation with an appropriate credit card, debit card, or smart card. Electronic money is invisible and silent. It knows no limits to its speed of transmission, nor any natural geographical boundaries.

Within these emerging global computer networks, electronic money is instantaneously channeled around the world. It is funnelled and controlled by the fingers of the public or the managers of corporations or the staff of financial institutions who access the keyboard of some computer.

The infrastructure is there to enable money to be paid out, deposited, withdrawn, transferred, and invested in seconds, from any location around the world, into any market around the world, by any person in the world.

## The Transformation of National Geography and Political Jurisdictions

The new computerized money and payments infrastructure transformed the industrial landscape of America throughout the eighties by eroding the boundaries that separated commercial banking, retailing, and other nonbanking industries. They opened markets and created an industrial explosion by enabling retailers and other nonbanking corporations to engage in banking. They broke down the boundaries that protected the banking industry, forcing its members to compete in an ever more competitive world. They also made the distinctions between intrastate and interstate banking obsolete, and they wore away the geographical boundaries that separated federal and state regulatory and legislative jurisdictions.

The new infrastructure heralded the emergence of a dual, complementary, electronic computer- and paper-based money and payments system in which computers were used to dispense money in paper form for out-of-pocket transactions while enabling money to be deposited and invested in interest-bearing instruments, automatically managed from shopping centers and convenience stores, and channelled instantaneously among national and global centers and into those markets with the highest rates of return. In these ways computers have fundamentally changed the nature and opportunity cost of money.

## Notes

1. *Economist*, "A Survey of International Banking," 24 March 1984, p. 73.
2. Ibid.
3. Shamoon, "The Sharing of ATMs," p. 126.
4. Garsson, "Easy Money," p. 34.
5. Ibid.

# 4

# The Evolution of an Electronic Trading Infrastructure

## The Development of Electronic Trading Infrastructure

Trading and the exchange of goods and services form the pillars of the market economy. Indeed, economic textbooks define a *market* to be a place where buyers and sellers meet to engage freely in trading and exchange activity. In the past, markets were actual physical locations where people watched one another, engaged in debate and discussion, grimaced, shouted, shook their fists, smiled, and signaled and communicated with one another about prices, quality, and payments, all in the interest of getting the best deal.

In the eighties, some of these physical markets began to disappear because individuals could communicate information, make decisions, execute trades and exchanges, and follow up with payment and settlement through the medium of the computer. Just as the emergence of markets represented a fundamental development that redirected the course of history and civilization, so has the emergence of computers as a medium for trading and exchange forever altered the future of mankind. Once a computer-mediated trading infrastructure is in place, neither the marketplace nor society will be the same.

## A Brief History and Principles of Electronic Trading

In many respects, electronic trading and brokerage are not new at all. Indeed, certain kinds of electronic trading have been taking place for some time, although not with the same degree of sophistication as the fully electronic or computer-mediated trading we see today. Since the advent of the telephone, for example, major banks, retailers, and brokerage houses have been selling merchandise, securities, and services directly by phone. They have also used telex machines to order merchandise and record and communicate their sales information; in fact, the telex has evolved as a special trading medium wherein a purchase or sale by telex has been considered a legal document for many years. When computers came along, they were used simply to keep track of the accounting and other details of the sale. Together, these practices were the preliminaries to electronic trading.

Brokerage houses, banks, and finance companies also had been selling services for some time at local retail outlets (through point-of-sale systems) in which the records of transactions, payments, and associated accounting were automatically processed and communicated to the head office, where information was permanently recorded, accounts processed, and transactions transmitted to and reconciled with other institutions. This constituted a form of intra- and intercompany computer-mediated trading. As described in the previous chapter, some banking and financial service companies were purchasing automated teller machines and configuring them into networks so that they could operate in a completely automated way as a computer-mediated trading and brokerage system.

On yet another front, several brokerage companies and consortia of banks, retailers, and communications interests, such as Sears, Roebuck, Knight-Ridder, IBM, AT&T, and Citicorp, were attempting to develop a complete package of electronic retail services for the home market, and electronic banking, information, and securities brokerage services were part of the package that was being tested to determine how much subscribers would pay for them. These systems permitted securities, merchandise, and certain other services to be sold automatically to homeowners and businesses electronically. In some of these tests, the credit card was one of the most popular and sometimes the only accepted means of payment. Indeed, people could purchase goods and services such as hotel reservations over the telephone simply by giving their credit card number to the business.

All these were forms of electronic trading, as they involved electronic media to varying degrees to mediate trading activities. In some, the trading consisted simply of communication by telephone between two individuals agreeing to make a trade, for what we might call telephone-augmented trading. The sales person or broker could then use a computer to initiate the trade automatically, perhaps best described as computer-augmented trading. In the case of the automated teller machine, the entire transaction was automatically mediated and executed by the computer. The degree of sophistication in each case, however, was small compared to completely electronic trading, where all the interaction between buyer and seller and even with third parties is mediated by computer systems and communications networks.

The microcomputer and the personal computer revolution accelerated the trend toward completely electronic trading by making it attractive for all traders to interact with one another on a continuous basis. "Versatile, powerful desktop computers," wrote *Business Week* in 1985, enabled "investors to make smarter decisions than they ever could with the old 'dumb' terminals, which could only display unvarnished numbers," and traders were also "using analytical packages [to] help them move employers' millions into more profitable pockets."[1] Some brokers were using sophisticated custom software to perceive patterns in stock market data, in turn "selling" it to their clients through the management of their computerized portfolios. As alternative telecommunications services proliferated together with growing uses of computers, options, and information, the once placid securities business soon became "hyperactive."

**An Industrial Metamorphosis**

Throughout the seventies and early eighties, the nucleus of a computer-mediated trading infrastructure was being created, and a number of companies in several different industries were converging from a variety of directions and strengths. All of them were attempting to develop electronic trading as a means of taking advantage of new growth and profit-making opportunities, invading new markets, and becoming more efficient and competitive. The situation was analogous to the formation of the electronic payments and information infrastructures, described in the previous two chapters. The most important industries in this new infrastructure are illustrated in Figure 4.1.

Companies in the computer services and telecommunications carrier industries, and systems developers—companies such as AT&T, IBM, Automatic Data Processing, and I. P. Sharp—were approaching this market as suppliers of network facilities, computer and telecommunications systems, sophisticated software, and related services. Banks and brokerage companies, such as Citicorp, E. F. Hutton, and Merrill

Figure 4.1. **Industries Influencing the Evolution of Computer-Based Trading.**

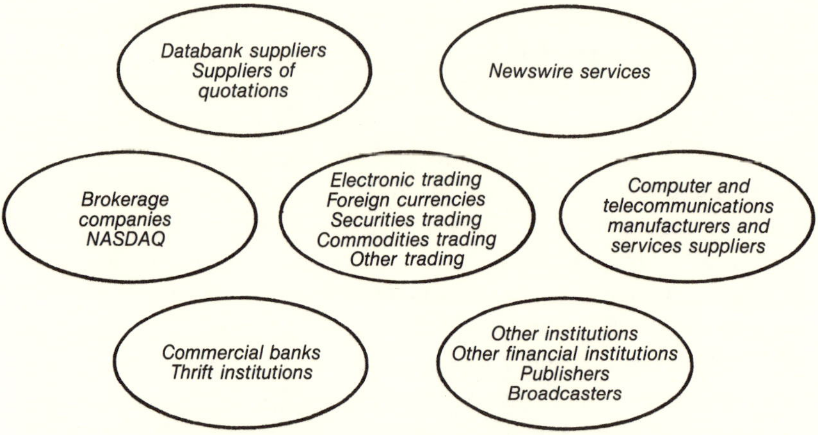

Lynch, were using the computer to automate and increase the efficiency of the brokerage function, to internalize transactions activities that would otherwise be done through the market, and to sell directly to the customer. The brokerage industry as a whole was innovating and experimenting with the use of computers to improve the efficiency and timeliness of the services it supplied to its members.

Some stock exchanges were introducing computers in increasingly sophisticated ways as a means of improving the efficiency of their trading floors and the services they provided to their customers. Publishers and suppliers of databank and quotations services, such as Dow Jones, Instinet, Reuters, and Quotron, were coming to the market as suppliers of content, particularly financial information and quotations, for which a financially viable and stable market was developing. Banks, increasingly dependent on computer systems to automate the more complex segments of their business operations, were being drawn into this force field created by the metamorphosis. Electronic trading was intrinsic to all.

Every company faced enormous technological, financial, and managerial challenges, and the competitive risks were indeed great. Each company needed significant systems expertise, and since the technology was still in its infancy, each company had to develop the very sophisticated software, systems, and other expertise to launch the business. Each required a national computer and communications network, which each had to develop, acquire in some way, or lease from others.

Ultimately, global linkages would be essential. Companies would also need to tap into large amounts of capital to finance all these activities. Finally, they would need a large base of customers buying and selling commodities, information, securities, or currencies to make the venture profitable. All these together represented formidable obstacles and challenges, preventing any single company from developing a truly electronic trading infrastructure on its own over the necessary time scale.

No individual company had strengths in all these areas, and few had any combination of them. The more of these strengths a company had, however, the more significant its advantage over its rivals. Several of these assets were more important than the others. For example, even though having a national computer and communications system was critical, it was even more critical to have a large base of customers. After all, it was customers who were the ultimate sources of revenue.

Two major player groups, in particular, had this advantage. Companies in the brokerage business had the large base of customers buying and selling securities, but needed to develop the systems, the facilities, and the infrastructure to support electronic trading. Companies in the information services business not only had a large base of customers, but also had access to national computer and communications networks. But they, too, would have to design the computerized trading technology. On top of this, the players required security and operational trading features and the management talent necessary to operate these systems.

The stage was set in the early eighties for a flurry of corporate acquisitions, mergers, and joint ventures to develop national and global computer-based trading systems. Either as a matter of offensive or defensive strategy, it made sense, in one way or another, for banks, brokerage companies, computer service companies, telecommunications carriers, systems integrators, and information suppliers to team up and combine their strengths. AT&T, Citicorp, Reuters, Merrill Lynch, Quotron, Instinet, and Dow Jones, to name a few, entered the fray.

But electronic trading could not come into being without significant deregulation and relaxation of the antitrust laws that kept companies from crossing long-established industry boundaries. Eliminating these boundaries was essential to give companies in one segment of the business the opportunity to diversify and develop strengths in other areas. Fortunately, deregulation was well under way in the late seventies, and electronic trading was under rapid development.

## The National Association of Securities Dealers
## and Electronic Trading

One of the first and most significant developments in electronic trading was initiated by the National Association of Securities Dealers (NASD) Inc., an association of securities dealers organized during the thirties and registered with the Securities and Exchange Commission. The goals of NASD were to provide a self-regulatory environment for the brokerage industry, to promote cooperation among its members, and to promote standards and fair trading practices for its constituents. In the late sixties, the association was looking at automation as a means of improving the efficiency of over-the-counter (OTC) trading in securities for its members.

In 1971, it embarked on a program to develop a sophisticated computer and communications network connecting all its broker and dealer firms trading in OTC securities. This system was called NASDAQ (National Association of Securities Dealers Automated Quotations). It provided up-to-the-minute bid-and-ask quotations on OTC securities for all its members as well as providing NASD with a means of automatically monitoring and checking trading activity. Formerly, this had been done manually using a decentralized, paper-based system. Now the activity could be done automatically, efficiently, and in a timely manner with computers. Once the bugs were ironed out of the new system, it became an unqualified success all around.

In order to enhance the attractiveness and efficiency of the NASDAQ system, broaden its functions and services, and make it operate more like the securities exchanges, clearance and settlement facilities for OTC transactions were added. NASD negotiated to make it possible to clear OTC transactions made on the NASDAQ system through the same facilities, in the same manner, and at the same cost per transaction as on the stock exchanges. NASD members were able to do this through such organizations as the National Securities Clearing Corporation, regional exchanges, the Depository Trust Company, and other depositories. In 1980, NASD introduced "inside" quotations to its NASDAQ service, i.e., automatic information on the highest bids and lowest offers on OTC stocks. This improved the attractiveness of the service to the public and gave it a small edge over the services provided by the stock markets. Inside quotations significantly narrowed the spreads on its securities, making the quality of its markets more visible and attractive. This information was also made available to its representatives and to newspapers throughout the nation.

After 1980, a significant upgrade of all NASDAQ facilities was undertaken. In 1981, a computer-based central registration depository (CRD) was completed, and an automated order routing and computer-assisted execution system was soon added. The CRD system enabled individuals to become licensed or registered with any of the participating states or exchanges and with NASD by filing a single form and making a single payment through NASD. The new computer-assisted execution system was designed to route and execute orders automatically, and it significantly improved trading activity in a variety of ways. It was superior to the old manual system of executing orders, which was considered unfair because brokers could obtain certain advantages for their favorite clients. The new system prevented abuses of this nature, increased the efficiency of the NASDAQ trading system, and speeded up the entire process.

Eventually, the NASDAQ system was upgraded until it provided three levels of interactive services for three primary markets. Level I, delivered through terminals to brokerage offices, was designed primarily to obtain prices on listed stocks. Level II was for brokerage agents to use in their retail services. Level III, called the market maker service, was designed for the specialist in "making markets."

NASDAQ's performance and growth was nothing short of spectacular. In 1983, for example, trading volume on the NASDAQ system reached a record of 62.9 million shares per day, or 74 percent of the 85.4 million recorded on the NYSE, up from 40 percent in 1981. In terms of the dollar volume of shares traded, the NASDAQ system recorded $188 billion in 1983, or 25 percent of the NYSE dollar volume, up from 18 percent in 1978. Much of NASDAQ's growth, however, was at the expense of some exchanges. In the preceding decade, for example, the number of stocks listed on the American Exchange declined from 1249 to 804, although the NYSE remained essentially the same.

A significant feature of the NASDAQ system for many companies and institutional traders was the higher liquidity it provided. Liquidity can be measured, for example, by the number of dollars required to cause a one percentage point change in the price of a stock. The higher the liquidity, the more orderly and stable the market. Higher liquidity means that a stock will be able to withstand heavy trading with minimal price changes. Institutional investors like it because it means that they can move large amounts of money in and out of a stock very close to the current market price. Companies, which depend on institutional investors for capital, like the higher liquidity of NASDAQ because it attracts institutional investors. Statistics supported the higher liquidity provided by the NASDAQ system in 1984. In all ten groups of stocks listed, liquidity was higher on the NASDAQ system than on the American Stock Exchange. And NASDAQ scored higher liquidity in eight of the ten groups than did the the New York Stock Exchange.

As we have seen in previous chapters, information is as important as money and securities, and NASD has always recognized information's importance to its own business. Through the facilities of the NASDAQ system, everyone involved in the OTC market can gain access to its information services, including its broker-dealer members who retail OTC securities to the public, as well as professional traders and investors. They all can gain immediate access to the quotations of all the dealers making markets in the securities displayed on the NASDAQ system. And NASD provides information to newspapers and wire services for daily publication.

## NASDAQ, Instinet, and Reuters

The big securities dealers such as Merrill Lynch were making progress in the late seventies in developing the computerized infrastructure that would enable them to provide electronic trading on a nationwide basis, but so were other companies. In addition to NASD, at least two other companies were making rapid strides in developing fully electronic, computer, communications, and network-based trading systems. One of these was Instinet and another was Reuters, which, as we saw in Chapter 2, was rapidly diversifying into the whole field of financial and information services.

These new infrastructures, with their very peculiar but superior economics, their efficiencies, and their multifunctional capabilities, quickly evolved until they began to compete directly with the traditional stock exchanges, the majority of which were sticking to their so-called marble-walled buildings and their paper- and people-based trading systems. It was only a matter of time before electronic trading systems such as the NASDAQ and Instinet systems seriously threatened the old stock exchanges and their long-established manual methods and procedures for doing business. Eventually, these dinosaurs would have to evolve themselves, but that is the subject of the next chapter.

Other factors were involved, however, and other events were taking place in the world that proved to be important to the development of electronic trading. Computerization had at least as great an effect on the development of electronic currency trading, which in turn had as great an impact on the operation and organization of the national and global economic system as computers were having through the emergence of electronic securities trading, the buying and selling of information, and the movement of money throughout the economy via the new electronic payments infrastructure.

Under the combined pressures of innovation, entrepreneurship, technological, institutional, and free market forces, one of the pillars of the old economic order collapsed. It brought to an end the old order in which national governments controlled the flow of money between and among nations and set the values of currencies relative to one another and to gold. The series of events and the factors and forces involved were prime ingredients of true Schumpeterian capitalist dynamics, and they represent another step in the march to a computer-mediated economy.

## The Breakdown of the
## Bretton Woods Agreement

Up until 1972, the rules and regulations for managing international currencies were set down in the Bretton Woods Agreement of 1944, named after the town in New Hampshire where it was signed. In this agreement, the rates for exchanging domestic currency into foreign currencies were fixed and pegged to gold, the standard for measuring the value of every currency at that time. The International Monetary Fund (IMF) was also set up to administer this fixed exchange rate system, with gold as its primary reserve asset. The value of the U.S. dollar was based on a price of gold of $35 an ounce, and the United States assumed the role as the main reserve currency country. Furthermore, the U.S. currency was the only one that could be convertible into gold. These arrangements constituted the gold standard for international monetary exchange and control.

Bretton Woods was the symbol of the old world, the precomputer world in which exchange rates were managed by governments. Once governments allowed markets mediated by computers to take over this function in the early seventies, they were unable to get control back again. Today, governments have very little say in determining exchange rates, which move up and down in conjunction with supply and demand factors in an atmosphere of global information, speculation, fear, and greed, all of which are mediated by computer-based infrastructures.

The Bretton Woods Agreement was designed to facilitate and encourage an active international trading system by ensuring that all exchange rates were stable and constant. Floating exchange rates, as the prevailing philosophy of the day went, were anathema to an active international trading system because they would lead to instability and therefore inhibit international trade. If the prices of international currencies were allowed to float freely, then traders would be loath to make international agreements because they could not rely on the prices that prevailed at the time the agreement was made. The solution, therefore, was to fix the price of all international currencies. Bretton Woods, in turn, made it necessary for the governments of every country to control and regulate the price of all international currencies.

This control, in turn, was delegated to the commercial banks, which had the sole right to buy and sell currencies at the fixed rates set by the government. The U.S. Treasury bought and sold gold to commercial banks, foreign central banks, and other licensed dealers at $35 per ounce.

In the years leading up to 1972, the U.S. dollar was coming under increasing pressure because of several factors. One of the most important was the decision to finance the Vietnam War by increasing the money supply rather than by raising taxes. The high cost of the war required an enormous increase in the supply of money and it led to a sharp rise in the rate of inflation. It also meant that a growing volume of U.S. dollars was floating in international markets.

Another factor was the huge flow of U.S. investment overseas during the sixties and the early seventies. Speculators' capital was running from countries with high inflation rates to those with lower inflation rates. All these factors together put mounting pressure on the U.S. dollar in the very early part of the seventies at a time when computer and telecommunications networks made it possible to transfer money efficiently and rapidly around the world as demand required.

As the situation worsened, the Nixon administration found it more and more difficult to support the dollar, and subsequent efforts by members of the International Monetary Fund to establish a new system of rates failed. Finally, in December 1971, the United States suspended the convertibility of the dollar into gold, and in 1973 the link was severed altogether. In the same year, the major central banks decided to allow their currencies to float rather than try to negotiate new rates. With these events, the era of the gold standard was over.

## Chicago and Foreign Currency Trading

Capitalism has always bred a strange mixture of people. It breeds those who play markets to win using the traditional rules. It breeds those who depend on their smarts to get ahead, and it breeds innovators and entrepreneurs. But it also breeds those people who will do anything to get ahead—particularly those who are willing to speculate and gamble on anything and everything in the market. They were all present as the wraps were taken off the Bretton Woods Agreement. The market was rife with speculation about currency realignments as pressure mounted on the dollar.

One individual wanting to speculate was Leo Melamed, a trader with a seat on the Chicago Mercantile Exchange. Another was Milton Friedman, a leading monetary economist, whose theories on the link between monetary policy and inflation had become very popular. Both wanted to speculate on a revaluation of currencies, particularly the British pound and the U.S. dollar, which they felt were overvalued and would soon be devalued by their governments. However, they were unable to enlist the cooperation of commercial banks on which they depended to sell them the quantities they wanted. So the two men became entrepreneurs. Melamed, who understood the mechanics of the stock exchange, obtained the financial backing of Friedman and opened his own market to buy and sell foreign currencies in Chicago in May 1972. The new market was called the International Money Market (IMM).

The idea was simple enough. Why not treat currencies just like securities or commodities? Why not open a market for currencies just like a securities market or a commodities market? There were certain advantages for all business groups to participate actively in the new market. Importers and exporters of commodities and services could hedge against currency fluctuations by buying and selling foreign currencies three to six months before they needed them at an agreed-upon price, and traders could take the risks that rates might change. Importers and exporters would be able to conclude a deal at a fixed price independent of changes in future exchange rates. Currency traders would provide a sort of insurance to commodity traders by assuming the risks while charging a fee for their services. Theoretically, all of them would have significant incentives to participate in the new market.

The timing of the Melamed venture could not have been better. When the U.S. dollar was allowed to float and find its own level against other currencies in 1971, it gave birth to an instant world market in foreign currencies and the IMM was open and ready for business. Better still for the IMM, it didn't have to worry about competition because there wasn't any. Bankers and traders, formerly loath to deal with the IMM, could no longer afford to ignore it and they soon became enthusiastic members. The IMM subsequently grew to become a world center for international currency trading.

During the seventies, other centers for currency trading sprang up in the major cities of the world including New York, London, Tokyo, Frankfurt, Zurich, Singapore, and Hong Kong. The players in this new market included multinational corporations, commercial banks, national governments, professional traders, and speculators. The interbank market where the big banks dealt with one another became the largest currency market in the world. It is here where big banks satisfy most of their money requirements. All these developments stimulated the need and demand for instant global trading, and computer-based infrastructures were on the way to accommodate these needs.

## Reuters as a Global Power Broker in
## Electronic Foreign Currency Trading

During the seventies, Reuters was developing an international reputation as a supplier of news and financial information services, including its automated stock quotations service. In the eighties, it began to strengthen, consolidate, and round out its financial services portfolio. Electronic trading was one of the most important targets of its new strategy, because it would complement its collection of financial news, quotations, and information services and make more strategic use of the company's vast capital investments in computer systems and telecommunications networks. It would also make very effective use of its worldwide network of offices and agents in many countries. Reuters was utilizing synergy in all these ways.

In 1981, Reuters introduced its now-famous Monitor Dealer Package, an instantaneous, global, computer-assisted trading and execution system for dealing in foreign currencies. It became an instant hit with banks, currency traders, and speculators, who were already subscribers to the Monitor Service. Members, which included multinational corporations, banking institutions, governments, traders, and speculators, could now buy and sell currencies to each other on the spot market or purchase futures contracts on various currencies. Subsequently, in 1983, Reuters added the software to enable arbitragers to automatically collect data that would allow them to spot opportunities more quickly, then to engage in financial transactions in currencies, bonds, and bullion.

Reuters made frequent use of acquisitions throughout the eighties to expand and sharpen its competitive edge over rivals such as Quotron, Telerate, and Dow Jones. In 1985, it signed an agreement with Instinet, which provided automated trading of equities and options in the United States, to complement its own strengths. Reuters wanted to market this stock trading service outside the U.S. through its own facilities and networks and to add stocks of non-U.S. exchanges to it as well, thereby strengthening its U.S. content, specifically the stock quotations of major U.S. companies.

The match had advantages to Instinet as well. By allowing its subscriber base to make transactions via the Instinet network, it would strengthen its own position and increase its efficiency by taking advantage of economies and synergies in computer processing, network facilities, and integrated services. In late 1986, when Instinet was trading about 8000 stocks, Reuters agreed to buy the remaining shares of Instinet for $102 million.

In March 1987, Reuters announced its intention to purchase all the stock of I. P. Sharp Limited, a Canadian-based computer services company that had an international computer and communications network with offices in over twenty-five countries. Sharp was also heavily involved in the development of software for electronic trading, electronic mail, database, and information and quotations services.

## A New Management and a New Culture

Electronic trading transformed the management and culture of brokerage companies, stock exchanges, investment banks, mutual and pension funds managers, and insurance companies in the eighties. It revolutionized their internal operations and organization, and it transformed their behavior and their profitability. It eliminated much of the paper and many of the people in both the back and front offices, the way automation did in banking. Computerization, particularly electronic trading, put systems people, engineers, programmers, mathematicians, and physicists on the payrolls of major brokerage companies, commercial banks, and organizations engaged in currency trading.

But computer mediation of the trading function has had, and is having, an even greater effect on the overall organization of the financial community. Theoretically as well as practically, it has made it possible for everyone and anyone who has anything to buy or sell to become a trader. The ultimate effect of electronic trading has been to make it possible for new players to bypass traditional financial intermediaries and institutions, and to create a competitive world where near-monopolies had previously existed.

A new electronic computer-mediated brokerage house is likely to resemble a video game arcade, an air traffic control center, the control room of a NASA space center, or the war room of a modern military center. The players are in rooms that are wired up and connected to all parts of the world, standing before banks of computer displays, some of which hang from the ceiling, while screens flash the latest price quotations from all over the world.

The traders interact continuously through these machines with hundreds like themselves, sending messages to one another, accessing various databanks and other sources of information, performing complex simulations and decision analyses, issuing commands and signals, and executing trades all over the world.

## Changes in the Balance of Corporate, Economic, and Global Power

By the mid-eighties, the new computer-mediated trading infrastructures were affecting people, organizations, and global activity. They were creating new power structures in corporations and in the world economy and altering the balance of power between governments, markets, and political states. Alternatives to the traditional financial institutions—in existence for centuries—were proliferating. The interbank market was no longer the only way to speculate and deal in foreign currencies, and more efficient ways to bypass them were coming along each year.

New suppliers such as Merrill Lynch were offering small and medium-sized corporations and even individuals an opportunity to engage in currency trading. NASDAQ was challenging the New York Stock Exchange and other stock exchanges. New players such as Reuters, Quotron, Citicorp, Telerate, and Dow Jones were elbowing their way into new markets to profit from the enormous opportunities that arise when any sector of the economy undergoes a transformation.

Every player was bypassing the traditional supplier-client relationships. Advancing computer mediation had created a vortex that was pulling in every major financial institution and company from many other sectors of the economy and creating a global electronic trading hyperstructure.

Foreign exchange dealing and the proliferation of new instruments such as futures have made speculation respectable, even by some of the most conservative financial institutions. Foreign currency trading is supposed to lubricate international trade, but perhaps nine out of ten deals are estimated to be speculative, which means that it constitutes a "zero-sum" game. In such a game, there are no net beneficiaries because for every winner there is a loser. Every trader, every speculator, and every country can be at risk in the new foreign currency trading game, and indeed, some countries fare as badly as some traders. Small countries are definitely far worse off than large ones because of the amount of currency being traded. On the one hand, it might take a 1000 trades to move the pound, for example, and 3000 to shift the dollar, the yen, and the West German mark, but trades of this magnitude help to keep the movements of these currencies orderly in the mid-eighties.

On the other hand, much smaller trading volumes than this can have a devastating effect on what traders call "exotic currencies," as the government of Italy found out on July 19, 1985. That day is known in Italy as Black Friday. The lira was valued at 1840 to 1 U.S. dollar when trading opened in the morning. When it was suspended six hours later, the lira was down to 2200—a decline of 19.6 percent. The Italian Government had been thinking about a formal devaluation, but not of this order. "A dollar purchase of . . . [$135 million] in London would cause only a tremor," wrote the *Globe and Mail*. "In Milan, the market erupted, especially when it became clear that the Bank of Italy would not intervene to stop the slide. . . . [The lesson drawn from this incident was that foreign exchange markets] effectively removed from the Italian Government the power to determine the value of its own currency."[2]

## Notes

1. *Business Week*,"Today's Stock Quote Machines," p. 144.
2. *Globe and Mail*, "The Man Who Rocked the Money World," p. A7.

# 5

# Transformation of the World Stock Exchanges

## The Bastions of Free Enterprise Capitalism

Stock exchanges are the bastions of capitalism. They are the "free markets" where the ownership of capital and wealth and the corporate enterprises of a capitalist society are freely traded according to certain rules. They are also the places where capital is allocated throughout the economy and between enterprises, industrial sectors, and economies of the world.

Theoretically, it is here that the public-at-large directly participates in the capitalist system, and determines, through its decisions, which companies are rewarded for their performance and by how much. It is in the stock markets that the executives of major corporations are held accountable for their actions, where the public can vote to hire and fire them as it pleases. Stock markets also represent the barometer and the psychology of capitalism. The sentiment and the confidence of the public are registered in the day-to-day operation of the stock exchanges, and trading can manifest the fears, joys, and wrath of the public at any time.

Stock markets are also among the most efficient markets in the world. There are more players dealing in the various traded instruments in the stock markets than in any other market in the world. Here everyone—individuals of all ages and income levels—theoretically can participate and compete with corporations, large and small, for the opportunity to make their wealth grow; where all can compete—again theoretically—with one another on a relatively level playing field, subject to what information they possess, or have access to, or can process, as well as to the rules of the game. All these features are integral to stock markets and to capitalism, and the rules and realities of stock markets make capitalism democratic just as they make it undemocratic.

Beginning in the seventies, traditional stock exchanges were challenged and threatened by competitors from outside the industry that had access to much more sophisticated technology. In a striking analogy to the banking industry, stock exchanges, in general, were managed by the most conservative of the conservatives, and they were highly regulated. Although these institutions represented the hallmarks of capitalism, unlike banking they did not have the same capitalist culture that spawned the revolution taking place around them. Most stock exchanges around the world, including the New York Stock Exchange, the largest in the world, had developed a corporate culture that simply was not open to new ideas or changing circumstances when the world around them was changing very rapidly.

In an age where innovation, opportunity, and expansion were predominant, most exchanges were oblivious to the waves of automation rolling about them. Whereas regulation, tradition, and natural factors had protected them from rivals in the precomputer world, intense competitive pressures, generated in a computer-mediated world, eventually compelled them to adopt wrenching changes in their management style, business practices, and procedures. They were forced to redesign their culture and reorganize themselves to compete in a new world dominated by computers.

## Stages of Automation in the Stock Exchanges

Although stock exchanges were very slow in reacting to the computer revolution, they did start to automate their back office activities during the sixties and seventies, as did banking. It was here that the really large volumes of information processing were concentrated, especially those activities relating to the capture and communication of information, as well as the accounting, reporting, and clearing of securities trading. Computers were perceived primarily as a means of improving the efficiency of administration in the stock exchanges.

During this time period, trading volumes were growing so rapidly that processing capacity had become a obstruction to efficient and timely trading and reporting. In some cases, the capacity limits of the computer system were reached anywhere from several months to a year of when an exchange had upgraded its operations with the latest generations of the most efficient, high-performance computer systems. Despite this snag, computer power and capacity did grow rapidly enough so that attention could focus on other activities amenable to automation.

Gradually, new applications focused on the needs of the trading floor itself, and with this a second phase of automation began. From then on, automation encroached more and more on the activities of the trading floor and eventually revolutionized the trading floor's operations.

On-line applications were developed connecting computers to the trading floor and giving traders direct access to the information contained in the computer databanks. Computer networks eventually enabled brokers and traders to communicate electronically their purchases and sales orders to the trading floor, where they were executed by people called "specialists," who administered all transactions in a particular security.

The stock exchange trading floor soon became a teeming concentration of high-technology gadgets, giant electronic screens, personal computers, video display terminals, and portable and hand-held devices for accessing and displaying information. Bid and ask pricing information on every stock could be instantaneously retrieved and displayed. Traders could interact with keyboards or touch-sensitive screens to obtain information. Some people began to think of the day when traders would use voice recognition and voice synthesis systems to communicate with the computer.

Some leading innovators began to develop and introduce highly sophisticated software packages that helped traders use their computers to spot trends in the markets better and more rapidly, and to make decisions within seconds based on complex mathematical and financial analyses. Traders also began to apply the latest advances in artificial intelligence and decision support techniques to enhance their speed, efficiency, and profitability. Gradually, it became evident that every player would have to use these new computerized tools and weapons to compete and survive.

Program trading began to proliferate throughout the major exchanges of the world, and some exchanges introduced fully automatic execution of trading in larger and larger volumes over geographic areas that were increasingly global in scope.

## World Stock Markets, Global Exchanges, and
## New Tradable Instruments

With computerization came greater economies of scale and greater efficiencies in the operation of stock exchanges. Exchanges could accommodate much higher volumes of trading, and the transaction costs associated with trading declined considerably, thereby stimulating increased demand. Exchanges became more accessible, more important, and more desirable places to do business. As competition became a more significant factor, exchanges were forced to innovate and market their services more aggressively and to look for further ways to innovate and modernize to cut costs and improve productivity.

Spurred by this competition, new kinds of tradable instruments and contracts were invented to take advantage of the increased capacity and superior efficiencies resulting from automation. Marketing became more important as competition heated up, and exchanges were forced to discover new markets. Pressures were brought to bear to relax significantly the tight regulations that inhibited competition among exchanges. Deregulation ensued; new markets were developed; trading volumes soared; and competitive forces on the exchanges strengthened. The only way stock exchanges could meet the increasing demand for trading as well as better compete was through further automation.

A major result of competition and computerization was the creation during the seventies of new marketable instruments and contracts, which significantly expanded the market and resulted in the opening of new exchanges. Automation played an important role in this as well, for it was only through automation that exchanges could process the much higher trading volumes and accommodate the greater number of transactions while increasing the efficiencies and lowering the costs of trading.

The most significant of these innovations were options and futures contracts, beginning with particular securities and extending to more exotic contracts. These would revolutionize stock exchanges everywhere.

Exchange volumes quickly soared in the seventies and early eighties with augmentation of computer capacity and efficiency. The emergence of new products and instruments represented considerable potential for expansion and new business. Resulting from intensified competition, these products ended up promoting even more rivalry among exchanges. The winners would be those exchanges with the most innovative, aggressive, efficient, and market-oriented strategies and corporate cultures.

## The Emergence of Options Trading

Until 1973, exchange trading was confined to securities, i.e., stocks and bonds, and to commodities contracts. In April of that year, the Chicago Board Options Exchange (CBOE) opened trading as the world's first and only exchange established expressly for trading standardized stock options, which offer the right or contract to buy or sell securities in specified amounts at specified prices for a specific duration of time. Options expire at a particular time, usually every quarter.

Their appearance was significant because of their flexibility and the advantages they bestowed on traders, investors, and the owners of commodities and securities. Options empower individuals to obtain significantly greater leverage with their investment funds by purchasing calls covering a much larger quantity or volume of securities or commodities, since the cost of an option is usually a fraction of the price of the underlying security or commodity. A margin payment of $6,000, for example, can qualify an investor to control contracts worth $120,000 in underlying stocks.

Options, therefore, enable investors to exercise control indirectly over many more securities without buying them outright, and in this way investors can increase significantly the probability of profit over what would have been possible by purchasing them outright. Options are also less costly to trade than securities because they involve less processing.

One of the real advantages of options is that they help individuals to manage risk better. For example, investors can hedge a short position against a price increase. An investor who intends to sell a security or commodity short in anticipation of a price decline can buy calls against a rise in its price. An investor can also fix the price of a future security or commodity purchase by buying a call option, which can be exercised at a future date when funds are available. The investor is thus protected against a price increase for the future period stipulated on the option.

After the emergence of options on the Chicago Board in 1973, other exchanges followed suit. The American and Philadelphia Stock Exchanges opened trading in options in 1975, and the Pacific and Midwest Stock Exchanges followed in 1976. In 1977, the Securities and Exchange Commission became alarmed at the proliferation of options trading activity, and imposed a moratorium on any further expansion of options exchanges while it undertook an investigation into the role and effects of options. Subsequently, in 1980, the moratorium was lifted, and the number of exchanges introducing options as well as the volume of options trading soared.

By 1983, more than 55 percent of all listed stock options trading in the United States was taking place on the floor of the CBOE, making it the nation's leading options trading center. Membership had grown to 1700, and trading was taking place in calls and puts on 145 of the most widely held and actively traded U.S. stocks as well as on U.S. Treasury bonds and Standard & Poor's stock indexes.

## Automation in Commodity Futures Exchanges

Until the early seventies, commodity trading and futures contracts were in existence but were unregulated. The largest exchange, the Commodity Exchange (COMEX), located in New York, was trading contracts in metals such as copper, zinc, silver, and gold, as well as in hides, raw silk, and rubber. Volumes were growing, and in 1974, commodity futures trading was brought under federal regulation with the passage of the Commodity Futures Trading Commission Act. The act established the Commodity Futures Trading Commission to regulate all activities relating to commodity futures and the exchanges trading them.

A commodity futures contract is a contract with standard provisions in which the seller agrees to deliver a quantity of a specific commodity under the definitions of the exchange, with the price and delivery month variable. Commodity exchanges usually provide for both spot or cash trading in commodities that reflect the values of existing commodities, as well as for commodity futures. As in the securities and foreign currency exchanges, computerization has increased the efficiency of commodity exchanges, making it possible for individuals and corporations throughout the world to play commodity futures markets in the major centers through advanced computer- and telecommunications-based facilities.

The primary purpose of commodity futures markets is to provide a mechanism whereby buyers and sellers can ensure themselves against losses due to price fluctuations during the period when their holdings of raw commodities are in the process of fabrication and sale to the ultimate customer. Hence, a commodity futures exchange is a means by which cash holdings can be hedged by the sale of futures, or vice versa. But a significant factor in futures markets is speculation rather than insurance. Futures markets have become inundated with speculators eager to exploit whatever information they may have for whatever financial gain.

But the insurance value of commodity futures is particularly attractive to producers of real goods. Futures allow farmers, for example, to sell crops and food manufacturers to buy the produce at a price that is agreed upon before the crop is harvested. This gives the farmer and the manufacturer security while transferring the risk of price fluctuations to traders willing and prepared to gamble on where the prices might move. Farmers and manufacturers are "hedging" while the traders are "speculating." Both buyer and seller gain from this transaction, both theoretically and practically.

## The Explosion of Financial Futures

Financial futures were also proliferating rapidly throughout the seventies. The history of the financial futures market goes back to 1972 when Leo Melamed opened the International Monetary Market in Chicago to trade in foreign currencies. In that year, trading began in futures contracts on the Italian lira, Japanese yen, Canadian dollar, Mexican peso, British pound, German mark, and Swiss franc. The Dutch guilder and the French franc were soon added.

Subsequently, the IMM merged with the Chicago Board of Trade (CBOT), which grew to become the world's largest financial market of its kind. In the meantime, many other kinds of financial futures instruments were introduced in addition to currencies. One of the most successful was interest-rate futures contracts, that is, agreements to buy and sell a specified quantity and grade of financial instrument on a particular future date.

The first interest-rate futures contract in history was the Government National Mortgage Association (GMNA) certificate, which was introduced in 1975 on the CBOT. In 1976, trading commenced on the IMM in ninety-day Treasury bills, one of the most successful contracts in its history. Treasury bond futures were introduced on the CBOT in 1977. Other short-term interest-rate contracts followed. In 1981, the IMM introduced contracts on domestic certificates of deposits and Eurodollar time deposits. All these instruments allowed easy arbitrage between contracts so that traders and institutions could move into, out of, and between securities in order to profit from price discrepancies. These were facilitated by the development of a cash settlement price for Eurodollars on the interbank cash market.

These and other actions paved the way, in 1982, for the introduction of a futures contract based on the Standard & Poor's 500 stock index. The new contract price tracked the upward and downward movement of the actual index; at expiration date, its price would converge with the cash index. Settlement of the contract could be in cash as well. More sophisticated financial contracts, including other kinds of index futures, the options on these, and other kinds of contracts were under development in one form or another throughout the eighties.

## Automation Throughout U.S. Stock Exchanges

Even the Congress of the United States recognized the importance of automation to the future of the stock exchanges in the seventies, and the Securities and Exchange Commission was convinced that computer-assisted trading held significant benefits for all the exchanges. So in 1975, amendments to the Securities Act were passed by Congress, which directed the commission to facilitate the development of a national system in securities linking all markets.

This new national market system was intended to be a computer-based system capable of disseminating last sale and quotation information for all qualified securities. The system was perceived to be desirable because it would "foster efficiency; . . . enhance competition; . . . increase the information available to brokers, dealers, and investors; . . . facilitate the offsetting of investors' orders; and . . . contribute to the best execution of such orders."[1] This was great, in theory, but the complete system was never realized.

Automation was gaining momentum, however, throughout all stock exchanges. In 1976, the New York Stock Exchange introduced its designated order turnaround system (DOT), which equipped a member firm to transmit standard types of orders in virtually any unlisted stock directly from its office through an electronic switch to the trading floor. There, it was handled manually by specialists on the floor who executed it and sent a confirmation out electronically over the same circuit.

In 1978, a key element in the national market system, called the Intermarket Trading System (ITS), came on-line. ITS interconnected the trading floors of the American, Boston, Cincinnati, and Midwest stock exchanges with the New York, Pacific, and Philadelphia exchanges. It provided a composite quotation system of bids and offered prices with the number of shares sought or offered at those prices at each of the centers. It made it possible for brokers, specialists, and market makers to participate in other exchanges and to execute a trade whenever a better price was available.

In 1979, the Cincinnati Stock Exchange commenced a trial of a computer- and communications-based automated securities execution service enabling its members to engage in trade without maintaining a physical presence on the floor of the exchange. The system automatically executed bids and offers by queuing orders first by price (highest bid and lowest offer), and second by time of entry (between orders of the same price). Once the bugs were ironed out of the new computerized system, it became fully operational.

In 1980, the Securities and Exchange Commission tried once again to implement a national market system by linking the Intermarket Trading System and NASDAQ system, and once again it failed. At that time, the NASDAQ system had just been enhanced to provide the capability for automated execution against "third market" maker quotations. Traders on the new NASDAQ system could select the best bid or best offer whether on an exchange floor or in the trading room of an off-exchange market maker.

The New York Stock Exchange, under pressure from rivals, also was improving and upgrading its computer-based facilities. In 1980, it introduced OARS (Open Automatic Reporting System), which permitted member firms to send to the computer of the exchange smaller orders that were entered before the market opened, and it used these to establish a fair opening price for the stock. In many respects, however, and in spite of the sophisticated use of computers and communications networks, the trading floor of the NYSE remained virtually the same because the actual processing and execution of a trade was largely a manual and human affair. When a broker in a brokerage office wanted to buy or sell a stock, he or she would telephone it in to a floor broker, who would hand-carry it to a specialist in that stock. Specialists were responsible for initiating, processing, and executing transactions in particular stocks, and kept a handwritten ledger to pair off the buy and sell orders received.

Before computers came along, this was the simplest and most efficient method of executing trading. Even though computers could do the job much more rapidly, efficiently, and perhaps democratically, computerization was not possible until the SEC abandoned a regulation known as Rule 390, which protected the specialists system. Until this rule went, trading on the New York Stock Exchange remained in human hands.

## Computer-Assisted Trading in the Stock Exchanges

In a modern computer-mediated stock exchange environment, the manual methods for executing trading became severe blockages interfering with the rapid and efficient execution of very high volumes of trading. Completely automated trading systems, like those of NASDAQ, were perceived by many as the direction of the future. These new exchanges had no trading floors and no "marble buildings." They had only a network of personal computer terminals in the offices of thousands of brokers and institutional traders worldwide, and computer-processing centers of the new exchanges, all interconnected by telecommunications networks.

These networks were rapidly becoming the new infrastructure of the new securities industry. Some in the industry still had their market makers whose job it was to actually initiate, execute, and conclude a trade. A broker would use a terminal to list the latest bid and ask prices, review them, and choose the market maker with the best price. The broker would then either telephone the market maker to conclude the deal or send a computer message to accomplish the same thing. Smaller orders could be executed automatically and instantaneously without human intervention.

In *Gentlemen of Fortune*, Paul Ferris described how the operations of brokerage houses and stock exchanges were managed in the mid-eighties:

> "Specialists" stand at positions under banks of hanging television sets, making markets in whatever stocks are their line. Bonds are traded elsewhere, out of sight on a lower floor, in as much as they are traded in the building at all. Essentially the bond market is electronic and has no center; it exists only in the telephone and computer networks linking buyers and sellers. The same thing is happening with equities. . . .[2]

He goes on:

> Institutions want instant liquidity on ten and twenty million dollar blocks. A lot of trading has switched upstairs [to the trading rooms of investment

banks] . . . because the specialist system is not capable of accommodating it. . . . In effect, the deal is done on the telephone and endorsed on the floor of the exchange. . . . [An order to trade more than 2000 shares would be] . . . professionally handled by the traders [upstairs]. They are on the pulse all day long. . . . [An order below 2000 shares] . . . goes down through the machines to the floor [of the New York Stock Exchange]. It's just fill-'em-and-bill-'em. . . . All they do is take the order off the machine, present it to the specialist, he writes down a price on it, and it comes back. It's automatic. . . . Above two thousand shares, [investment bankers] . . . would bid for it a little. . . .[3]

## Toward Full Automation and Global Linkages

In the mid-eighties, stock exchange administrations around the world were fully cognizant that computers were crucial to their long-term survival and growth. If systems such as NASDAQ continued to flourish, the very existence of the traditional stock exchanges could be in jeopardy. When NASDAQ began to investigate international linkages with stock exchanges in Europe and other countries, the New York Stock Exchange began to worry.

For the first time in their almost two centuries of existence, stock exchanges around the country and around the world experienced the greatest challenge to their future health and prosperity. The solution was either automate or face extinction. Automation was no longer a choice for stock exchanges, but a necessity for their survival. "The writing [was] . . . on the screen," commented *Fortune* magazine.

Most responded by embarking on crash programs to automate their operations to the degree necessary to compete. The New York, Tokyo, London Stock Exchanges, and others like them around the world, began to use the latest generation of computer and telecommunications systems as agents to increase their efficiency and to introduce new services. Some, like the Toronto Stock Exchange—one of the first to use computers on the exchange floor in 1962—went so far as to construct a new building and an entirely new trading floor.

In 1985, the Amsterdam Exchange began providing its traders with hand-held computer terminals to execute trading more quickly. In that year, the Tokyo Stock Exchange was trading more than 80 percent of its 1450 listed stocks by computer, with brokers executing buy and sell orders from terminals in their offices.

By 1985, NASDAQ and Instinet were both offering fully automated trading. NASDAQ offered automatic execution on small orders of a selected number of actively traded stocks as the initial step in a plan to ultimately transfer half its total volume off the telephone lines and onto its computer network. Instinet offered spontaneous execution of deals of up to 1000 shares of companies at the best price quoted on U.S. markets, including those on the NASDAQ system. Deals of up to 20 million shares worth $50 million were being executed automatically.

Since major competitors such as NASDAQ, Instinet, and Quotron operated networks spanning the nation, and were about to form international ones, stock exchanges were forced to do the same. Liquidity, which is what all individuals and corporations were looking for, and national and global computer trading became inextricably joined, and stock exchanges had to accommodate or lose out.

So in the mid-eighties, a new era began in stock exchange history. The interwiring of national and global stock exchanges began. In December 1984, the Montreal Exchange hooked up with the Boston Exchange and began investigating links with the Intex–Bermuda-based electronic futures exchange. In June 1985, the Toronto Stock Exchange began investigating links with Amex and, subsequently, with the Chicago Midwest Exchange. The New York and London Stock Exchanges began discussions to unite their exchanges. A new, more aggressive and forward-looking NYSE emerged. It developed a multipronged thrust including trading in the stocks of several hundred of the largest companies on its exchange seven days a week. It also considered lengthening daily trading hours, taking over a West Coast exchange, and entering into joint ventures with other major world exchanges.

## Computer Infrastructures' Threat to Trading Floors

It became evident by 1985 not only that did stock exchanges had to automate to survive, but also that automation could lead to the elimination of the trading floor altogether, since it could be an obstacle to competing effectively with the likes of NASDAQ and Instinet. If this were the case, stock exchanges would have no choice but to adopt the same computer-based infrastructures as their competitors, even if this meant making their trading floors redundant.

Global computer-mediated trading threatens medium- and small-sized stock exchanges, in particular. With the power and performance of computers continuing to increase, and the economies of networks continuing to provide more efficient global coverage, much of the global trading may eventually be done in the big three global centers of Tokyo, New York, and London. Since communications networks can efficiently link all traders in the world with these global centers, the only possible role for the other exchanges may be as regional centers or local nodes, in which limited or perhaps no trading takes place. In other words, today's smaller centers may become simply electronic switching centers in the future, in the same manner as computers are making all telephone exchanges completely electronic.

One of the first to realize this was Pearce Bunting, president of the Toronto Stock Exchange. In the TSE quarterly report to its members in 1985, the president said, "The Toronto Stock Exchange faces the prospect of losing further trading in Canada's major companies to foreign trading systems and of eventually becoming a backwater exchange. . . ."[4] Mr. Bunting went on to say that the march of technology would eventually lead to the demise of the Toronto Stock Exchange's new and expanded trading floor.

The same experience and fears began to plague even the London Stock Exchange in the aftermath of the Big Bang on October 27, 1986 (see Chapter 8). The London Stock Exchange's main attraction was its newly installed computerized trading network, but traders were abandoning the floor in large numbers for their own newly wired dealing rooms. Within six weeks of the October event, the regular crowd on the floor of the LSE had dwindled from 1000 to fewer than 100, and speculation was that it would soon be abandoned entirely. *Business Week* wrote, "Available soon. Prime location in historic City of London. Nearly 25,000 sq. ft. Equipped with latest telecommunications technology. Inquire at London Stock Exchange."[5]

In the latter half of the eighties, stock exchanges everywhere confronted an incredible irony that few businesses would want to face. Competitive forces were compelling them to automate to survive. The same set of forces was pressuring them to enter the international marketplace and link up, so that they could trade in stocks around the world and around the clock. But this could mean eliminating the floors altogether. If this happened, there was no telling where trading would take place: it could be in major centers, or it could be distributed throughout the world with no physical centers whatsoever. In any event, the world would probably not need as many regional exchanges.

When conditions such as these loom before an institution, the only thing it can do is to perform as well as it can and hope for the best. Even a minor mistake could be disastrous.

These are the ironic consequences of the peculiar economic forces that are at work in the global computer-mediated village. But this also is how great social and economic transformations occur. There is no place for companies or institutions to hide from the tides of change. There is no big brother or institution that is able to protect them from the technological and economic transformation that is taking place. They must adapt to survive and prosper. They are either the casualties and victims or they are the survivors and winners in the process of creative destruction.

## The Realities of Computer-Mediated Global Trading

People, managers, corporations, and institutions must fit in as best they can in the emerging computer-mediated global financial village. People must alter their habits and their life styles to adapt to the new realities of instantaneous, round-the-clock global trading. Brokers and traders must accommodate themselves to the various time zones in New York, London, Tokyo, and Hong Kong, where the bulk of trading is processed these days. As stock exchanges around the world extend their trading hours to compete and gain business, brokers and traders are forced to use their computers to play the stock exchanges in the major world centers at any time of the day.

Securities firms such as Merrill Lynch and Nomura claimed that they were trading around the clock in the mid-eighties, making use of a desk in New York or London, and carrying a ''book'' of securities. The ''book'' is the term used to record the positions that the firms hold in all the securities they handle, together with the strategies they follow. At that time, it was embodied in computer printouts and telex messages, and it was being communicated around the world from east to west, following the sun—New York to the Far East, back to Europe, and on again to New York—every twenty-four hours.

As Paul Ferris wrote:

> When the book leaves New York in the early evening, it is breakfast time next day in Tokyo: branch offices in different time-zones across the United States may also be involved. When Tokyo passes the book back to the West at the end of its afternoon, the morning's work has just begun in

London. London has the book to itself until 3 pm, give or take an hour for daylight-saving time, when Wall Street begins to trade. It is then 10 am, New York time. Until London closes, the two trade side by side.[6]

It would be only a matter of time before this "book" was completely mediated by computers.

The pace of events and the march of computerization take their toll on people and institutions. The subject came up in the aftermath of London's Big Bang in October 1986. It had become evident by that time that one of the biggest casualties in the automation of the stock exchange was people, particularly the traders, whose culture in London was well known to be polite and gentlemanly and whose pace of activity was leisurely. Long coffee breaks, fine food, and nice clothing were commonplace in the profession, and most enjoyed a good family life, unlike their counterparts in Chicago and New York. Computers changed the lives and the culture of London's financial community. Work overload, fatigue, exhaustion, and burnout became more pronounced.

"The problem with the stock exchange computers will probably be followed by far more serious ones suffered by the people who operate them," warned Malcolm Carruthers, who ran a stress clinic in London at the time. "We haven't anticipated . . . the workloads people will have to bear. Stress is the spice of life, but when you get an overload situation, then you can blow a fuse and have a heart attack or . . . a nervous breakdown."[7]

J. A. Bonn, a psychiatrist at the Stress Research Unit of St. Bartholomew's Hospital in London, put the problem this way: "The problem with computers is the lack of communications with other people. . . . Under pressure, people can become more work oriented and less able to cope. They become isolated. They cut down on family life, good food, exercise. They . . . blame it on the computers. . . ."[8]

## Principles and Dynamics of
## the New Computer-Mediated Stock Exchanges

Computer-mediated stock exchanges behave in a completely different manner from stock exchanges of the past. This behavior was no more evident than in the Great Stock Market Crash of October 19, 1987. To understand the role computers played, and the role of stocks, options, mutual funds, and pension funds, for example, one must examine the microfoundations of the operations of computerized stock exchanges.

First of all, computers made possible the proliferation of *derivative instruments* (the term used to describe the new instruments such as options, futures, and stock index futures, as well as options on futures), which act as substitutes for securities, and which have enormously complicated the strategies that traders can play. Second, as described above, all the major traders were linked to the computers in both the New York and the Chicago Stock Exchanges, as well as to other major exchanges of the world, so they knew what was happening in all the exchanges at all times.

A decade or more ago, stock exchanges around the world operated relatively independently of one another, but this is no longer the case. Computers synchronize them by the hour, by the minute, and perhaps ultimately by the second. This enables traders to buy and sell on any exchange as if they were right there. In New York, you can buy and sell securities belonging to major corporations, but when you want to deal in derivative instruments, you trade in Chicago, and since these instruments are designed to better manage risk, Chicago is known as the world capital of risk.

Traders can now more easily and inexpensively engage in speculation, and they can hedge their portfolios against increases or decreases in the market. Their use of a technique called *arbitrage*, which consists of buying instruments in one market and selling them in another, makes it imperative that they have electronic access to as many markets as possible.

Traders can also protect their entire portfolio through a technique known as *portfolio insurance* by buying stock index futures or options on them, for example. To the extent that stock index futures represent a basket of securities making up an index such as the S&P 500, buyers cannot be worse off than the market itself. These new instruments can protect a trader from volatility but they also can increase volatility at the same time because they demand playing large blocks of securities.

Traders can also engage in a technique called *program trading*, which is a special way of playing stock markets. The computer serves as a medium for accessing, processing, and analyzing vast amounts of information from all over the world, and assists traders in making decisions on what, when, and where to buy and sell. Using computers in this way, traders can play incredibly more sophisticated strategies in multiple instruments and markets. Trading in this way speeds up the pace of stock market activity as well as the speed of adjustment, and it increases trading volume enormously.

This highly publicized technique involves programming computers automatically to take the best position in a variety of stocks, options, futures, and stock index futures by drawing on artificial intelligence, sophisticated mathematical techniques, and game strategies. The computers can calculate the probabilities of profitability resulting from various strategies, and can prove a crucial instrument and superior to manual methods, especially in volatile stock markets. (There is a widely held view that computers were the source of most of the volatility that was taking place on the stock markets throughout the eighties.) Once they have made these rapid calculations and figure out the best strategy to play under the circumstances, they issue commands to buy and sell the appropriate combinations of ''goods'' in the different markets.

In fully automated environments, computers can even initiate and execute trading without human intervention, based on their decision-making software. Program trading techniques are particularly popular with big institutions that manage billions of dollars and buy and sell huge blocks of securities at once. Pension and mutual fund managers, insurance companies, and investment houses make extensive use of portfolio insurance and program trading techniques; when they act in concert, they can dictate and control the behavior of the market.

Program trading and portfolio insurance techniques can be used to explain much of the chaos on the stock exchanges in 1986 and 1987. Traders play options, futures, and stock index futures, as long as the price of the underlying stocks in their portfolio remains within a certain range. When the price varies outside these so-called ''trigger prices,'' the computer issues commands to buy or sell the underlying stocks in their portfolio.

To make these new techniques profitable, it is important to buy and sell large blocks of securities, which can have a dramatic impact on the price of the securities as well as the price of the derivative instruments. When the effect is quite significant, it can stimulate rapid trading in derivative instruments, particularly options and stock index futures as traders try to protect themselves. This in turn can affect the price of the underlying stocks once again. A price spiral begins to develop, and it can grow in hours or even minutes to have a roller coaster effect on the entire stock exchange.

Since options and futures are traded on exchanges such as Chicago's, while the securities themselves are traded elsewhere, most likely in New York, an effect of program trading and other techniques is that the two exchanges sometimes are synchronized by the minute. Other stock exchanges around the world can be synchronized in the same way.

In the absence of the computer, it normally took many days for stock exchanges to adjust to changing economic conditions or trigger-happy speculators, but today these adjustments are made in a matter of hours, and in some cases minutes. At some point stability is restored, because computers are also programmed to reverse their strategy when there is profit to be made.

What worries many people is that stability might not be restored quickly enough because no one will have confidence that the market will turn profitable. Once the amplitude of the swing becomes great enough, there might not be any price in which people are willing to buy. Portfolio insurance and program trading techniques simply exacerbate a plummeting market, forcing a delay in and indeed inhibiting a correction. When this happens, there can be a domino effect on all the stocks on a single exchange, which can spread to other stock exchanges around the world in a matter of hours. There may be nothing to stop it.

After all, if investors and institutions in Tokyo, London, and other major centers are participating in a great sell-off, the chances are that no buyers will be found anywhere. When this happens, many fear that it can lead to a collapse of the world financial system.

Consequently, people can no longer play the markets on a day-to-day or even a week-to-week basis without being connected to a computer in one way or another. They need computers to keep them informed, to enable them to buy and sell in the market, and to make decisions about what to sell, where to sell it, and for how much.

The global marketplace and the proliferation of new instruments are simply too great for individuals to cope with any longer using manual techniques. People need computers to tell them when and where opportunity exists, to enable them to capitalize on opportunities, and to protect themselves from risk. The reality is that people can no longer depend on their innate mental powers to keep track all of the events, to analyze all the possibilities, and to make all the calculations necessary to play the markets. They need to be mediated by computers. Some people even suspect that the computers may some day play the markets by themselves. This is the direction trading appears to be heading in the late eighties and there may be little anyone can do about it.

## The First Warning: The Stock Market Crash
## of September 11–12, 1986

It was factors such as these that caused a so-called crash of the stock market on September 11 and 12, 1986, when the Dow Jones plummeted a then-record 86.81 points, or 4.6 percent, the largest drop since the Great Depression. In Chicago, activity was just as hectic as it was in New York as trading in futures broke all records. Trading volume in Standard and Poor's 500 stock index futures contracts soared to a record $36 billion, about twice the value of stocks on the New York Stock Exchange. The trading became so volatile, particularly on the eleventh, that one trader was reported to have lost $10 million that single day. Five members of the Chicago Mercantile Exchange did so badly that they had to sell their seats on the stock exchange the same night. The stock markets in London and Tokyo were experiencing similar shocks.

Trading volumes were surpassing all records. On the eleventh, volume reached 237 million shares; the next day it hit 240 million. In another market swing, on January 23, 1987, the Dow rose 64 points and then dropped 110 points in the span of one hour. Trading volume soared to an unheard of 320 million. This volatility didn't cause all the panic that many were predicting, however, because traders had gotten used to it. They had reprogrammed their computers to make the appropriate adjustments in their calculations. Speculation was mounting that the Dow could drop 150 points, or even 250 points, in a single session. Of course, nobody really thought it would surpass this.

## Black Monday: The Greatest Collapse
## in the History of the Stock Exchange

October 19, 1987 is known as Black Monday around the world. On that day, all the major stock markets in the world crashed so badly that, for a day or so, it made 1929 look mild in comparison. The chairman of the New York Stock Exchange called it a "financial meltdown." The Dow fell 508 points, a drop of 22.6 percent, and the volume of shares shot to over 604 million. (In comparison, the market dropped 12.8 percent on October 28, 1929.) More than half a trillion dollars in wealth evaporated in a few hours.

*The New York Times* reported that the fifty-two specialists on the NYSE, whose job it was to maintain an orderly market, lost $750 million. The biggest loss was $40 million, and one specialist firm did so badly that Merrill Lynch had to take it over. Three other firms had to arrange immediate bank financing.

The following day the NYSE made one of the greatest gains in history. It jumped 186.8 points.

Shock waves hit Chicago, London, Tokyo, Hong Kong, and other international centers. Within hours, the Tokyo Stock Exchange had dropped an unprecedented 14 percent, wiping out $400 billion. The next day it roared back with its biggest one-day gain ever of 9 percent. The Hong Kong Exchange was hit harder than any other exchange. It had actually plummeted before the New York Stock Exchange and probably triggered the panic in New York to some degree. After New York fell, Hong Kong closed its doors altogether for four days.

The Sydney Stock Exchange slipped 25 percent. Stock exchanges in London, Frankfurt, and Paris fell in synchrony with the other exchanges. For two weeks, the shock waves reverberated around the world. Sometimes, they took their lead from London, at other times from Hong Kong, at other times from New York.

None of the exchanges had ever witnessed anything like this. Some blamed it on the computers and program trading. Others blamed it on the Reagan administration, especially its inability to stem the tide of growing budget and trade deficits. Still others blamed it on the big institutions that, in their eagerness to protect themselves, overreacted. The New York Stock Exchange blamed Chicago and Chicago blamed New York. The specialists on the New York Stock Exchange were also blamed. In truth, in one way or another, all of them were to blame.

On that day, computers were ready with their program trading and portfolio insurance techniques, and when the market began to become more volatile than usual, they began telling their masters, the big institutions, to sell. When the sell-off picked up in the late morning, the computers kicked in and took over. The techniques, which were supposed to protect computer trading under volatile conditions, did not work. They did the reverse. There was nothing to do to protect themselves except sell, which effectively exacerbated the fall. About 20 percent of the trades that day were triggered by the computers, with critical results at a critical time.

The crash shook the confidence of the governments and central banks of all major industrialized countries. Finance ministers were in constant communication with one another, and they agreed to coordinate their actions to restore confidence in the market and their economies. Since a few days before October 19 there had been fears of an outbreak of inflation, central bankers were already in agreement on the need to increase interest rates. On the evening of the nineteenth, there were widespread fears that the crash would initiate a recession. The Fed chairman, Alan Greenspan, pumped so much money into the financial system that three-month Treasury yields dropped three-quarters of a percentage point. In Canada, the Bank of Canada lowered its key interest rate by 157 basis points, the largest in its history. Central bankers in other countries followed suit.

President Reagan also went on national television promising to cooperate with Congress to cut the budget deficit even if it meant raising taxes. A week afterward, confidence in the U.S. dollar waned and it fell below the psychological barrier of 140 yen. One week later, it reached a then–all-time low of 134.45 to the yen when it was clear that the United States was not going to support the dollar and that Japan and West Germany were not going to stimulate their economies.

A month after the crash, however, the statistics on how the economy had performed were published and they surprised everyone. The Crash had had little effect on the real economy. Computers had fundamentally altered the links between the psychological economy, the intelligent economy, and the real economy.

Essentially, however, October 19 will be remembered in history as a turning point in world economic affairs. On that day, the full impact and significance of global computer-mediated stock markets hit home. No stock market in the world could be insulated any longer from what was happening in the other exchanges. No national economy, no national government, and no individual would be insulated from events in the global marketplace.

Global computer-mediated securities and currencies markets and options and futures markets were integrating all national markets into a single global *hypermarket*.

## Notes

1. *Encyclopedia of Banking and Finance*, 8th ed., p. 696.
2. Ferris, "Gentlemen of Fortune," pp. 122–124.
3. Ibid.
4. *Globe and Mail*, "Computerized Trading Poses Threat," p. B3.
5. *Business Week*, "The New Exchange Floor," p. 60.
6. Ferris, loc. cit.
7. *Globe and Mail*, "Computers Have a Chap Working," p. B28.
8. Ibid.

# 6

# Strategically Managing Computer Systems Synergies and Integrated Service Financial Supermarkets

## Computer System Synergies

*Synergy* is defined as the effect of various organs, drugs, or forces that, when combined, exceed the sum of their individual parts: an important but invisible component of all corporate and economic activity, one that American banking and financial services companies found in their growing arsenal of computer-based assets. Synergy enabled these companies to bundle more and more financial services under their respective corporate umbrellas to build what have become known as financial supermarkets. They captured the synergies in their massive computer-based processing, distribution, and communications systems by using them to better manage money, capital, information, systems, and human resources on a national and global scale.

Computer networks enabled them to concentrate these resources and dedicate them to satisfying the entire range of services demanded by each customer. They became sources of greater efficiency and productivity, higher-value services, and growth and profit that gave these companies strategic advantages in the battle for domination of the entire financial services sector of the United States.

Before computerization, financial markets were highly fragmented, having many isolated local markets, each with several distinct products, services, and customer classes. After computerization, financial markets were integrated, forming multiple-service markets with diverse customer classes distributed over national and global territories.

It was the synergy derived from their computer-based assets and their financial, capital, and human resources that enabled financial corporations to grow to such a size that they began to internalize what used to be entire markets.

Synergies enabled a few of the largest corporations in America to form highly diversified conglomerates encompassing the entire range of banking, financial, information, telecommunications, and other services. Companies such as American Express, Citicorp, Merrill Lynch, Bank of America, and even Sears, Roebuck and General Motors used these synergies to try to dominate banking, brokerage, retailing, travel and entertainment, and insurance. Their weapons were computer systems and networks, sophisticated software and artificial intelligence–based products and services; telecommunications and satellite systems; computerized debit and credit cards; automated teller machines, personal computers, databanks; and an expanding variety of related assets, systems, and services.

## Strategic Management, Capital, and Human Resource Assets

To prosper in the computer age, corporations must use every asset and resource strategically, including their computer systems and networks; information and communications resources; and their human, capital, and financial resources. They must have large amounts of capital to finance enormous investments in systems, networks, software development, telecommunications, and related infrastructures.

Capital, for example, is essential for financing the regional and national distribution networks that have become the backbones of banking services, the automated teller machines, credit card–processing systems, brokerage services, and mortgage and insurance services. Capital is also integral to bankrolling innovations in the development and marketing of new financial instruments, which are of crucial significance to all companies. As competition from other large corporations heats up, margins are eroded and companies find that they need vast sums of capital to survive. Huge capital resources can finance expansion through acquisition, thereby taking advantage of synergies in various markets. Capital is necessary to fend off takeover bids from competitors and raiders.

In addition to capital, corporations depend on an ever-widening portfolio of human resources. They need leaders capable of exercising strategic vision. Highly trained technicians, systems specialists, programmers, and managers have to cope with extreme complexity in systems design, planning, development, and implementation. Innovators and strategic planners must spot opportunities far into the future and devise ways of grabbing them. Professional marketing people are important to effectively determine rapidly changing customer needs and market conditions, and assess ways of meeting them.

Professional sales people have to be capable of satisfying diverse customer needs, using corporate system resources in satisfying these needs, and effectively promoting each of the many kinds of financial services offered by their company. Experts in banking and finance are needed to advise on and manage complicated money, capital, and securities assets and services in an electronic environment. Trained staff have to be able to utilize corporate systems, networks, information, and decision support systems to maximum advantage.

Finally, the portfolio of human resources includes the generalists, the strategic planners and managers, and those who can manage human resources to create the necessary corporate cultures and people synergies to complement the all-important system synergies. All of them need to be in place for entry into the world of computer-mediated banking and financial supermarkets.

## The Window of Opportunity Opens Up

In the late seventies and early eighties, the window of opportunity for exploiting the potential of full-service financial supermarkets opened up. Several very large American corporations not only took advantage of it but also staked their future on it. The result was a scramble for position and fierce competition between formerly separate and noncompeting industries and sectors of the economy. The race was on to dominate all of the information, financial, banking, and other sectors of the United States—and international—economy.

Acquisitions was one of the most important strategies for obtaining the critical mass of computer systems and customers necessary to realize the all-important economies of scale. Diverse customer classes could be reached by these integrated corporate infrastructures, and the resultant national and global multiservice, multimarket financial conglomerates could wring enormous computer systems synergies from these procedures.

Figure 6.1. **Stakeholders in the Financial Supermarkets Game.**

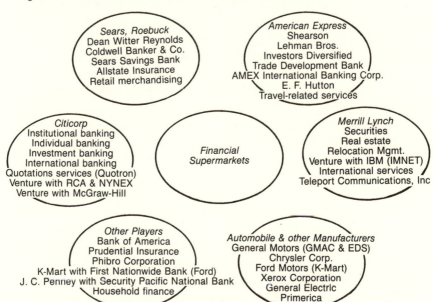

Leading contenders in the banking industry began purchasing insurance, real estate, or brokerage companies. Every major nonbanking corporation, it seemed, became interested in acquiring banks and thrifts. Brokerage companies began buying banks, finance and insurance companies, and giant retailers began snapping up banks, thrifts, brokerages, and insurance companies. Corporate titans began to emerge in America and around the world in this way.

Acquisitions were not the only route to success, however, and the action was not confined to the banking and financial industries. Several joint ventures were launched across seemingly unrelated industrial sectors including the financial, telecommunications, and computer industries. These gave strategic advantage to companies with complementary strengths, including those with great technological strength and systems expertise, those with enormous network assets, and those with strengths in various segments of information, securities, and financial services. Merrill Lynch, for example, engaged in joint ventures with IBM, as Sears did with IBM and CBS, and as Bank of America did with Time and AT&T. Companies with substantial credit card services, data processing services, or automated teller networks, for example, had an incentive to pool their resources through joint ventures, although some of these became targets for acquisition by larger companies. Figure 6.1 illustrates some of the corporate holdings of the major players in the financial supermarket.

The enormous synergies possible and the profit potential attracted the major automobile, computer and equipment leasing, and oil companies with subsidiaries in finance. As the decade of the nineties drew near, companies from all sectors of the economy became drawn into a vortex of change, mutation, metamorphosis, and conglomeration. The result was a proliferation of corporate acquisitions and joint ventures that, together with other factors and forces, completely restructured the industrial landscape of America.

## Strategic Management Vision at Citicorp

Citicorp is often cited as an example of how computer technology and banking were melded together in a more organized fashion than in most other companies. Under the leadership of Walter Wriston, its president in the late seventies and early eighties, and John Reed, in charge of consumer banking, Citicorp was transformed from a mediocre bank holding company into one of the most innovative, growth-oriented, competitive companies in the world. Under these two visionaries, Citicorp grew and overtook Bank of America as the largest bank holding company in the United States. This transformation is often cited as a lesson in leadership, strategic vision, corporate cultural building, and the integrated management of technology, automation, and change.

The challenges facing Wriston and Reed in the seventies were considerable. Both commercial and consumer banking were coming under increasing competitive pressures at a time when banking was supposed to be highly protected by regulations. The wholesale bank's base of deposits from corporate borrowers had been eroded by competition for a decade. At the same time, allowing deposits to sit at fixed interest rates over long periods was not the right thing to do when automation permitted the more efficient use of deposits through the creation of cash management networks.

Citicorp also foresaw that banks would eventually face the loss of demand deposits to higher-yielding transaction vehicles such as commercial paper and money market certificates. According to Reed, the solution was to shift Citicorp's assets away from structurally unattractive prime wholesale lending to more productive activities such as computer-based services. Computer technology could be used to significantly increase the value and productivity of these financial assets, thereby gaining advantages over the competition.

Another problem faced by Citicorp was regulatory. Regulations and geographical restrictions prevented the company from making a foray into computer-based services and the creation of a national branch banking network. The company would have to overcome this problem as well, and it realized that technology could also provide the solution. Reed argued that "technological improvements in the delivery of financial services had enabled nonbanks to compete with banks through money market funds and mortgage pools. . .[and that] technology had made country, state and regional boundaries artificial constraints."[1] If nonbanks could use computer technology in this way, then so could commercial banks.

Reed, an MIT-trained computer expert, initiated many of the technological and management innovations at Citicorp that changed the corporate culture of the company and positioned it for maximum leverage in the marketplace. He initiated Project Paradise to install minicomputers in the company wherever possible, even at the expense of mainframes, to distribute better the power of the computer. The company's Technology Caravan was designed to encourage managers to try various kinds of hardware and software to improve their productivity, to educate workers having little or no familiarity with computers, and to overcome resistance to the new technology. Reed's think tank, Transactions Technology Inc., was created, among other reasons, to design software that would enable IRAs, deposits, loans, and the administrative procedures for branch management to function from one database. This would enable managers to make more effective use of the information resources of the corporation.

In the late seventies, Citicorp began to make several moves to break out of the regulatory straightjacket that constrained its future growth, using all the managerial and technological tools at its disposal. It created a time-sharing subsidiary called Citishare to lead the company into nationwide banking. Trying out these services internally at first to gain the necessary experience and to develop the necessary expertise while testing, Citicorp lobbied the regulators intensively and eventually persuaded them to permit the venture to go commercial. The newly created subsidiary immediately set out to build a nationwide electronic network. It built a "thin branch distribution network" relying less on traditional brick and mortar and more on telephones, mail, credit cards, and automated teller machines.

One of Citicorp's advantages was that its operating costs were about one-third lower than those of its competitor's brick-and-mortar branch systems. It developed one of the first comprehensive ATM networks to serve the New York area and used a variety of low-cost techniques to ensnare consumers across the country into doing business with the bank. In these ways, it was able to devise end runs around laws limiting U.S. banks to operating in a single state, thereby making it an interstate bank in all but name.

Citicorp targeted the credit card business because it was a key to electronic banking and a wide variety of new business services that were necessary to its future. In 1977, the company made a major foray into the credit card business by mailing out 20 million credit cards; almost overnight, it became one of the largest issuers of credit cards in the United States. It purchased Diners Club and Carte Blanche, which were directed at the market dominated by American Express. Citicorp also bought a third card company, which it renamed Choice, and proceeded to market the card aggressively as an all-purpose card. It promoted the card with a line of credit, no annual fees, rebates on certain purchases, and the choice of several interest-bearing accounts with attractive rates. These multiple features, it hoped, would enable it to gain rapid acceptance by the public.

In 1983, Citicorp promoted Choice heavily in Colorado, one of the few states that allowed limited-service, out-of-state banks to collect consumer deposits and that required banks with ATMs to share them with others in the state. In the same year, Citicorp petitioned Maryland to pass legislation allowing out-of-state bank holding companies to set up shop; subsequently, it established a subsidiary in the state to process credit card transactions. Citicorp then used Maryland to launch Choice nationwide, signing up ATM networks in Florida, Texas, and California and expanding into Washington, Delaware, Virginia, North Carolina, and Pennsylvania by using the enormous economies in its huge credit-card processing operations.

In Virginia, Citicorp started a price war with state banks by offering to process merchants' Visa and MasterCard transactions at one-half a percentage point below that of the other banks. The banks eventually capitulated and offered to promote Choice as well as Visa and Master-Card. Altogether, Citicorp was estimated to have 16.7 million card holders and 10 percent of the U.S. card revenues in 1984.

In the late seventies, Wriston began to position Citicorp as a global, diversified company capable of competing in just about every segment of the emerging integrated electronic financial marketplace. He replaced the old matrix management structure with a simpler one, which can be summed up as the three I's: the Institutional Bank, which handled worldwide business with corporations, banks, and governments; the Individual Bank, which dealt with worldwide consumer accounts; and the Investment Bank, which functioned somewhat like a Wall Street investment house. As a result, the company became highly decentralized and distinguished by a competitive, entrepreneurial spirit. The company also positioned itself in the emerging market for global information services. Wriston became convinced that "information about money has become almost as important as money itself . . . [and he set out to turn the company into a] . . . preeminent distributor of financial database services worldwide."[2]

Citicorp's so-called five-I strategy—calling for activities in institutional, individual, investment, insurance, and information sectors— emerged in the late 1970s as a means of preparing the company to play a preeminent role as an integrated financial supermarket. It used the enormous economies of scale offered by the new technology to great advantage. It also created synergies and scale economies by a process of acquisition and diversification into nonlending sectors.

Citicorp was the first federally chartered bank to buy an out-of-state thrift, California's 92-branch Fidelity Savings and Loan Association, in 1982. In 1984, it added a 60-branch thrift in Illinois and a 34-branch one in Florida. By 1984, Citicorp offered in most states consumer and sales financing, mortgage banking, discount securities brokerage, and some insurance and data processing services, and, as already noted, it had a sizable domestic base of customers in credit cards. In the mideighties, it became a communications common carrier and a supplier of computer services, teaming up with RCA and NYNEX to provide electronic services to the home. It also entered into a joint venture with McGraw-Hill to provide a twenty-four-hour trading venture called Global Electronic Markets Company so traders not only could get information instantly, but also could make deals and transfer money in minutes using Citicorp's financial services and McGraw-Hill's commodity data.

In 1985, Citicorp's forward-looking, innovative style of management and its leadership in the entire financial services field were showing results. It overtook Bank of America as the bank with the largest base of deposits in America—$94.4 billion, up from $79.6 billion the year earlier. In 1985, it consolidated its huge foreign exchange and money market trading operations into a new investment bank with $425 million in revenues, and in 1986 it bought out controlling interest in Quotron, one of the largest suppliers of automated stock quotations. In 1987, Citicorp began offering a national money transfer service called Express Money in competition with Western Union. It also became determined to break into the Japanese market and started stalking the Japanese marketplace to purchase a bank. In ways such as these, superior management, leadership, and aggressiveness made Citicorp one of the most powerful financial supermarkets in the United States.

## American Express: From a Credit Card Company to a Financial Supermarket

American Express, one of the most successful financial empires in the world, was able to reach its pinnacle in a period of four years through a series of well-targeted acquisitions in the early part of the eighties. The transformation of American Express in such a short period of time is a lesson in planning. Before 1981, the company managed primarily a credit card business and sold traveler's checks to the public. After 1984, it had strengths in securities brokerage, investment banking, and insurance that together rivaled that of any competitor in the financial supermarket business. It was able to raise and manage billions of dollars in capital to buy its way into this market, and to make money at the same time. Perhaps no other company could have done it the same way.

The flagship of the American Express financial empire is its Travel Related Services Company (TRS), which dominates the high-end segments of the traveler's check and credit card business. Between 1979 and 1984, its circulation of credit cards had grown from 10.5 million to 17.7 million. Although this represented only about 6 percent of the market, it comprised the most profitable segment of the business consisting of those high-income individuals and corporate users who were the biggest spenders and the users of traveler's checks and credit cards.

The company was able to use the technological and marketing strengths of TRS to branch out into other segments of the financial services business. Its Funds Access Services, for example, gave customers access to an increasing number of computerized services, including bank-operated automated teller machines and traveler's checks dispensers. These machines were accessed by using the American Express credit card as well as proprietary bank cards, and they enabled customers to quickly replace lost or stolen traveler's checks. It also operated one of the most up-to-date reservations systems in the world, which it provided in conjunction with the American Airlines Sabre System. This system, the core of its travel control and reporting service, provided information about the most advantageous fares for travelers, and automatically printed tickets together with itineraries and hotel reservations.

American Express already had a presence in the property and casualty insurance services field through a subsidiary called Fireman's Fund Insurance Company, which it purchased in 1968. But it wasn't until 1981 that it began its drive to transform itself into a full-service financial empire. In that year, it purchased Shearson Loeb Rhoades, one of the largest securities firms in the United States with over 300 offices within the United States and several outside. With this, American Express gained an enormous retailing operation, which it vitally needed to exploit its supermarket mission, and was able to sell credit cards, credit card services, and Shearson products directly to consumers for the first time. This was significant, for in the past American Express had relied more on third parties such as banks, trust companies, brokers, and insurance agents to market it to the public.

Shearson itself had a history of successful acquisitions. In 1979, it had acquired Loeb Rhoades for $83 million and integrated it into its financial empire. The synergy between Shearson and Loeb Rhoades was tremendously beneficial for both companies. By absorbing Loeb Rhoades, Shearson was able to achieve a cost savings of $124 million in back office costs alone. Subsequently, Shearson acquired four regional brokerage houses, a major real estate syndicate, and a large money management firm. Shearson became the catalyst for the transformation of American Express into a financial supermarket.

In 1983, American Express paid $773 million for Investors Diversified Services (IDS), which sold life insurance, annuities, and mutual funds to middle America, the market served by Prudential Insurance, Sears, Roebuck, and others. IDS's main attraction to American Express was its ability to tap into new markets comprising millions of people that few competitors had access to other than through direct marketing. It had 4500 salespeople, 1.1 million customers, $17.5 billion in assets under management, and $13.5 billion in life insurance.

IDS complemented American Express in a number of ways. As noted above, American Express had a major presence in property and casualty insurance through Fireman's Fund, but it was weak in life insurance. IDS, however, was just the opposite—its strength was in life insurance. American Express also had only had a modest stake in the fast-growing money management field while IDS was one of the nation's largest managers of stock and bond mutual funds as well as a major institutional portfolio manager. The match seemed unbeatable.

The next move of American Express was further into investment banking in 1984, when it acquired Lehman Brothers Kuhn Loeb, a blue chip investment firm, for $360 million. Lehman was to become part of the Shearson unit and would more than double Shearson's presence in the investment banking business. Together, Shearson Lehman/ American Express became almost equal in size to the brokerage industry leader, Merrill Lynch Pierce Fenner & Smith. The acquisition had major benefits to both Shearson and American Express in the form of major synergies and economies of scale.

Shearson had such large processing capacity that it could incorporate Lehman's operations without any additional costs in its back office. When you combine the revenues of two companies in this way without having to absorb the cost, it can have a mind-boggling effect on the bottom line. That is what synergy is all about. Shearson planned to absorb Lehman's trading operations in bonds and money market instruments as well as its equity arbitrage unit, reflecting the increasing importance of investment banking to American Express and the financial supermarket business in general.

But American Express was expanding aggressively in the international marketplace as well. Its subsidiary, American Express International Banking Corporation (AEIB), had 85 offices in 38 countries and had become a major player in private banking with $4.5 billion in deposits and fiduciary accounts. In 1983, AEIB purchased Swiss-based Trade Development Bank (TDB) for $520 million. The TDB and American Express deal meant further synergies and mutual benefits for both sides, both in terms of the kinds of services they provided and of the geographical markets they served. The TDB had branches throughout Europe and its clients were very wealthy. American Express wanted both.

Other synergies were evident as well. The TDB owned a sizable commercial bank in New York, while its original owner, Edmond Safra, controlled a bank in Brazil called Banco Safra, which accepted international deposits, engaged in gold trading and foreign exchange, and moved bank notes, the physical cash, around the world. These complemented the American Express Asian operations and its Shearson subsidiary operations in commodity markets and gold. With these strengths and these assets, American Express was well on its way to becoming a powerhouse in the domestic and international financial marketplace.

It topped these off in April 1987 by selling a 13 percent stake in Shearson Lehman to Nippon Life of Japan for $508 million in exchange for the right to offer the entire range of Amex products to Nippon's customers. Then, in December, it announced that it was purchasing the E. F. Hutton Group for $960 million. The company was close to its goal of overtaking Merrill Lynch as the biggest brokerage company in the United States.

### Sears Corporation: From Socks, Tools, and Home Appliances to a Financial Supermarket

The name "Sears, Roebuck" has become as synonymous with finance in recent decades as it has been with merchandising and retailing throughout this century. In some respects, the company has been a financial supermarket for many decades. Early in its history, in 1931, the company established Allstate Insurance, and in 1958, it formed Sears Savings Bank, now the nation's twenty-third largest thrift. When American Express and Citicorp began executing their plans to build financial empires in the early eighties, Sears was ready with its own.

Besides its financial and insurance holdings, it had unparalleled massive retail distribution and merchandising operations. It enjoyed direct access to the large mass market in the United States through its national network of retail stores. It was able to build on this foundation by acquiring companies in retail banking, brokerage, real estate, insurance, credit cards, and automated teller machines. By 1983, Allstate had built a network of 1,950 offices throughout the United States. Sears had also acquired 87 savings and loan association offices and had diversified into real estate.

In 1981, the same year that American Express acquired Shearson, Sears made a double play by acquiring Dean Witter Reynolds, the fifth largest securities brokerage company in the United States, and Coldwell Banker and Company, the nation's largest real estate broker. Together, these acquisitions significantly increased the company's stake in the rapidly growing and changing field of integrated financial services. Sears then had a substantial presence in insurance, consumer credit, brokerage, and real estate to complement its even greater strengths in retail merchandising.

By early 1982, everything was in place for Sears to embark on an ambitious plan to develop a Sears Financial Network. The undertaking would entail opening 33 financial centers at first in its vast retail network across the United States, increasing these to 250 by 1984. Through these centers, the company planned to capitalize on its large, almost captive customer base, cross selling a growing array of financial services. By suitably managing its credit and financial services portfolio, using the synergy gained from merchandising and financial services, Sears hoped to achieve cost advantages, market advantages, and quality and service advantages over its rivals.

With this portfolio of assets, the synergies would come from many sources, from vertical as well as horizontal integration of its diverse activities. It began originating, insuring, and packaging its loans, and selling them through Dean Witter to investors. It started selling mortgage-backed securities and introduced tax exempt unit trusts and a line of credit that allowed homeowners to borrow against their home equity. It distributed these through its massive distribution network of 831 retail stores, 2,388 catalog outlets, 1,950 stand-alone Allstate Insurance sales offices, 355 Dean Witter offices, 87 Allstate Savings & Loan Association branches in California, and several hundred real estate locations. In so doing, Sears was "eliminating the middleman up and down the line, so each profit they internalize puts them a step ahead."[3] The company gained by cutting its costs as well as by increasing the value added to its services, thereby gaining significant advantages over its competition in the financial supermarket game.

After 10 months, Dean Witter brokers were piling up almost four times as many accounts in the centers as at its other offices in the same cities. According to Allstate Chairman Donald Gaib, Jr., the productivity gains of agents stationed in the new centers were double those of other agents. One source of the synergy lay in areas such as using credit information available on Sears's customers to prequalify them for home loans or for cross-selling financial products.

One of Sears's strengths was its long-range strategic planning. As the momentum of the eighties increased, the company made a number of moves to further strengthen its position in the evolving financial supermarket business. It initiated nearly two dozen task forces to explore "possible synergies in areas ranging from mortgage banking to telecommunications . . . [to] figure out how . . . [to] attract its 40 million-strong customer base to its financial services."[4] Its annual telecommunications bill, which amounted to about $500 million, made it the largest private customer of AT&T and IBM. As a result, it created a new unit to leverage its huge data processing and telecommunications capabilities and tie together the data processing facilities of its various subsidiaries.

One of its top-priority ventures was to link the systems of its several operating companies so it could later sell a multitude of information and transactions services. It also planned a nationwide electronic payments system for financial institutions that was much less expensive than those provided by the banks. In all these ways, the company was taking advantage of its internal economies and making itself more efficient and competitive.

Sears continued stalking the savings and loan industry for acquisitions to increase a nationwide deposit base throughout the eighties. Its potential in this regard was summarized by Visa president Charles Russell: "Sears has what is tantamount to a nationwide retail bank today. . . . If even a small percentage of Sears's customers begin banking with them, it will become a giant bank almost overnight."

In September of 1986, Sears announced what many competitors had been waiting for, its entry into the general service credit card business. The card, called Discover, was designed to be the link between the assortment of banking, investment, and insurance products offered by the various Sears units. According to Sears President Edward A. Brennen, "Discover is the glue that will pull together our banking, insurance, brokerage, and real estate products. . . . We're going to change the way people think about plastic."[5]

## Merrill Lynch Plays for
## Supermarket Supremacy

Merrill Lynch was a financial supermarket before the name was invented in the eighties. The company had always maintained a department store approach to the securities brokerage and investment business, and was more successful at this than any other company in the United States. To win big as a financial supermarket, a company had to be measured against Merrill Lynch in size and distribution capability and had to be capable of successfully competing with it.

The company had acquired a foothold in real estate financing in 1968, and, in 1969, it purchased a company in the asset management and economic consulting business. But it was Donald Regan, later

President Reagan's Treasury Secretary, who saw the financial super-market as an important natural outgrowth of the philosophy of the company. The company's size and its national distribution network made it a natural winner and pacesetter in the evolving marketplace. It was Regan who converted Merrill Lynch to the concept of the financial supermarket, blazing the logical path to future growth for the company.

Throughout the seventies and early eighties, Merrill Lynch began to expand and diversify its financial interests through acquisitions and joint ventures, as well as by offering new services via its existing organization. A formal Capital Markets group was established in 1976, and strengthened in 1978 with the acquisition of White, Weld. It diversified into the life insurance business, into the employee relocations business, and into real estate brokerage, principally through acquisition. One of its new subsidiaries, Merrill Lynch Relocation Management, developed such a complete set of relocation services that it was said that an executive could give the Merrill Lynch agent the keys to his home in one city and pick up the keys to his new home in another city within days.

In order to better position itself as a financial supermarket, Merrill Lynch moved toward a customer-oriented rather than a product-centered structure, seeking to provide an integrated package of services "wrapped around the customer." The company was able to successfully make the necessary adjustments in the investment area to meet the growing and changing demands of its customers—particularly individual investors who were demanding more flexibility and more sophisticated products and services in convenient packages—and the increasing institutionalization and globalization of the markets. Its expanding assets of computer systems and networks played an essential role in transforming Merrill Lynch into a financial supermarket.

Many companies the size of Merrill Lynch have difficulty being innovative, but this is not true of this company. In 1977, for example, it unveiled one of the most successful new financial services in American history, which brought the company into direct competition with commercial banks. The new service was called the Cash Management Account (CMA). It had a variety of very attractive options that no other financial institution offered, all packaged into one account. Three unique features were the ability of investors to borrow against their own securities; the automatic reinvestment into money market funds of the proceeds from the investments and any other surplus funds; and the ability of investors to borrow on the account up to an agreed-upon amount. Customers received a consolidated monthly statement of all transactions made on the account. This CMA could not have been developed by Merrill Lynch without major investments in its computer and information systems and without designing them in ways that were strategic to the environment.

The CMA was an unqualified success for Merrill Lynch. Instead of the one hundred thousand accounts it had expected, the company got one million. The triumph of the CMA gave the company an even greater advantage over its rivals. In the eighties, Merrill Lynch continued to dominate the service even though other companies had by then developed their own.

Merrill Lynch depended on computer technology to transform itself into a financial supermarket. It used its nationwide computer network to tie its brokerage and trading operations together, enabling it to distribute new securities issues throughout the nation more rapidly and to get more penetration than any other brokerage company. This, in turn, gave the company major competitive pluses in the brokerage and underwriting business. But the company also continued to be innovative in other areas as well.

In 1983, for example, it unveiled what amounted to a foreign currency trading service for small- and medium-sized corporations that could not afford to use the interbank market. The new service provided a low-cost means by which companies could buffer their earnings against exchange rate volatility, and gave currency traders another way to speculate on currency movements. The service was made possible by the enormous base of computer assets owned by the company. This was reinforced in 1984, when it announced a joint venture with IBM to develop IMNET, a new financial brokerage and information service based on the IBM PC.

The 1984 Annual Report of Merrill Lynch spotlighted its success as a financial supermarket. Revenues from its investment underwriting and advisory services amounted to $746 million, and its trading operations were worth $675 million. In comparison, First Boston's were $198 million and $176 million, respectively. Gross revenues of Merrill Lynch were $5.6 billion in the same year, with earnings at $230 million and capital at $1.9 billion. Through its subsidiaries, the holding company employed more than 45,000 people, mostly in the United States. Its retail brokerage activities were conducted through Merrill Lynch Pierce Fenner & Smith, the largest securities firm in the world, which served 4.5 million customers through more than 9000 salespeople and account executives operating in over 430 offices in 49 states. It was this distribution system that was so vital to the company's strength. It could market and distribute securities locally, regionally, and nationally and tailor its marketing to meet the special circumstances of each client and each market. Merrill Lynch International Inc. includes the trading, sales, and capital-raising activities outside the United States, with more than 50 offices in over 30 different countries.

Merrill Lynch is actively involved in telecommunications as well. It is a majority shareholder in Teleport Communications, Inc. of New York in a joint venture with Western Union. The teleport, completed in 1985 and comprised of a 250 mile optical fiber network extending throughout New York and into New Jersey, is advertised as the world's first fully digital, end-to-end, optical fiber telecommunications system in the world. The nerve center on Staten Island houses high-capacity satellite facilities connecting all the corporations on its network to the major financial centers of the world. This operation is complemented by extensive real estate and related business services holdings associated with the teleport. The company is involved in an increasing number of telecommunications ventures such as this, including one across the Pacific.

Telecommunications and computers have played no small part in the ascendancy of Merrill Lynch to its national and global position. The company has always made extensive use of telephones, teleprinters, and computers in all its operations. With its large national retail base and its use of rapid and efficient computer, communications, and network facilities, it was unrivaled in its distribution network and became one of the strongest financial supermarkets in the United States.

## Other Stakeholders in
## the Financial Supermarket

There was an increasing number of other corporations in the United States making plans to transform themselves into financial supermarkets in the eighties. Many of these took the form of alliances among large and smaller competitors of American Express, Citicorp, Merrill Lynch and Sears, Roebuck. They included major retailers such as K-Mart and J. C. Penney, insurance companies such as Prudential, and even the major U.S. automobile and other manufacturers.

In 1987, K-Mart and Ford Motor Company, through Ford's subsidiary, First Nationwide Bank, announced a five-year plan to set up banking stations in 1000 of K-Mart's 2200 stores. In the same year, Security Pacific National Bank and J. C. Penney reported plans to market a variety of loans and investment services through 17 California retail stores of J. C. Penney. Elsewhere, Household Finance Corporation was putting together a national network through a group of thrifts it had rescued. General Electric, Primerica, and Kemper Corporation, an insurance company, were also building financial empires.

Prudential, one of the largest life insurers in the United States, had ambitions of becoming a financial supermarket as well. By 1981, it had more than 20,000 agents throughout the United States. Meanwhile, Bache Securities, a retail broker with a network of several thousand securities salesmen, was experiencing some financial difficulties in the early eighties and was fighting a takeover bid. Prudential and Bache complemented one another enormously, and a deal was struck in 1981 whereby Bache became a subsidiary of Prudential. The new company was called Prudential-Bache Securities.

This set Prudential well on its way to becoming a financial supermarket. Another Prudential subsidiary, PruCapital, provided loans and investments for industrial clients. Prudential soon bought a commercial bank that it named Prudential Bank & Trust Company, which offered financial services to insurance and brokerage clients. Eventually Prudential's insurance agents and Bache's brokers would cooperate to offer an integrated set of financial services.

Although the Prudential-Bache deal was not primarily intended to trigger a race for the financial supermarket, it did just that. Within several months of the Prudential-Bache deal, Salomon Brothers became part of Phibro, the trading conglomerate; Dean Witter Reynolds was bought by Sears, Roebuck; and American Express bought Shearson Loeb Rhoades.

Xerox Corporation, the giant copier and office equipment supplier, also grew to become a financial supermarket entity. In some respects, it had been in the finance business for some time through its leasing subsidiary, Xerox Credit Corporation. But in the early eighties, the company moved to place itself in what was to become a growing business. In 1981, it purchased Crum and Foster, which sold home, auto, and business insurance; Xerox also set up to sell another subsidiary called Xerox Financial Life life insurance and annuities. Yet another subsidiary, Van Kampen Merritt, which is in the investment banking business, was purchased in 1984 for $150 million. In 1987, Xerox purchased Furman Selz to sell institutional brokerage research and investment banking and equity expertise. These are all part of the Xerox Financial Services empire or what the company calls the Xerox Financial Machine.

### The Major U.S. Automobile Manufacturers Get into the Act

Throughout the sixties and seventies, the large American automobile manufacturers, Ford, General Motors, and Chrysler, had created financing arms to promote car sales and to take advantage of the growing profit in making loans to their clients. By the eighties, these subsidiaries had evolved into successful finance companies in their own right and become the means by which the automobile manufacturers would play an increasingly important role in the evolving financial and banking sector. Although they could offer cut-rate financing to promote the sales of automobiles independent of the banks, more significantly they were transforming the automobile manufacturers into financial service companies.

By the mid-eighties, General Motors Acceptance Corporation, Ford Motor Credit, and Chrysler Credit were gaining market share in the automobile loan business at the expense of the traditional lenders such as banks and credit unions. They offered cut-rate financing to spur the sales of automobiles, and at the same time came to be an acceptable source of credit for their clients' other purchases. By 1986, GMAC was servicing about $22.5 billion in mortgages through the purchases of Colonial Mortgage Service Company and the servicing portfolio and facilities of Norwest Mortgage Inc.

At the same time, its rival, Ford Motor Company, began to issue Visa cards through a thrift it owned to 20,000 of its employees who were frequent travelers. In 1987, First Nationwide Bank, its thrift subsidiary, which operated in eight states, negotiated an agreement with K-Mart to set up 53 kiosk-size branches in K-Mart stores. It planned to open 150 more of these stores before the year was out and to buy thrifts in six other states. Another rival, Chrysler, was studying the cross-marketing of some financial services through its consumer loan operations. These were some of the steps the automobile companies' financial subsidiaries were undertaking to establish themselves as prime providers of credit to American families.

One of the major advantages enjoyed by these financial subsidiaries was that they could afford to make loans at rates well below those of the banks because the loans were essentially subsidized by the auto companies themselves. By the mid-eighties, these subsidiaries were offering loans at rates of about 5.5 percent while the banks were keeping loans at about 11.5 percent. There was no way the subsidiaries couldn't win. The banks' share of automobile loans declined from 56 percent in 1981, when Detroit's cut-rate financing first appeared, to about 43 percent in the spring of 1986. The market share of the financial companies had gone up from the range of 20–30 percent to 35 percent. Overall, bank auto loans rose 4 percent in the year ending June 1986, while those of finance companies rose 40 percent.

General Motors had particularly ambitious plans in financial services as well as in other sectors of the economy, and computers played a major role in these plans. The company had developed the idea that computer-based services could offer enormous advantages in a variety of sectors of the economy. In 1984, it purchased Electronic Data Systems (EDS), one of the largest computer services companies in the United States, for $2.5 billion. GM used the technical and systems expertise of EDS and its national computer-based network to tie its national and international operations together as well as to play a strategic role in its ambitions in the evolving financial services market.

## The Formation of Hypercorporations and Hypermarkets

The term "financial supermarket" has been used to describe the phenomenon of conglomeration that was taking place in American industry in the eighties. This term significantly oversimplifies what was happening. Something akin to a "black hole" was drawing more and more corporate interests and entire industries into a new orbit. That force was the synergy that could come only from the development and strategic use of a supersophisticated intelligent infrastructure, which I have called a *hyperstructure*. So it is more appropriate to call these new forms of industrial organizations *hypercorporations* and *hypermarkets*. They are unique because they are increasingly mediated by computers in all their internal and external activities.

### Notes

1. *Datamation*, "Citi's Techno Boss?" pp. 32–34.
2. *Fortune*, "Citicorp After Wriston," p. 146.
3. *Business Week*, "Synergy for Sears' Financial Supermarket," pp. 116–117.
4. Ibid.
5. *Business Week*, "Sears Tests Its Clout," pp. 62–63.

# 7

# And the Walls Came Tumbling Down: The Erosion and Obsolescence of the Four Pillars of the Financial Community

## The Institutional Foundations of the Banking and Financial Services Sector

The tide of technological, industrial, and economic change that swept across America in the seventies and eighties ultimately destroyed the regulatory and institutional foundations of the financial community by making obsolete the four pillars that separated the banking, thrift, securities, and insurance industries. Computer-based infrastructures were incompatible with the older institutional order, and they made anachronistic its regulations and management practices. They did not recognize geographical boundaries to states and industrial markets, and their enormous synergies and efficiencies made it possible for companies to form financial supermarkets that supplied the complete range of financial services under one corporate roof.

Nonbanks, not subject to the same strict regulations as banks on their geographical operations and the kinds of services they offered, were able to use computers to perform many of the activities on which banks had a monopoly, but to do so in nontraditional, computer-based ways and under different names. As a result, commercial banks came under increasing competitive pressures from nonbanks. Legislatures at both state and federal levels were besieged by banks for relief, and by nonbanks for permission to expand further into banking territory. Deregulation ensued and allowed corporate executives to use their computer-based infrastructures to redesign the banking and financial playing fields of America.

## The Plight of the Commercial Banks

Commercial banks were constrained by a multitude of federal and state regulations, the three most important being the McFadden Act, which prohibited banks from crossing state lines; Regulation Q, which set ceilings on the interest rates banks could offer their customers for money on deposit; and the Glass-Steagall Act, which prohibited banks from engaging in securities underwriting and brokerage services. These and other regulations and legislation had the effect of putting commercial banks in a straightjacket, paralyzing their management, and creating a corporate culture immune to innovation and change.

Strategic management, marketing, leadership, and competition were foreign to the commercial banking industry of the fifties and sixties. As a result, it was among the last to recognize and use computer technology strategically, while other companies in other industries applied the technology and mastered it as it developed and evolved.

Before the computer, commercial banks had a virtual monopoly on checking accounts, and since literally every individual, household, and corporation used checks, this gave the banks enormous power. Customers were charged a fee for checking privileges, but they received no interest on their account balances. Interest rates on savings accounts were low. Commercial banks were able to take these deposits and account balances and invest them at much higher rates in loans to individuals and corporations. As long as they were able to continue in this way, they enjoyed a guaranteed secure and profitable business. The banking and financial legislation and regulatory institutions were in harmony with the underlying technological infrastructure of the day. Each aided and abetted the other. Eventually, however, computer technology and computer-based infrastructures destroyed these old infrastructures and the institutions that went with them.

The McFadden Act of 1927 represented a landmark in banking legislation. It permitted national banks to operate branches other than where the banks were based if a state law allowed their state-chartered counterparts the same freedom. The effective result was that all national banks were constrained by the branching laws of individual states. Since state laws prohibited state-chartered banks from crossing state lines to accept deposits, they also prohibited federally chartered banks from doing the same. This act became an albatross to the banking industry because it prevented it from building truly national banking systems and computer networks, which were needed in order to compete. This exclusive geographical franchise resulted in a unit banking system with over 15,000 commercial banks.

In an article of legislation know as Regulation Q, the Federal Reserve controlled the ceilings on interest rates that banks could charge to attract deposits. Banks borrowed money from the Federal Reserve at considerably below the market rate and loaned it to their customers at much higher rates, although subject to limits set by Regulation Q. This, and the fact that competition among banks was prohibited, provided them with an enormous advantage over other financial institutions and guaranteed them revenues and profit. During the late seventies, however, inflation rates hit the double-digit levels and interest rates quickly followed.

As interest rates on loans soared, banks, prohibited from raising the rates they paid their customers for cash on deposit, found themselves unable to compete with nonbanks, which were not subject to the same regulations. Nonbanks were able to attract a significant portion of the deposit base of commercial banks through innovative new services such as money market funds and cash management accounts, both products of the computer age. These had a devastating effect on the banking industry.

The third important piece of legislation that became an albatross around the necks of many banks was the Glass-Steagall Act of 1933. This act was designed to separate the operations of commercial banks, which accepted deposits from and loaned money to businesses, from those of investment banks, which engaged in underwriting and dealing in corporate securities. The legislation was introduced in the wake of a series of bank failures in the 1930s and was meant to discourage speculation, prevent conflicts of interests, and ensure the soundness and stability of banks.

The Glass-Steagall Act was constructed to prohibit a number of conflict-of-interest situations in the banking industry. For example, it prohibited any bank engaged in both accepting deposits and lending money from also engaging in the underwriting and brokerage of securities, since a conflict of interest might arise when the bank could put its corporate interests in investment banking ahead of that of its commercial banking customers. This piece of legislation had the effect of protecting the public from potential abuse by the commercial banks, but it also protected the commercial banks and investment banks from competition. This act and the boundary between commercial and investment banking was made obsolete by the computer.

## Erosion of the Commercial Banks' Monopoly on Checking

Technology eroded the monopoly that banks enjoyed over checking accounts during the seventies as a proliferation of substitutes to checks emerged to reduce their importance. The credit card was one of these, and it was followed by the magnetic strip card, which had many more practical uses than the ordinary credit card—such as obtaining cash from automated teller machines, paying bills, and transferring money between accounts. The appearance and proliferation of automated teller machines also meant that other nonbank institutions could begin to offer bank-related services. Cash was to become more convenient and universally available with the spread of ATMs. Credit card companies were attracting more of the payments-related business, originally enjoyed by the banks, and for some time, banks were prohibited from offering credit cards and credit card services. The credit card enabled its users to avoid writing perhaps several hundred checks on their checking account each year, and also gave its users a variety of additional convenient services such as a line of credit.

These and other credit card services empowered the public to reduce the cash in their checking accounts, thereby depriving banks of the use of these funds. Credit cards could also be used across state lines whereas checks could not. This, too, gave an edge to credit cards and nonbanks.

As the trend to electronic banking gained momentum, insurance companies, savings and loan associations, and mortgage companies were able to develop check and check-related services that competed directly with the banks, but differed only in name. On the horizon were new payment media such as debit cards and smart cards. The proliferation of check alternatives seemed endless, and if it wasn't for the fact that computer technology made it possible for banks to process checks efficiently, the check may have disappeared altogether.

Most of the new alternatives had some commonalities: for example, they were electronic or made extensive use of electronic media rather than paper; and they enjoyed the superior efficiencies of computer processing and communications.

## Erosion of the Barriers to Geographic Markets

During the sixties and seventies, as America became an even more mobile society with a growing demand for financial services that could be accessed in more than one state, banks found themselves at yet another disadvantage. Improvements in transportation, particularly more accessible and efficient highways, railroads, and airlines, also made it relatively easier and more convenient to conduct business with a bank in one state while living in another.

However, the development of electronic infrastructures also made it even easier to circumvent the regulations that prohibited interstate banking. Customers, for example, could use a telephone to perform certain banking transactions, such as funds transfer, at a bank in one state while living in another state. Automated teller machines and computer networks enabled banks in one state to conduct some banking business in another even though they had no branches in that state—at least by the legal definition of a bank branch.

Networks of computer systems also made the laws obsolete because money in electronic form was being moved across state lines daily. It was possible, for example, to conduct business in one state using a computer system in another state. Some banks had opened up nonbranches in other states that they called loan production offices (LPOs) to circumvent the regulations. Credit cards issued by institutions in one state could be used in other states and payments could be made to a bank in any state.

Moreover, the location of the business and the question of whether a transaction or banking business was intrastate or interstate were becoming increasingly irrelevant. Geography was becoming unimportant in a world of efficient, nationwide, computer-based and network-based anking. National banking networks; national automated teller machine networks operated by banks, nonbanks, and retail department stores; and the increasing use of electronic funds transfer services, magnetic strip cards, and debit cards—all these were making the distinctions between state and out-of-state banking obsolete. Indeed, all geographic distinctions, whether they were state or national, were being made nonapplicable in the evolving global electronic financial village.

## The Commercial Banks Take a Hit from Securities Dealers

Innovations from outside the banking industry sapped its profitability in other ways as well during the seventies and eighties. Three of these were money market funds, commercial paper, and cash management accounts. All of them were made possible by the new economics of banking. Computerization significantly lowered the cost of managing and investing money, created more efficient alternatives to attracting money and deposits, and opened up opportunities for investing in new instruments in national markets with higher yields. It was no longer efficient to let cash balances sit idle when they could be channeled instantly into national markets and invested in high yield instruments through the use of electronic computer networks. The opportunity cost of money was simply too great to leave it inactive anymore.

Securities dealers took advantage of these new economics, but the commercial banks could not. The regulations that had always favored them had become a burden to their growth. For sums of the order of $100,000, investors could obtain significantly better rates of return than those offered by the banks to their smaller customers.

Money market funds were a form of investment offered by securities dealers through the seventies, particularly to small investors unable to gather sufficient funds of their own together to obtain premium rates offered by the banks. Money market funds were pooled investments that were like mutual funds, only they offered high liquidity, low risk, and high yields. Securities dealers sold them in small units to the public at attractive rates, pooled the funds together, and placed them in Treasury bills and higher-yielding instruments from banks. They also invested heavily in commercial paper, which consisted of short-term notes placed with institutional investors. Investors could cash their funds and obtain their money within hours. People with as little as $500 to invest could purchase money market funds, thereby enjoying better rates than those offered by the banks for their certificates of deposit.

Certificates of deposit had been a fine investment until inflation soared into the double digit range during the seventies. With these inflation rates and with a ceiling of 5.5 percent on bank deposits imposed by Regulation Q, people with deposits in bank accounts were taking a real beating. Depositors were actually losing money because the real rate of interest on bank deposits was around −5 percent. Suddenly, money market funds became very popular. Bank customers withdrew billions from their savings accounts and put them in money market funds offered by the securities dealers. This siphoned billions of dollars out of the banks and into their competitors' accounts, and there was nothing banks could do about it because Regulation Q prevented them from competing by raising their rates of interest.

The banks suffered in two ways, first from the loss of interest on deposits, and second, from not having sufficient funds to meet the demands for loans, on which there were no ceilings.

The second setback for the commercial banks was to come from the ash management account (CMA), introduced by Merrill Lynch in 1977 and described in the previous chapter. The CMA offered the benefits of a combined investment, credit, savings, and checking account, all in one. It had convenience and flexibility, the advantages of higher rates of return on investment, accessibility to credit, competitive and variable rates of interest on account balances, as well as checking privileges.

The returns accruing from securities and other investments were automatically reinvested by Merrill Lynch. Each day the account was rolled over automatically and invested in money market funds. The account holder could also use his or her securities as collateral for borrowing funds up to a certain agreed-upon limit using a magnetic strip card or debit card. CMAs were possible only in the computer age.

The effects of money market funds and cash management accounts on the banks were devastating. According to Paul Ferris, by the end of 1982, "more than two hundred billion dollars had shifted over from [the banks] to money market accounts of one sort or another. Merrill Lynch had $47 billion of it, nearly half of it in CMA accounts."[1] "Banks made money by hanging onto depositors' funds as long as possible," wrote *Business Week*, so they were "practiced in the arts of inhibiting liquidity." The securities dealers, on the other hand, were in the business of "providing liquidity" and they were able to exploit this advantage. By promoting money market funds, they "sucked an ocean of deposits out of the banking system. And by pushing commercial paper . . . the Street took a bite out of the banks' bread-and-butter business of making loans to corporations."[2]

## Computerization Begets Deregulation

It was not until 1980, after years of lobbying by the commercial banks, that legislation was finally passed by Congress that recognized some of the new realities of the banking system. The Depository Institutions Deregulation and Monetary Control Act of 1980 repealed Regulation Q. The Act provided for a six-year phase-in of decontrol to minimize any dislocation in the industry. It also legitimized what the thrift institutions had been doing for some time. It allowed the savings and loan associations, mutual savings banks, and credit unions to offer negotiable orders of withdrawal (NOW) accounts (which were actually checking accounts that could be used to pay bills), get cash from third parties, or facilitate most other financial transactions.

In 1982, President Reagan signed into law the Garn–St. Germain Depository Institution Deregulation Act, which was described by the president as the most significant piece of financial legislation to be passed by Congress in 50 years. It significantly expanded the safety net of deposit insurance available to depository institutions and made capital assistance available to them for losses suffered (primarily as a result of their mortgage-lending activities). It also provided for increased investment powers for federally chartered thrift institutions, enabling them to invest in all types of government securities and domestic and international commercial, agricultural, and corporate loans. Lending limits and the authority of member commercial banks were also amplified under the act.

### Shake-Up in the Securities Brokerage Industry

If the banking industry was coming under increasing pressure from the securities industry during the seventies, the securities industry itself was experiencing pressure not from competitors but from the Securities and Exchange Commission. The SEC started to clamp down on the industry in the early seventies because of its cartel-like practices. Brokerage fees were fixed, ruling out competitive pricing; it turned out that there was little competition on nonprice grounds as well.

A complicated system of cooperative dealing had evolved over decades, precluding effective competition. Companies in the underwriting business "club," for example, had cultivated long-standing relationships with certain clients, and when one member received an offer to float a new issue, it would share the issue with others in the club by distributing a portion of the shares to other members depending on their position. Other members were expected to reciprocate when they received an issue from their favorite clients. Although the industry maintained that collusion of this nature was an essential part of their business, its behavior made it a target for reform by the SEC on the grounds of price fixing.

Finally, on May 1, 1975, on what is now referred to as "May Day" in financial circles, the SEC abolished the practice of fixed commissions. Brokers were then free to charge their clients whatever fees they wished, and their clients could look around for the best deal. Rates for brokerage services were soon unbundled, and they plummeted for such basic services as buying and selling securities, which involved no selling of advice or advisory-related services. Deregulation benefited clients but it dealt a devastating blow to the brokerage industry. Fierce competition in the industry cut commissions drastically: between 1975 and 1985, for example, brokerage commissions declined from 55 percent of total revenues to 21 percent.

A shakeout overtook the industry, and mergers, takeovers, and consolidations followed. Very large corporations such as Prudential, Sears, and American Express moved in, and the race to develop financial supermarkets began. In the ten years following May Day, the market share of the top ten members of the New York Stock Exchange increased from 38 percent to 63 percent. During the same period, the capital base of the average member firm on the NYSE increased by 700 percent. Terry Arnold of Merrill Lynch summed it up in the following way: "Back in 75, when we had full commissions, an IBM trade would pay us sixty-five dollars a hundred shares. . . . Today on a block trade it may pay us ten cents a hundred."[3] The era of discount brokerage had arrived.

## Deregulation and Competition in the Underwriting Business

Having experienced an unqualified success on the brokerage front, the Securities and Exchange Commission turned to the underwriting business. Pressure had been mounting for some time to break up the old-boy network that dominated the underwriting business and prevented the public from benefiting from more competitive practices. So in April 1982, the SEC introduced Rule 415, whereby a company wishing to raise capital could simply register the deal and leave the securities "on the shelf," deciding itself on the right timing of the issue.

Up until then, the company handling the issue was in complete control of everything, including the timing. Rule 415 meant that the underwriters would have to compete for the issue. The corporate client could then sell the entire issue to the investment house with the highest offer. The balance of power between the industry and its clients was now reversed and the high profits that were so common in the past soon dissipated. Rule 415 also caused a shakeout in the industry the way deregulation did in the brokerage industry, and the industry became more concentrated. Between April 1982 (before Rule 415) and September 1984 (after Rule 415), the market share of the top ten underwriters in U.S. debt issues increased from 31.6 percent to 42 percent.

The contrast in the culture and behavioral practices of companies in the securities underwriting business before and after Rule 415 was as significant as the effect on the bottom line. The *Economist* captured this contrast in the following way:

> Less than a quarter of a century ago, companies would still approach their investment bankers cap in hand when they needed capital. Certain banks, such as the blue-blooded Morgan Stanley, loftily declined to participate in any new issues unless it was given the position of lead or co-lead manager. The business of raising capital, conducted at a leisurely pace, would take several weeks. The "lead" bank would: Design a suitable issue of bonds or shares . . . ; Go through the appropriate regulatory hoops . . . ; Guarantee that the money would be available to the issuer on time, while putting together a group of underwriting institutions, each of which promised to buy a slice of the issue in return for a small commission—thus eliminating the lead bank's risk . . . ; Distribute the newly-created securities to the underwriting group and to investors in the market. Today . . . this lengthy process is telescoped into a matter of hours. . . . The introduction of this [Rule 415] speeded up the trend towards bought deals [in which the successful firm takes the whole issue on its books] . . . the underwriters must concentrate on selling to big wholesale investors, such as pension funds and life insurance companies, which can decide quickly whether they should or should not buy large blocks of stocks. . . . In an age of high speed communications and an inquisitive financial press, competitors are busy dismembering an innovative deal almost before the ink is dry. The half-life of new ideas has shortened dramatically. To keep ahead, innovation must not only be good, it must be continuous."[4]

## The Banks in the Brokerage Business

Deregulation in the brokerage industry created opportunities for commercial banks, and it was only a matter of time before they retaliated for the loss of business they suffered from money market funds and cash management accounts. Large commercial banks, in particular, had an extensive retail network with a large client base and began offering discount brokerage services, in spite of the Glass-Steagall Act, on the grounds that they were merely offering their customers access to brokerage services rather than actually offering advice, which was the real source of value added by the brokerage industry. In spite of vigorous lobbying efforts by securities dealers, discount brokerage became a legitimate business for commercial banks in 1981.

It was about this time that the race began to develop financial supermarkets; commercial banks, especially the big ones, didn't want to be left out. In 1983, Bank of America paid $52 million for Charles Schwab, a discount broker, although the deal was challenged under the Glass-Steagall Act. In the same year, Chase Manhattan bought Rose & Company Investment Brokers Inc., and Security Pacific National Bank bought the brokerage firms Kahn & Company and Kenneth Kass & Company. This was taking place in spite of the Glass-Steagall Act.

## The Scramble for Nationwide Banking: Breaching the Laws Prohibiting Interstate Banking

By the early eighties, commercial banks were seeking legislative remedies to their competitive limitations. Competition from nonbanks had eroded their markets. New innovations from outside the industry had proven very popular with the public and profitable for their competitors. Some of the largest banks had big loans with developing countries and they were being threatened by default. All this combined to weaken them financially. Many small banks, in particular, were facing bankruptcy because, unlike their competitors, the giant retailers and securities dealers, they lacked the national banking operations and networks that were essential in a world of computerized banking and financial services.

Banks strenuously lobbied their legislators for the freedom to compete. In particular, they needed the right and the freedom to develop truly national banking operations.

The decision to let out-of-state banks cross state lines was left up to individual states. However, since the banks in most states were very small, most states were concerned about being dominated by the big banks, particularly those based in New York, California, and Texas, where 18 of the 25 largest bank holding companies were located. Some state legislatures, recognizing the plight of banks in their state, began to pass banking legislation that permitted the entry of banks from other states as long as those states passed reciprocal legislation. By June 1985, seventeen states had passed reciprocal regional banking legislation and five other states had passed similar legislation but with various conditions attached. Few of these bills, however, named New York for reciprocity because of its high concentration of big banks.

Nonbanks joined the scramble to set up nationwide banking operations. As the trend toward financial supermarkets was gaining momentum, banking assets became highly desirable property, even if the banks were on the verge of collapse. One way in which the acquirers could circumvent regulations was by exploiting a technicality in the definition of a bank. The Bank Holding Company Act (BHCA) of 1956 defined a *bank* as any institution that accepted deposits and also made commercial loans. The act was supposed to protect banks from competition from other financial institutions.

Some banks as well as nonbanks got around the provisions of the act by buying a bank and selling off the commercial loan portfolio to another bank while retaining the deposit and consumer loan business, thus staying technically within the law. Other companies kept the commercial loans portfolio while selling off the demand deposit portion. These so-called "limited-service" banks offered the only hope for banks to expand nationally, but this also meant that nonbanks could set up what were effectively banking operations without being subject to the same regulations as banks.

By the mid-eighties, the pressures to allow interstate banking were too great to ignore. In 1984, the Comptroller of the Currency, which regulated the operations of national banks, granted charters to 250 limited-service banks, and 24 limited-service banks were soon operating with insurance from the Federal Deposit Insurance Corporation. Citicorp took over ailing thrifts in California, Illinois, and Florida and won the right to open a bank in Maryland in return for a credit–card processing center there (see Chapter 6). Attempts to break the deadlock in Congress failed to resolve the situation, and finally, on June 10, 1985, the Supreme Court voted 8–0 to ratify regional banking. Two days later the House Banking Committee voted to require states with regional banking laws to permit entry by banks from any other state within five years.

According to *Business Week*, by unanimously ratifying interstate banking on a regional basis, "the court has unleashed a process of consolidation that would make full nationwide banking a virtual certainty by the end of this decade."[5]

## Breaking the Glass-Steagall Act

The boundaries that separated the investment banking and commercial banking industries had been eroding for some time. By the mid-eight-ies, securities dealers had entered commercial banking in a big way with money market funds and cash management accounts. They had also moved aggressively into commercial paper, competing directly with corporate lending, the traditional preserve of the commercial banks. Corporate lending used to be a significant source of revenues for the commercial banks, but many companies with good credit ratings now found it cheaper to raise money by issuing commercial paper. The amount of commercial paper issued ballooned over the years, growing from $13 billion in 1963 to an estimated $320 billion in 1986.

In the search for new business, commercial banks found themselves lending to companies whose inferior credit ratings prevented them from issuing commercial paper. Besides initiating a determined drive for the freedom to set up banking services on a nationwide basis, commercial banks were lobbying legislators for the right to set up financial supermarkets so they could compete across the entire range of the growing securities and investment business.

By 1983, legislatures in over a dozen states were considering legisla-tion giving state-chartered banks that were not part of the Federal Reserve broader powers to underwrite securities. In the same year, South Dakota allowed state-chartered bank holding companies to en-gage in out-of-state insurance underwriting even though federal regula-tions maintained a separation between banking and insurance. Com-mercial bankers began to toy with the estates-agency services and to move more forcefully into discount brokerage services. They began offering their clients liquidity in the form of commitments to make loans, to buy and sell foreign currency, and to guarantee the obligations of a creditor. The banks introduced floating-rate financing as a way of diminishing the risk they faced by shifting the burden of rising interest rates to borrowers. International banking looked like an attractive future prospect as well because, unlike the domestic scene, there were few, if any, laws prohibiting them from offering securities services or any of the growing number of other financial services.

Wall Street was beginning to be nervous of the growing aggressive-ness of banks, particularly if the barrier that separated them—the Glass-Steagall Act—was repealed completely.

Commercial banks began to turn to a new weapon called *securitiza-tion* as a means of competing with the investment banks. Securitization was a means whereby lenders in general, and commercial banks in particular, were able to replenish their loan-making capacity by packaging their loans as securities and selling them to investors. Securitization was another way of raising money, although not through the usual route of underwriting, which is associated with bonds, stocks, and commercial paper.

Commercial banks were prohibited from underwriting securities, mutual funds, or commercial paper, which were the preserves of investment bankers. Nonetheless, commercial banks were attracted to the business of municipal revenue bonds and securities backed by home mortgages and consumer loans. A handful of Wall Street firms, notably Salomon Brothers and First Boston, dominated the packaging, underwriting, marketing, and trading of mortgage-backed securities. By the end of 1986, the largest pool of securities from all sources was based on mortgages and amounted to about $600 billion. Banks and thrifts had entered the business, and commercial banks, in particular, had securitized an estimated $50 billion of their loans, up from nothing four years earlier.

Commercial banks also wanted to get into the business of packaging securities backed by consumer debt such as credit card balances. Although the Glass-Steagall Act did not explicitly allow them to underwrite and trade general obligation bonds backed by state and local governments, regulations effectively prohibited them from doing so. Commercial banks wanted this restriction lifted.

To many, it seemed that the investment dealers were making more money off the securitization business than the banks themselves because the commercial banks had to engage the services of investment dealers to sell their securities. But the banks gained significant advantages from securitization in any event. They were getting a fee for servicing loans and they didn't have to shoulder the cost of holding additional capital to back their loans. In essence, securitization had the effect of increasing their return on equity.

The efforts of the commercial banks began paying off in the eighties. In February 1987, the Federal Reserve Board began hearings on applications by Citicorp, J. P. Morgan, and Bankers Trust to allow their affiliates to underwrite and deal in some securities, including commercial paper, mortgage-backed securities, and municipal revenue bonds; the Fed approved the applications on April 30. In July of the same year, a U.S. appeals court upheld a 1986 Fed decision allowing National Westminster Bank of New York to offer full brokerage services.

At the same time, the Fed made a decision allowing banks to underwrite and deal in the new consumer-receivable-related securities.

These were collectable debts of individuals and personal credit card accounts that could be bought and sold as securities. Together, they widened the already widening crack in the "window" of the Glass-Steagall Act.

## Securitization, Disintermediation, and Concentration in the Financial Sector

Securitization exploded during the eighties. Wall Street was exploiting all opportunities by working to transform almost every kind of illiquid loan agreement into marketable paper. Securities backed up by auto loans and computer leases premiered in 1985, and a secondary market emerged in commercial loans. By 1986, General Motors Acceptance Corporation was originating more than $7 billion of securities based on car loans, and it was growing rapidly each year. Securitization of credit card loans also began in 1986.

In addition to the words "securitization" and "deregulation," the words "disintermediation" and "concentration" crept into the jargon of the financial industry during the eighties. Disintermediation meant that commercial banks were displaced from the privileged and powerful position they once enjoyed in the economy. They were bypassed and sidelined by other purveyors of financial instruments and services. Insurance companies, retailers, and investment banks were luring away their consumer and business customers.

When the securities companies began marketing money market funds, cash management accounts, and commercial paper, they were in effect displacing commercial banks as financial intermediaries. And because a number of them were able to concentrate a complete range of financial services in financial supermarkets on a national scale, they were able to achieve greater efficiency and attract a growing segment of customers. But securities companies themselves were being bypassed as well by large companies that raised money selling commercial paper directly to institutional investors.

In all these developments, computers were pervasive. They let companies lower the costs of transactions and doing business over regional and national markets. They helped companies increase the efficiency and capacity of trading and doing business, and made it possible for them to concentrate the entire range of financial services under one corporate roof. They made it possible for companies to develop innovative new services. Finally, they made it possible to circumvent commercial banks and displace them as the intermediaries of the financial community.

## The Elimination of Geographical, Functional, and Jurisdictional Boundaries

The Glass-Steagall Act was slowly being obliterated altogether, and the walls were coming down. The time was coming to consider imposing a new order on the U.S. banking and financial services and, indeed, the entire economic system. A proposal to do so was made on January 29, 1987, by Gerald Corrigan, the president of the Federal Reserve Bank of New York. In a 54-page essay entitled "The Longer View," he laid out some of the most comprehensive proposals ever made to reform the entire banking industry. He proposed to create a level playing field for all financial services in which all the traditional separations between commercial banking, thrift activities, investment banking, and insurance were eliminated. Securities and insurance companies, for example, could own commercial banks and vice versa.

He did put forward a new line of demarcation, however, this time between banking—by which he meant taking federally insured deposits—and commerce—by which he meant concerns such as retailing and manufacturing. The Corrigan proposal, if implemented, would inhibit the expansion of companies such as Sears, Roebuck and General Motors Acceptance Corporation into financial services.

He also suggested giving investment banks and other financial institutions access to the payments system, while giving the commercial banks the expanded powers they were seeking in dealing in securities. Corrigan's "think piece" would in effect transform the U.S. financial community.

In August 1987, Congress passed the Competitive Equality Banking Act, which barred federal regulators from granting banks any further powers to engage in activities in the securities business until March 1, 1988. This provided Congress with time to review and make recommendations about the future of the entire financial services sector of the United States, whether it should be restructured, and whether the Glass-Steagall Act should be repealed. The Act closed the nonbank loophole by bringing nonbank banks, their parents, and affiliates under the Bank Holding Company Act. It also permitted national banks to engage in leasing.

In October 1987, Alan Greenspan, the incoming chairman of the

Federal Reserve Board, urged Congress to revamp the entire banking system. On March 2, 1988, the Senate Banking Committee approved a bill which, if enacted, would repeal the Glass-Steagall Act and give banks the power to underwrite any type of security except corporate equities within six months of enactment.

The erosion of the boundaries separating the banking and securities industries revealed yet another serious problem that plagued the financial system of the United States. The solvency and the future of many thousands of banks and thrifts were at stake. Many large companies, domestic and foreign, and many industries, including manufacturing, retailing, insurance, brokerage, and banking, would be directly affected by the solution. The jurisdictional power of state and federal governments was also at stake, as was the entire economic system of the United States and the relationship of all of these with the rest of the world. All the boundaries depicted in Figure 1.5 of Chapter 1 were being erased.

Global economic issues were indeed perhaps as, if not more, important as domestic ones in all industrialized countries. The banking and investment business everywhere was moving rapidly into the international arena, where competition was open and fierce. Huge conglomerates with headquarters in Japan and elsewhere were moving into global markets, where no Glass-Steagall Act restrictions existed.

The governments of Japan and Great Britain were dismantling the controls, restrictions, and regulations on their entire banking and financial communities in the hope of attracting more business, or, more aptly, in an effort to become a global hub for international banking. The U.S. market, on the other hand, had a different structure. Its unit banking system and its obsolete regulations prohibited banks from growing and diversifying like their counterparts in other countries. In short, if the regulators did not do something soon, all but a few very large U.S. banking and finance companies might be left out of the scramble for domination of national and global banking and finance.

## Notes

1. Ferris, *Gentlemen of Fortune,* p. 128.
2. *Business Week*, "Playing with Fire," pp. 78–84.
3. Ferris, p. 127.
4. *Economist*, "International Investment Banking: A Survey," pp. 6, 9–10.
5. *Business Week*, "Nationwide Banking: A Welcome Mat," pp. 90–91.

# 8

# The Making of a Computer-Mediated Global Economic System

## Deregulation and Concentration at the Global Level

In the seventies and eighties, all industrialized and many leading industrializing countries were experiencing the same transformation as the United States. Computer technology was being applied in strategic ways in information, banking, and financial services sectors; in stock markets; and in retail services, publishing, and manufacturing industries.

Automated teller machines, credit, debit, and smart cards, and retail point-of-sale systems were proliferating. Computerized infrastructures were emerging to mediate an increasing volume of trading and exchange activity in markets and corporations. Automation was advancing on an ever-widening front, and change and transformation were accelerating. Economic activity was being concentrated in a handful of global corporations, which took advantage of the synergies and efficiencies of computers to increase their profitability and internalize increased market activity. Disintermediation and securitization were in full swing.

In Europe and Asia, computers were eroding the barriers that existed between the banking and financial services industries, retailers, and other sectors of the economy. Deregulation was afoot, particularly in the United Kingdom, and it too was spreading to the Continent and Asia. Computer-based infrastructures held the distinct possibility of concentrating and centralizing global financial activity in several centers, and if this continued, many existing world centers would lose out. European cities on the Continent were concerned about London. London was concerned about the growing strength of New York and Tokyo. Tokyo thought it could displace New York and London as the leading financial centers in the world, but it was concerned about the growing aggressiveness of other Asian centers, such as Singapore and Hong Kong. Global competition was heating up everywhere.

A global hyperstructure was eliminating all space, time, and geography in the economic affairs of nation-states and pitting them one against the other. Major world cities were eyeballing one another across the Atlantic and Pacific. The old institutional order was deteriorating, and a new one was emerging.

## The Big Bang in Britain, and
## Little Bangs in Japan, Canada, and Europe

The term "Big Bang" was coined by scientists and astronomers to describe a theory of the origin of the universe, that it was created with one great event from a single concentration of matter rather than by evolving slowly. But the term was adopted by Britain to describe what was scheduled to happen to London's banking and financial community on October 27, 1986. In 1983, the British government and London's financial community described their plan to transform London into the premier world financial center by completely deregulating its entire financial community with one great blow, rather than by doing it slowly.

London was the center of the European financial community, and it was one of the three dominant financial centers in the world. It was also the center of the Euromarket, the market in deposits, loans and securities denominated in European currencies held outside home countries. In 1985, the Eurocurrency deposit market held $2.75 trillion, and the Eurobond turnover was $2.25 trillion. London had about 31 percent of the Eurocurrency lending market in 1985, while Japan was in second place with 11 percent.

London was also the world's leader in insurance and shipping contracts and commodities trading, although its lead was diminishing. Many blamed this slippage on the more liberalized markets in the United States. As in other countries, the banking and financial community in the United Kingdom was still highly regulated, fragmented, and segmented. Merchant banks handled corporate finance and underwrote securities. Jobbing firms monopolized trading and made markets on the exchange floor. Brokers were limited to acting as agents for investors. Brokerage commissions were fixed, and limits were set on the commissions that could be charged.

This set the scene for London to pioneer Big Bang politics. It all began in 1983 when the Office of Fair Trading was threatening to take the London Stock Exchange to the Restrictive Trade Practice Court to justify its commission fee structure. The Exchange agreed to drop its restrictions if the case were dropped. But subsequent discussions centered on how London might capture a major share of the rapidly growing securities market, and how it might become a more formidable international financial center. The result was the Big Bang, a plan to deregulate London's banking and financial sector within three years.

The *Economist* described the event of October 27, 1986 in the following way:

> . . . the formal and informal barriers which kept stockbrokers to buying and selling as agents for clients, stockjobbers to making markets for brokers, merchant banks to underwriting new issues and foreigners to looking wistfully over their shoulders will disappear. Banks and merchant banks, money brokers and discount houses, Americans and French, Germans and Swiss will be allowed to . . . join the London Stock Exchange. Fixed minimum commissions will disappear, in one "big bang." What is likely to emerge . . . is the most broadly based big financial market in the world, with fewer internal divisions than America's or Japan's and fewer external walls than West Germany's or, again, Japan's.[1]

A wave of mergers and consolidation preceded the Big Bang, and many more took place afterward involving British, American, Japanese, Canadian, and European institutions. Barclays Bank paid 110 million pounds to buy the jobbing firm Wedd Durlacher and the stockbroker Zoete & Bevan, merging them with Barclays Merchant Bank to form Barclays de Zoete Wedd. Natwest laid out 35 million pounds to purchase the smaller firms Bisgood Bishop and Fielding Newson–Smith, and spent two years building them into larger operations. Midland Bank bought stockbroker W. Grenwell & Company which it merged into Samuel Montagu, its merchant banking subsidiary. Mercury International Group purchased the jobbing firm of Akroyd & Smithers and the brokers Rowe & Pitman and Muller & Company, merging them with its merchant banking subsidiary, S. G. Warburg, to create a major investment bank encompassing strengths in securities and corporate finance.

Following the Bang, large American companies descended on London and bought up what was available. Citicorp purchased the stock-brokers Vickers da Costa and Scrimgeour Kemp–Gee for 75 million pounds. American Express–Shearson Lehman acquired L. Messel for 20 million pounds. Merrill Lynch bought Giles & Cresswell and joined the stock exchange. By the end of 1986, Citibank had a staff of 3400 in London and Chase Manhattan had 2500.

Canadian banks also were active in London. The Canadian Imperial Bank of Commerce teamed up with broker Grenfell & Colegrave, while the Royal Bank of Canada joined with Orion Royal Bank, brokers Kitkat & Aitken, and market maker Orion Royal/Kitcat. Royal Trust combined with brokers Savory Millen, Arbuthnot Securities, and market maker Dow Scandia Savory Millen.

Japanese and other Asian companies weren't caught napping. Nomura Securities joined the stock exchange. The Hong Kong & Shanghai Banking Corporation bought James Capel for 100 million pounds. Japan was going through a revolution of its own, but more or less at its own pace. The years 1985 and 1986 made a big difference in the way Japan managed its internal banking and financial sectors and its relationships with the rest of the world. A U.S. banker described the change in the following way: "Two years ago [in 1984], everything here was banned unless it was specifically permitted. Now precisely the reverse is true."[2] Government control over the Japanese financial system had consisted of two pillars, the first being the regulation of interest rates, and the second the separation of financial institutions into compartments of long-term credit, short-term finance, investment management, and securities. These pillars were now being eroded by technological change, competition, and deregulation, very much like in the United States.

One reason for the change in Japan was that the rapid rise in government bond issues made it necessary for the government to relax underwriting rules and encourage greater freedom in primary and secondary financial markets. In March 1985, money market rate certificates were introduced, and in June a yen-denominated banker's acceptance market was created. In July of the same year, some foreign banks were allowed to engage in trust banking. In September, the Tokyo Stock Exchange called for applications for 10 newly created seats on the 83-seat exchange, and American companies like Merrill Lynch, along with giant European financial institutions, eagerly lined up to pay $5.1 million for a seat.

Bond futures trading started in October 1985 and interest rates on large denomination deposits were liberalized. In 1986, the minimum size of a negotiable rate time deposit was reduced in two successive waves. Dealings in foreign currency fund trusts were also freed up. In November, stock exchange commissions were reduced by as much as 40 percent for the largest transaction, and in December, in response to competition from other Asian centers, the Tokyo Offshore Banking facility opened.

The rise of the Japanese yen in 1985 and 1986 strongly influenced the government to deregulate its capital markets to encourage an outflow of capital, thereby taking the heat off the yen. As Japanese firms pushed into foreign capital markets, other governments began to urge the Japanese government to grant reciprocal access. Pressure began to mount to eliminate the separations between the various financial institutions. The securities firms wanted part of the city banks' foreign exchange business, which wanted part of the business of the long-term credit banks, which in turn wanted part of the business of the trust banks.

Japanese banking and financial institutions began to burst aggressively into the international arena as the regulatory barriers were being dismantled domestically. There were even murmurings that Tokyo could challenge New York's position in terms of world market share sometime by 1995.

A "bang" occurred in Canada as well in 1986. Canada's financial community had its own pillars that separated banking, trusts, insurance, and securities, but the relationships between the sectors were becoming increasingly complex and blurred. Trilon Financial Corporation had Can$15 billion tied up in Royal Trustco Limited (in the banking and trust business), London Life Insurance Company, Royal Lepage (in real estate), as well as holdings in investment and merchant banking. The Laurentian Group controlled the Montreal City & District Savings Bank and Credit Foncier (in the trusts business), Imperial Life Assurance, Laurentian Mutual Life Insurance, and Northern Life Assurance Companies. Another of Canada's biggest conglomerates, Power Corporation, was also in the banking, securities, trusts, insurance, and real estate business. In 1984, the Toronto Dominion Bank created a real stir when it entered the discount stock brokerage business with its Green Line Investors Service.

Part of the problem in Canada was that it was not clear whether the federal government or the provincial governments had jurisdiction over the securities industry. After several federal proposals for deregulating the sector were made public and following several major bank failures, an announcement of an impending Canadian Bang was made in the fall of 1986. On December 4, 1986, the Ontario Government announced that as of June 30, 1987, banks, insurance, and trust companies (and foreign-controlled institutions) could acquire 100 percent of any investment dealer. The federal government reinforced this with legislation in 1988. "A giant 'For Sale' sign has been posted on the front doors of Canada's investment dealers," reported the *Globe and Mail*.[3]

The biggest of the big Canadian, U.S., British, Japanese, and European banking and securities giants thus were to meet in yet another national market. Shearson Lehman Brothers purchased a stake in McLeod, Young, Wier Ltd., and Security Pacific Corporation bought shares in the investment house of Burns Fry Limited. Deutsches Bank AG of West Germany acquired 50 percent of the securities firm McLean McCarthy. Sumitomo Bank Ltd. of Japan, Chase Manhattan, and Citicorp had subsidiaries in Canada and were contemplating acquisitions.

All over the world, the laws and regulations, the economic institutions, and the sovereignty of nations were becoming the victims of computerization and globalization.

## The Emergence of Computer-Mediated Global Stock Exchanges

The pace of events was speeding up in international stock markets as well. New York, Tokyo, and London were competing for control of their respective regions of the world and with one another. Reuters, Instinet, and NASDAQ were challenging the domination of the big stock exchanges. Reuters and the London Stock Exchange, which had always cooperated with one another, were finding themselves competitors. International linkages were proliferating throughout North America and across the Atlantic and Pacific Oceans.

All this activity posed a major threat to many smaller exchanges because computer and telecommunications networks enabled companies and traders to bypass them altogether. Fabio Basagni, deputy director of the Atlantic Institute in Paris, underlined this fear when he reported, "Regional centers are going to almost disappear, leaving only the major three centers of New York, London, Tokyo."[4]

*Business Week* in 1985 observed:

> Instant communications means that you no longer have to move around physically. And the major three [stock exchanges] can give you 24-hour-a-

day markets. . . . Right now, New York is the leader in the triumvirate of global financial hubs. Wall Street has 55% of the world's total equities market, [three times Tokyo's, and six times London's]. It dominates the institutional market with explosive growth in big block trading. More and more foreign companies are coming to the U.S. market to raise capital. Foreign stocks listed on [the NASDAQ system] rose from 99 in 1979 to 294 in 1983. The dollar volume of trading in these foreign stocks jumped from $5.7 billion in 1982 to $11.46 billion [in 1983]. . . .[5]

By 1985, Canadian stock exchanges were becoming increasingly worried. Cross-border investment flows from Canada to the United States reached Can$37 billion in 1985, up from Can$5 billion in 1980. Toronto and Montreal were losing their position as the primary markets for shares of large Canadian companies, and the New York market alone traded an estimated 52 percent of the shares of Canadian companies jointly listed in both countries by the end of 1986.

"If the NYSE becomes the prime market," Pearce Bunting, president of the Toronto Stock Exchange, was quoted as saying, "even our largest [Canadian] brokers will end up playing second fiddle to their U.S. counterparts and most equity underwriting in Canadian companies will be done by foreign dealers and many jobs in the Canadian investment industry will disappear."[6] The Montreal Exchange even went to the extreme of urging Canadians to band together to form a national market system. Donald Thompson of the University of Western Ontario, recognizing that it takes world-class players to compete in the global securities business, observed that "the alternative [to Canadian exchanges] . . . may be a very constrained and provincial future."[7]

## Computer Technology as a Strategic Weapon in Global Securities Trading

In the latter part of the eighties, computer technology was making a critical difference in the way the global financial marketplace was evolving. The way computers were designed and operated and the kinds of instruments they could trade, as well as the ability of nation-states and their industries to innovate and compete, could determine which companies would survive, where the global centers of finance would emerge, and which nations would become primary, secondary, or tertiary centers.

With proper management and the appropriate kind of institutional structures, computers could deliver instantaneous, efficient, 24-hour global trading. They could produce the means by which to create new financial instruments and dominate world markets. They could concentrate global power in a single center.

The importance of technology, evident in London's Big Bang, was to increase in the near future. In the language of stock markets and computers, there are various ways to design, organize, and operate stock exchanges depending on the intensity at which computers are used.

One format is the auction market or specialist market, in which every listed stock is assigned to a single specialist company; this is used by the New York Stock Exchange. The specialist company risks its own capital to make markets "fair and orderly," and in return the specialist is given an exclusive franchise to make a market in the security on the exchange floor and to execute customers' orders in that stock. Rule 390 of the NYSE protects the specialist system, prohibiting exchange members from dealing over the counter in listed stocks, and prohibiting them from making markets in listed stocks.

A second kind of operation is a screen-based system called a dealer market like the NASDAQ, which has been so successful in the United States. A third system, which goes back to 1962, is the Toronto Stock Exchange's Computer Assisted Trading System (CATS). CATS provides price negotiations, automatic execution, trade reporting, and continuous price quotations based on auction principles. According to Don Unruh, senior vice president of Toronto's international trading, CATS is superior to both the NYSE and the NASDAQ systems because every order in the system is executable and the system enforces strict price and time priority to ensure that it is a fully visible and fair market.

London chose a dealer market system, called SEAQ (Stock Exchange Automated Quotations) based on the NASDAQ model. This system consisted of a computer trading network that allowed market makers to display competing quotations to each other as well as to brokers and their customers. Transactions could take place over the telephone or on the exchange floor, leaving it up to the players to decide how they wanted to do it. London didn't seem bothered by the fact that most of the trading might take place in brokers' offices rather than on the floor.

According to an article in the *New York Times*, "The London Stock Exchange has in effect demolished the distinction between stock exchange and over-the-counter trading, while preserving the public advantages of a stock exchange as an organizing and regulatory entity for the securities markets. The result is a stock exchange without floors."[8]

The decision by the Council of the London Stock Exchange to adopt SEAQ was evidently based on the superior capabilities of the computer and what the London Stock Exchange had planned for its future. SEAQ had the advantage of placing all members on an equal basis; it did not rely on any one individual for the continuity of the market; and it lent itself readily to the concept of a 24-hour international market.[9]

The Paris Bourse licensed the CATS software from Toronto, and in June 1986 started a trial period by trading seven active stocks listed in Paris, using terminals linked to the computer system in Toronto. In February 1987, the Paris Bourse became operational using CATS. Stockholm, Amsterdam, and Madrid were negotiating for the CATS software as well. In September 1987, the Brussels Stock Exchange, worried about possible domination by London, announced plans to introduce CATS in May 1988.

The world obviously does not agree on how computer systems should be designed and programmed to mediate stock markets, or what democracy means in such an environment. There are advantages and disadvantages to the various schemes, but the NASDAQ, SEAQ, and CATS systems could very well win out over the NYSE's system as the world's exchanges continue to automate. This is because computer-mediated trading is more efficient, and it can be designed with the physical trading floors in mind—or without them. Trading on such exchanges can be transacted from the offices of the brokers around the world on a 24-hour basis.

According to some people, the New York Stock Exchange does not have these advantages. The fairness of the NYSE's specialist system has often been questioned as well. Norman Poser, former executive vice president of the American Stock Exchange, stated that the main problems with the specialist system of the NYSE were the absence of competing specialists, the need for a private profit-making company to perform what many people feel is a public function, and the need to regulate when and how specialists risk their own capital. He concluded, "The specialist system may have been well suited to the markets of 30 or more years ago, when a busy day of trading produced a volume of three million shares. But in today's vast international markets, the specialist system and Rule 390 may be anachronisms that the New York Stock Exchange cannot afford to retain."[10]

The decision by the London Stock Exchange to adopt fully computerized trading went with its decision to try to dominate the international marketplace. Just prior to the date of the Big Bang, the London Stock Exchange and a group of international securities dealers announced a venture to form a 24-hour electronic marketplace for stocks that would compete with exchanges worldwide. The London Exchange would merge with the International Securities Regulatory Organization (ISRO)—the self-regulatory body of about 200 companies in the Euro-bond market—and change its name to the International Stock Exchange (ISE). The *Globe and Mail* described the announcement by London authorities of their intent to proceed with 24-hour global trading as "the most important development to date in the evolution of around-the-clock, worldwide trading of major stocks."[11]

The new central electronic marketplace would trade leading international stocks when their home markets were closed and compete with the home markets when they were open. The NYSE retaliated by prohibiting its member firms from trading on the London Exchange in jointly listed securities during NYSE trading hours because, it said, it did not recognize foreign exchanges that did not have a floor.

By the fall of 1987, all major European countries, including West Germany, France, Spain, Switzerland, and Italy, were laying the groundwork for their own computerized Big Bangs. All these countries were concerned about the ascendancy of London in the securities business. In particular, Paris was preparing legislation that would permit banks to purchase stockbrokers; the Paris Bourse began examining buyout proposals; and large foreign banks were vying to snap up French brokerage companies.

## Global 24-Hour Trading Comes to Futures and Options

As the nineties neared, futures and options exchanges began experimenting with 24-hour trading as well. Some were linking their exchanges in different time zones so they could trade each other's products during their own time, and others were opening for longer hours; some were doing both. Up until 1987, the distinct trend was to form international linkages, but this was not very successful.

In 1984, the Chicago Mercantile Exchange, the world's largest financial futures exchange, interconnected with the Singapore International Monetary Exchange; in 1986, the London Financial Futures Exchange linked up with the Sydney Futures Exchange. In 1985, Philadelphia and London discussed establishing hooks-ups, but Philadelphia began to have second thoughts. It feared losing business to London, even though it completely dominated London in currency options contracts. For reasons such as these, a number of options and futures exchanges began looking for other ways to compete worldwide without establishing direct linkages and risking losing their position in global markets.

In 1987, the Chicago Board of Trade, the world's largest in options and futures on Treasury bonds, and the Philadelphia Stock Exchange, the world's largest in currency options, extended trading hours into the evening. Chicago was trying to overlap morning trading hours in Tokyo by staying open between 5 and 9 P.M., and Philadelphia was planning to offer five of its eight currency options contracts between 7 and 11 P.M. to coincide with trading in Tokyo. The Sydney Futures Exchange and the Singapore International Monetary Exchange already had entered into evening trading in November 1986. Most of these exchanges, however, were continuing to explore both extended hours and linkages since it was difficult to predict which trend would predominate. In a screen-based world, it may not matter to traders when and where trading takes place, but it does matter to the exchanges and the nations where they're located.

By the summer of 1987, the pioneering global linkages that the Chicago Mercantile Exchange had established and its extended trading hours were proving a disappointment, so it began seeking other means to compete in the global securities industry. In September of that year, it announced an entirely new approach to its bid to cope with the increasing demand for its products. It entered into an agreement with Reuters that would open the way for automated futures trading while the exchange floor was closed. The agreement would give CME members and their customers direct access to the Reuters Dealer Trading System early in 1989. One currency trader observed, "Within two-to-three years you'll be able to trade anything off the tube."

## Currency Trading and the Shift in the Balance of Power

The transformation of global banking and finance is nowhere more evident than in the foreign currency markets; the behavior of these computer-mediated markets staggers the imagination. It has been estimated that by 1986 the value of foreign currency transactions was running at about $150 billion per day and growing rapidly. That translates into about $35 trillion per year. In comparison, in 1986 the value of annual world trade in goods and services amounted to about $3 trillion, and the U.S. deficit was ''only'' about $170 billion.

Funds in these amounts were being moved into and out of currencies across national borders as rapidly as modern computer communications, optical fibers, and satellites could carry them. Since money effectively was traveling at or close to the speed of light, these vast sums were moving between global centers in milliseconds in response to the actions of national governments in setting their interest rates, increasing their money supply, or changing the size of their deficit—or in response to expectations and speculation thereof.

Although it was well known that currency markets were concentrated in the three major financial centers of the world, it wasn't known until 1986 what the pattern of growth and concentration was among these centers. In that year, the central bankers of the United States, Britain, and Japan coordinated a study to measure the size and distribution of international currency trading in leading banking centers. It concluded that ''only a small part of the trading is related to expanding world trade and travel,''[12] which had been the traditional reasons for currency trading. The bulk stemmed from capital flows as investors searched the world for safety and high returns from speculation.

According to the Federal Reserve Bank of New York, total interbank dealing in the United States reached an average daily volume of $50 billion, up from $26 billion in 1983. The Bank of England measured an average daily volume of $90 billion, 80 percent more. The Bank of Japan showed that trading had quadrupled over the previous three years to $48 billion. Clearly, the distribution of trading was changing. New York was no longer as big as it used to be as a global banking center, Tokyo was growing very rapidly, and London was pulling out in front.

## Global Securities Investment
## in the Eighties

The rise of electronic infrastructures in the eighties was a boon to international securities investment. Salomon Brothers estimated that total international equity business almost doubled from $400 billion in 1985 to $740 billion in 1986, small perhaps compared to the $300 billion per month in American Treasury bonds, but immense in its rate of growth. In European markets, international business had become a driving force. Foreigners accounted for 40% of total equity turn-over in West Germany, 35% in France, and 36% in Britain. Foreign investors were most active in the United States and least active in Japan.

In a major study of international investment conducted in 1987, the SEC determined that investments across international boundaries had soared since 1980. According to the report, Americans bought a record $102 billion in foreign stocks in 1986, but that amount was dwarfed by the unprecedented $277 billion foreigners invested in U.S. stocks. International bonds' gross mushroomed to $254 billion in 1986 from $38 billion in 1980, and of the 1986 total, only $44 billion was raised in the United States.

By the end of 1986, the total market value of U.S. stocks was $2.6 trillion, or 43% of the world total, down from 56% just two years earlier. Between 1978 and 1986, the Japanese market grew at an annual rate of 23 percent, and the Italian at 39 percent, but those of Britain and the United States grew at only 18 and 14 percent respectively.

### Pension and Mutual Funds Go Global

American pension funds were trading globally in the eighties as well. By the end of 1985, America's funded pension assets amounted to $1.5 trillion, or about half the net equity in all U.S. companies. World-wide, pension assets totaled $2.4 trillion. Funds invested overseas went from zero in 1981 to $32 billion by March 31, 1986, having grown 105 percent over the preceding year alone. In 1986, global investment of pension funds out of London, New York, and Tokyo grew two to three times as fast as domestic pension fund investment, which itself had grown 20 percent in the previous five years. Global pension fund investment reached $80 billion, nearly double the $42 billion recorded in 1983. By the 1990s, it was estimated to reach about $300 billion.

A clear trend developed in international mutual funds toward regional and country funds. Japanese, Asian, and Korean funds had emerged as had American, European, and other funds. In fact, the International Finance Corporation (IFC), an offshoot of the World Bank, had begun to encourage private investment in the third world through its international underwriting activities, which it carried out in conjunction with Wall Street investment banks.

## The Global Bond Market

The Eurodollar market, where the world's financial institutions borrow from one another, is a prime example of how the new global computer-mediated economic system is evolving and how it functions. In 1986, daily turnover reached about $300 billion per day, or $75 trillion per year. That was 25 times larger than the value of annual trade and about twice the value of the rapidly growing trading in foreign currency.

The Euromarket is typical of the emerging global financial marketplace. It has no physical location, no trading floors, just computers and computer screens displaying bits and bytes representing information, decisions, investment, and the flows of money and capital.

## Corporations as Global Titans

The corporate giants in the United States, Europe, and Asia continued to merge and converge in the global marketplace, gobbling up whatever they could in order to dominate. Already titans in their respective national markets, they were getting bigger all the time.

Having digested the best their home country could offer for the time being, they went off to foreign lands seeking new acquisitions, new opportunities, and new sources of profit. It was reminiscent of the sixteenth and seventeenth centuries when the great European nations sent out explorers to claim and conquer new lands for their king and country. This time, it was global corporations invading new markets for their shareholders.

The number of foreign banks operating in the leading industrialized countries increased as a result. In the United States, they rose from 50 in 1970 to nearly 800 in 1987. Over the same period, in Britain the number grew from 95 to over 300, and in Japan it grew from 38 to more than 100.

Size is obviously one of the most important prerequisites for survival and participation in these global banking and securities markets. The 1986 figures illustrate this point. For example, in that year Merrill Lynch, the largest U.S. brokerage company, had a capitalization of $2.3 billion, as much as the three largest British brokerage companies combined and more than the entire brokerage industry in Canada. But it was small compared to Nomura Securities of Japan, which was 50 percent bigger with equity at $3.4 billion, and ten times

Merrill Lynch's size when measured by market capitalization.

Nomura alone earned just over $3 billion in profit in 1985, which was about the same as the capitalization of Shearson Lehman, Salomon Brothers, and Goldman Sachs combined. Nikko Securities and Daiwa Securities of Japan were both larger than Salomon Brothers, the number two U.S. brokerage company. Yamaichi Securities was bigger than Shearson Lehman Brothers, Prudential-Bache, Dean Witter, or Goldman Sachs. Seven of the ten largest commercial banks in the world were Japanese; Dai-Ichi Kangyo was 10 percent bigger than Citicorp, while Fuji, Sumitomo, Mitsubishi, and Sanwa were almost as large.

It's not easy playing in these big leagues, but it helps when you are one of the giants in your respective national market. These giants can command virtually all the capital they need, and they need all the capital they can get. They need it to invest in the most sophisticated corporate computer and communications infrastructures to gain the efficiencies of processing and distribution that are essential to compete globally. They need it to purchase and develop the portfolio of assets in the various industries. They need it to be able to pay the high salaries that attract the very best corporate managers and executives.

The average capital base of the member firm on the New York Stock Exchange, for example, grew 700 percent in the 10 years following May Day (1975) with the entry of corporate giants such as Prudential, Sears, and American Express. The ten largest member firms on the New York Stock Exchange accounted for 38 percent of the total capital base in 1975, increasing to 46 percent in 1980 and 63 percent in 1985. Shearson Lehman, of course, was one of the most successful examples of these, having been the product of over 30 mergers. At each step, as described in Chapter 6, the firm increased its capital base and its market share.

These giants also need capital to fight off competitors and to develop new services. In the early seventies, for example, the firms on the New York Stock Exchange offered about a dozen services. By 1986, the number had risen to 100 and was still going up.

Size was on the mind of the U.S. Treasury Department in 1987, when it concluded that the U.S. government should encourage the creation of massive banks to help U.S. financial institutions compete more effectively with their rivals in Europe and Japan. The Treasury also wanted to abandon a major pillar of financial regulation preventing industrial companies from owning banks. By then, only two U.S. banks ranked among the 25 largest in the world, as compared to only a few years earlier, when U.S. banks were among the largest in the world. The proposal, if implemented, would allow five to ten U.S. banks to attain the size of the leading financial institutions in Europe and Japan.

It was only one of the many ways the United States was considering as a means of competing in the new global economy.

## An Open, Integrated, Interactive, Volatile Economic System

A global economic intelligence system now interconnects and integrates stock markets, currency markets, and commodity markets and, indeed, all markets directly or indirectly throughout the world. The entire global economic system is rapidly becoming one in which people and computers operate as one enormous economic intelligence, decision-making, and control system.

The new infrastructure is integrating markets and synchronizing economic activity on a global rather than a national scale, and it is transforming the distribution of world economic power and wealth between nations. It is as if the entire world, all its markets, all money and capital, and all traders were concentrated at a single point in space and time with instant access to almost perfect information and with the ability to make decisions and invest money and capital accordingly.

This intelligence infrastructure is creating what is close to the textbook definition of perfect markets, but it is also creating such volatility and disorder that at times many players can no longer cope with it. Volatility is the result of the collapse of time, distance, and information in the decision-making and trading processes, and it can be triggered by speculation, program trading, information—be it fact, fiction, or rumor—or just about any world event.

As we saw in 1986 and 1987, volatility can originate from the publication of a report on changes in the projected budget deficit or the balance of payments deficit of the United States; the threat of default on the loans of Brazil or Mexico to major world banks; the failure of OPEC to come to an agreement on the price levels and production quotas for crude oil; a threatened increase in the rate of inflation; or a slackening of economic growth in West Germany, Japan, or the United States. Instant information, instant trading, and instant money and capital flows alter the ways markets operate and how power and wealth are acquired, wielded, and manipulated in global markets.

Volatility affects everyone directly or indirectly, from those dealing in the stock, commodity, and currency exchanges to those buying foreign goods and services. It influences the interest rates we receive on our savings deposits and the rates we pay for mortgages and loans. Speculation, volatility, information, and instant trading create a situation of dynamic tension in which minute changes or perceptions anywhere in the world are registered in and magnified throughout the global economy. These trigger huge flows of money and capital between international financial centers and put pressure on international currencies, which in turn affect exchange rates and result in a lower dollar or a higher yen or mark, with corresponding movements in other currencies.

Volatility in currency markets is registered in global stock markets as investors and institutions rearrange their portfolios to accommodate exchange rate changes by switching capital among the shares of multinational corporations in various countries and between global stock exchanges. These adjustments bear on currencies' levels as well and can further increase volatility.

The prices of global commodities are also sensitive to exchange rates; volatility in the latter triggers volatility in the former, and vice versa. Volatility makes its way throughout the national economies of the world, affecting the prices of imports and exports, interest rates for loans, mortgage rates, payment schedules, and the delivery of goods and services. Variable interest rates on loans, savings deposits, mortgages, bonds, and the new options and futures instruments have evolved to protect any single individual or corporation from risk and volatility, but at the same time they diffuse the risk to everyone.

In these ways, the global hyperstructure or intelligence system is a finely tuned, almost perfect market that factors in information, supply and demand, and major and minor changes taking place everywhere in the world and responds and behaves accordingly. This global system can be stabilizing or destabilizing depending on factors such as the instructions programmed into the thousands and someday millions of computer systems, the confidence players have in the various markets, and the information and intelligence they possess.

### The Aftermath of Black Monday

The Great Crash of 1987, of course, is now history. But it does represent the time when all the forces that were changing the stock exchanges and financial markets around the world became synchronized to the breaking point. The realities of a computer-mediated global economic system were imprinted on the mind of everyone.

In response to the crash, President Reagan appointed Nicholas Brady, head of a respectable investment house, to chair a task force to investigate the causes of the crash and recommend ways of improving the system. The Presidential Task Force on Market Mechanisms made its report public on January 10, 1988.

The Commission expressed shock at how close the market came to a total collapse. It laid much of the blame on overzealous computerized trading and a misuse of portfolio insurance strategies by the big institutional investors. The combination, according to the report, turned a falling market into a panic-driven rout when the links between the New York Stock Exchange and the Chicago options and futures markets overloaded and snapped. It pointed out that the prevalence of portfolio insurance and the rise of computer-directed index arbitrage had transformed what were once three separate stock, options, and futures markets into a single integrated entity.

The report also noted that the problems on the exchange floor and between the exchanges triggered problems at the clearinghouse at the Chicago Mercantile Exchange. The Merc was slow in making margin payments of over a billion dollars to two major investment houses and this almost caused their collapse. But the financial side of the markets also began to seize up as banks cut their lending to some brokers, thereby slowing down the billions of dollars that were traversing the electronic networks. Several bankers complained that the Fed's system for transferring sums between banks broke down completely on October 20 for about an hour.

The report also criticized the specialist system of market makers on the New York Stock Exchange. "Market makers possessed neither the resources nor the willingness to absorb the extraordinary volume of selling demand that materialized," the report said. It also had some criticism for the market makers on the OTC market.

The Task Force made a number of recommendations for improving the system. It proposed a coordinated system of "circuit-breakers" operating across all three markets when trading in one threatened to get out of control; and the creation of a unified clearing system for all three markets. Another important recommendation was to boost futures margin requirements to near the 25 percent level, thereby discouraging stock speculation via the futures market. Finally, it recommended a single agency to regulate the interplay between the stock and futures markets.

There was a great deal of protracted fallout from the crash. The dollar went below the 120 yen barrier in January 1988. Further shakeout and consolidation took place in the securities industry. Shearson Lehman Brothers agreed to take over E. F. Hutton for $960 million. A wave of ayoffs took place in the brokerage industry as thousands got their notices, sometimes on the day they were dismissed. Fear, confusion, and lack of confidence in the entire system ran rampant and persist today.

On other fronts, the New York Stock Exchange undertook to expand its trading floor by 20 percent. The Toronto Stock Exchange, on the other hand, dismissed 5 % of its employees and undertook a reorganization. Fearing a loss of more business to London and to New York, Toronto began preparing to abandon its trading floor altogether. In Hong Kong, a massive firing of senior executives at the Hong Kong Stock Exchange and a complete reorganization followed.

Some of the recommendations of the Brady Commission were immediately implemented. On January 13, the CBOT set permanent daily price limits on its stock-index futures market, and two days later the NYSE announced that it would curb program trading when the Dow moved more than 75 points in a single session. The other recommendations require more time to put into effect because they involve a complete regulatory, organizational, and operational overhaul of the entire financial system of the United States. But these are prerequisites to similar changes at the global level.

## Economic and Political Power, Control, and Sovereignty of the Nation-state

The ultimate effect of the emergence of a computer-mediated global economic system is that it erodes the control that nation-states and national governments have traditionally exercised over economic activity within their economies, and between themselves and other national economies. This power is exercised to an increasing degree in global markets beyond the reach of any particular national government. The new relationship and global power structure are illustrated in Figure 8.1. Global hyperstructures and hypercorporations have superseded the nation-state as the focal points of global economic power and control.

Figure 8.1 **Hierarchical Power Structures and the Economic Order in Traditional Society and a Computer-Mediated Society.**

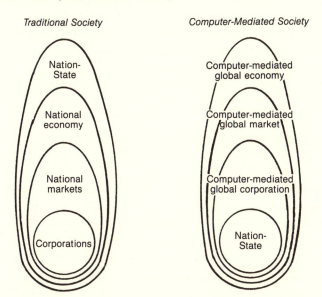

The implications of this new reality are enormous, but they are particularly relevant to the manner in which central banks and nation-states have exercised control over their national economies since the formation of the banking system several centuries ago.

The essentially free and uncontrolled flow of investors' and speculators' capital across national borders now represents a force over which few if any national governments have any control. Central banks and national governments are in a position whereby they are forced to look for new ways to accommodate and cope with this new world. They no longer have the discretionary fiscal and monetary power they once had, and they cannot operate as they have in the past to pursue and achieve their previous noble social and economic objectives. Instead of activist policies, they are forced to take reactive policy measures.

The rise of the computerized global infrastructure even jeopardizes the power exercised by national governments through their ability to tax their citizens and their businesses. Global invisible money, capital, wealth, and other factors of production are highly mobile and know no political or geographic boundaries. They move to political regimes where their rate of return is highest and at the least risk. They put governments in a position of having to compete with one another for tax revenue, investment, and growth.

National governments no longer have the effective control they once had over domestic investment, employment creation, and economic growth. They no longer can control exchange rates and interest rates in the ways they did in the past. The best they can do is coordinate what power they have left over the thousands of individuals, traders, institutions, and corporations that are playing their games, doing business, investing capital, and speculating in the global computer-mediated marketplace.

## Political Leadership and Policy Coordination in a Computer-Mediated Global Economy

Computerization and globalization are affecting politics in other ways as well. For the greater part of the twentieth century, for example, particularly since the Second World War, economic and political hegemony over the world economy has been exercised by the United States more than by any other nation. Sometime after the war, perhaps in the sixties, the power of the United States in the world economy reached a peak, only to wane ever since.

The United States is no longer the global superpower it used to be in terms of its technological or economic strength, nor in its military or political power, for all four go hand in hand to some extent. The scuttling of the Bretton Woods Agreement in 1971 was a milestone in the decline of U.S. control over the global economy, and most people concede that that control is now beyond the power of the United States or any other single country, for that matter. It is distributed instead among many nations of the world, including the United States, Japan, and the European Economic Community.

That is the reality of the new global economic power structure. Together, these countries share the leadership of the global economy, and they must share the responsibility for managing it.

Recognition of this has been very slow in developing, but in the mid-eighties it led to the setting up of formal and informal meetings among the leaders of the seven largest industrialized countries of the world to discuss some of the more urgent global economic problems facing them as a group and to try to find a basis of agreement on ways to better manage them. The meetings were held primarily at the request of U.S. Treasury Secretary James Baker, who wanted to arrive at a consensus among the leaders to lower and stabilize the value of the dollar relative to other currencies, particularly the Japanese yen and the West German mark, as a way of stemming the tide of growing trade deficits with these countries. The United States also wanted these two countries in particular to agree to stimulate their economies through fiscal and monetary policies, thereby taking more responsibility for governing the world economy.

The first of these meetings was held in New York in September 1985, and it was at this meeting that the Group of Seven (G7) agreed to cooperate and coordinate their central bank policies in such a way as to devalue the dollar. This so-called Plaza Agreement was the first of its kind since the Bretton Woods Agreement of 1944.

The ultimate goal of the Reagan administration was to get all members of G7 to agree on a system of target zones for managing their exchange rates, but it was unable to do so at this meeting. Since then, the Group of Five, Six, or Seven largest industrialized countries have continued meeting periodically; staff meet much more frequently to collaborate on policies and economic strategies, and to provide whatever leadership they can in the computer-mediated global economy.

The reality of the new economy is that even the largest industrial power in the world, by itself, cannot stimulate the world economy as it has in the past. The United States economy (and that of Japan and West Germany, for that matter) is too leaky and too intricately integrated with the rest of the world for domestic economic policies alone to be effective instruments in domestic economic control. The domestic problems and policies of each member of the group more often than not directly affect and even exacerbate the domestic fiscal, monetary and other policies of other members of the group. Both the benefits and the adverse effects of the U.S., West German, and Japanese economic policies, for example, are felt in each other's economy and in those of other countries of the world.

To be effective, the policies in each country need more coordination, and this, in turn, implies some form of global cooperation and perhaps regulation. The costs of the alternatives are just too great now.

These periodic meetings of the heads of state of G7 have not turned out to be an overwhelming success, but they have not proven a failure either. The fact that they are still held provides some basis for optimism, and it proves that all parties regard them as necessary. Evidently, nation-states and national governments, acting together, can have some effect on the direction and performance of this global economy simply by meeting and talking. In doing so, they can send signals to all the markets, traders, and institutions of the world. They are able to instill confidence in world markets, in the world economic system, and in themselves. In this way, it is now possible to "talk" the exchange rates up or down. Meeting together, the members of G7 can exert some "soft" control because they are perceived as carrying a big stick.

If they hadn't met, it's difficult to tell what exactly would happen, but at the very least their exchange rates and economies would be left to the mercy of markets and traders the world over, with a resulting volatility that could lead to a collapse of the international financial system.

Information can lead to control and that's an important message in this new world, but this has been the case since ancient times. In a sense, the meetings have become more like show business. Members meet to assure the world of their presence and of their determination to coordinate their efforts and policies in case they are forced to intervene actively. But that may be all they can do in a computer-mediated global economy, unless they are prepared to make some sacrifices for the common good, if indeed they perceive there is some common good.

**Toward a New Global Economic Order**

The meetings of the heads of state are particularly important when viewed in a more global, historical, and evolutionary context. Seen in this perspective, the events taking place in the eighties take on a very different meaning. What was happening was nothing short of the evolution of a new global economic order. These colloquys could be the forerunners of the formation of a new set of global institutions and ultimately, somewhere down the road, some form of global government.

An examination of the options sheds some light on the possibilities and prospects for such a new global economic order. There are perhaps four options open to nations in the future. One is to regress to a world of less interdependency among nation-states so as to minimize the effects that countries, economies, and political systems have on one another. This option is an extreme one and would probably turn out to be too costly, because it would result in economic decline and backwardness.

The other extreme is some form of global government in which each nation is represented and votes on global economic policies. This option is unlikely as well because it is virtually impossible for governments to arrive at such an agreement. It would probably entail major transfers of wealth, and governments most likely could not agree to this.

A third option is the evolution of a global computer-mediated economic system operating with very little or no government intervention. This might be a self-regulating global economy with financial institutions, corporations, and other players in the market regulating the world economy in their own way. This is unlikely as well in a world that gave birth to insider trading, caused the greatest stock market crash in history in 1987, and causes volatility in every market but is incapable of managing it.

The fourth option is some form of limited but cooperative control, regulation, and guidance over the global economy by major nations of the world who meet to synchronize their policies to ensure that an acceptable course of international development is taking place. This is what appears to be taking place in the meetings of the heads of state, but there is other evidence pointing to the emergence of some form of coordinated regulation over the global economy.

In 1987, for example, the United States, England, and Japan initiated talks to regulate their global banking and financial institutions. They were afraid that unbridled competition together with the absence of limits placed on the reserves of international banks could set off a series of events that would result in a collapse of the international banking system.

On another front, the new global computer-mediated securities industry was increasingly vulnerable to those wanting to abuse their privileges, but it was difficult if not impossible to police the system. An international transaction, for example, could involve as many as 12 financial institutions, making it extremely difficult to trace and track transactions, much less obtain sufficient evidence for a conviction. One of the first steps, therefore, was to put into place a framework for exchanging information or to institute a written convention to monitor and police trading activities taking place across international borders. These initiatives were in progress by the end of the decade as the governments of leading Western countries moved to monitor and police insider trading.

A truly global financial and trading system threatens to be a nightmare for revenue authorities. It is difficult to pin down profits made by banks, financial institutions, corporations, and individuals when multiple jurisdictions are concerned, and to identify where they have made tax-allowable losses when securities are bought in one jurisdiction and sold in another. Other problems including third world debt and finding a means of making the global economic system more equitable, particularly for the poorer countries, are too serious to ignore any longer. They require global cooperation and coordination as well as a better regulatory system that has never before been conceived of on a global scale.

The new global economic order is only one small part of the challenges we face as a society mediated by computers. There are other far more serious problems facing our society and our political institutions. These are the result and consequence of living in a society such as was described in Chapter 1. Although it is not possible to detail how this society will evolve in the future and how it will ultimately be organized, it is possible to provide some general observations about how it appears to be evolving and what we are up against.

The remaining chapter describes some of the effects of computerization on people, power, and politics, for this new industrial revolution will have a greater impact on our work, our wealth, our institutions, our culture, and the choices open to us in the future, than any other revolution in history.

## Notes

1. *Economist*, ''Technology and the City of London,'' p. 9.
2. *Financial Times*, ''Japan's Genie,'' p. 9.
3. *Globe and Mail*, ''Banks Win Unrestricted Entry,'' p. A1.
4. *Business Week*, ''Why the Big Apple Shines,'' pp. 100–102.
5. Ibid.
6. *Globe and Mail*, ''Computerized Trading Poses Threat,'' p. B3.
7. Thompson, ''Big Bang,'' pp. 5–83.
8. *New York Times*, ''Can Wall Street Afford Specialist?'' p. 2F.
9. Finn, ''The Big Bang,'' *New York Times*, p. 12F.
10. *New York Times*, ''Can Wall Street Afford Specialist?'' p. 2F.
11. *Globe and Mail*, ''London Exchange Set for 24-Hour Trading,'' p. B15.
12. *Globe and Mail*, ''Traders Love New York,'' 21 August 1986, p. B21.

# 9

# Toward a Computer-Mediated
# Global Society

### The Computer-Initiated Economic
### Metamorphosis in Perspective

The massive iron and steel colossi, which constituted the factories of
the industrial age, are disappearing from the landscape. They lasted
several centuries and consumed and devoured enormous amounts of
material and energy resources. They were the focal points of an economic system dominated by long assembly lines of human bodies who
shaped and molded metal to form parts and assemble them into place.
This older industrial age is giving way to a new one that will predominate in the twenty-first century.

The machinery and the infrastructures of the new age are intensive in
computer processing and communications networks that contain silent
and invisible content. They are intensive in artificial intelligence, and
in some cases they run offices, factories, and defense establishments
almost by themselves. The new machinery communicates with its own
kind, its operators, and its environment. These intelligent machines,
with tiny computer chips as their brains, are the slave class of a new
society, and they are creating a new culture. They are making the
traditional strengths of mankind obsolete, and they are giving birth to a
new kind of civilization.

### Computerization and
### National and Global Wealth

As computer technology has diffused throughout the world, it has
initiated a global industrial and political revolution. Advancing factory

and office automation are enveloping every society; computers are mediating more and more corporate and economic activity; and computer-based products and services are proliferating. Computerized infrastructures are complementing the evolution of a global transportation infrastructure and these together are razing the barriers that used to separate national economies. In the process, they are influencing the composition of economic activity within nation-states and restructuring industrial economic activity between the highly industrialized and less industrialized nations of the world.

Growing computerization is integrating all national markets and fusing financial institutions and political states into one economic identity and sovereignty. It is altering the location and structure of economic activity and investment throughout the world, as well as the nature of the workplace in the manufacturing, resources, and services sectors at the national and global levels. In the process, it is redistributing and dispersing global economic power and influencing the economic prospects, growth, and wealth of every nation.

## A Rapidly Changing, Increasingly Obsolete, Complex, Hyperactive Society

Prehistoric man relied on runners to deliver messages and to communicate between villages. A thousand years ago, man relied on horses, carrier pigeons, ships, and the semaphore to relay messages over long distances. In the intervening centuries since then, an explosion occurred in the ways information and intelligence were relayed throughout the world. The invention of the printing press in the fifteenth century was one of these, followed by developments in transportation, particularly the steam engine and the railroad, and subsequently the automobile, the aircraft, and the jet engine. At the same time, communications were revolutionized by the telegraph, the telephone, the radio, and, more recently, the television and the satellite.

These media enormously increased the speed, capacity, and efficiency of transmitting information around the world, but the advent of computer-based media fundamentally changed communications media overall. They brought the added dimensions of programmed intelligence and information processing, and accelerated the speed, capacity, and efficiency of producing and distributing information. Computer-based communications media eliminated all the lags that formerly separated us from the real world. They created a universally accessible, instant, global information system.

The speed, capacity, and efficiency of our intelligence infrastructure stuns the most capable minds and leaves many in a state of shock. This sophisticated economic intelligence and surveillance system has become essential in keeping us informed about the state of the world around us. Satellites spy from the skies; on the ground, surveillance is conducted in computers, databanks, stock exchanges, payment systems, corporations, and law enforcement and military establishments everywhere. One result is that a seemingly minor event occurring in the world is captured within minutes by reporters and information mediators, who record it and send it into the collection arteries and networks of the computerized infrastructures of the global information system.

This information is distributed through the newswire services and databanks to individuals in the stock markets and the money, capital, and currency markets of the world. These individual markets use these and other intelligence arteries to shift money and securities throughout the world, again in seconds and milliseconds. The financial health of corporations, national currencies, and political parties can be changed within minutes by the actions of this computerized infrastructure, which in turn is affected by the organizations' decision support systems and the programs and instructions contained in the memory and operating systems.

Technological change is rampant in our computer-mediated society. Generation after generation of new technology and systems is born on an ever shorter time scale, each one augmenting the information-processing capacity and efficiency of our computer-based infrastructures. They transform the nature of our work and increase the demands on our workers, managers, and executives. Semiconductor technology undergoes fundamental redesign on a diminishing scale from years to months to increase its efficiency and capacity and to lower its size and cost. For all intents and purposes, the design and production of semiconductors, software programs, computer systems, and robots has become a continuous process.

Every office, factory, or organization that uses computers is in a state of continuous change. Organizations can be revamped within minutes simply by rewriting the software that controls their operations. The behavior of a corporate organization and ultimately an entire economic system can be altered instantly by revising a few codes or instructions in the computers that control them. This can be accomplished by electronically transmitting revisions to their operating systems over the telephone, whether the organization is located in New York, London, Tokyo, or Saskatoon, Saskachewan.

Obsolescence plagues the publishing industry. Not long ago, for example, most printed information and literature were classified either as books, magazines, or newspapers, and the distinctions among them were partially determined by the life expectancy of their content. In the computer age, the life expectancy of information and knowledge is diminishing to quite an extent, even though the distinctions still exist. Computerized databanks and other electronic media are forcing all publications toward the instantaneous end of the spectrum in production, print, and distribution. Annuals are becoming quarterlies, which are becoming monthlies. Monthlies are becoming weeklies, and weeklies dailies. Some textbooks are being updated and republished every year to keep them current. And it is increasingly the case that books are obsolete before they are printed.

Continuous innovation and the proliferation of variety are evident in other sectors of the new economy. In financial services, for example, new instruments are being created each week to help companies better compete in and dominate the financial markets. These new tools would not be possible without the computer. New products and processes are also in a continuous state of development with the help of computer-aided design and production systems that accelerate the life cycle of new products, machinery, and equipment.

Computer simulation, design, testing, and decision making speeds up all industrial processes, saving time, energy, and materials. New products and services, new knowledge, and new information are continually being introduced, making obsolete all that went before.

The volume of new knowledge continues to grow far beyond the capacity of most humans to cope effectively with it. It spews out of our newspapers, magazines, and databanks. It pours out of our computer systems, word processing machines, copiers, and printers. It flows from our television sets and radios, and it fills enormous libraries. It clutters our offices and our desks. We keep developing higher-capacity storage systems and disks to cope with it. On the one hand, this has become an enormous drag on our productivity. On the other, we could not manage without it.

We appear to be continually storing greater quantities of information on higher-capacity microfilm and microfiche. We look to new storage media such as optical disks to store the profusion of information and knowledge. We invest more capital in equipment to manage and administer this new world of intelligence and to filter, process, and distribute it as best we can. We deploy armies to produce more knowledge and information, and to research further how to manage and profit from it in one way or another. At the same time, it becomes obsolete at an increasingly rapid pace.

Seemingly, the more successful we are at keeping up, the faster and more efficient we have to become to stay abreast.

Without the human and computer infrastructures to cope with this information- and knowledge-intensive world, without computer systems to mediate, process, analyze, report, and communicate it, we would surely be lost in a sea of information. But without this global information- and communications-intensive infrastructure, we wouldn't have these problems.

We'll simply have to learn to cope with it, and we'll do so by deploying more efficient, higher-capacity systems, machines, and infrastructures.

## An Intelligent, Knowledge-Based, Cerebral Society

If the socioeconomic universe of the past was driven by muscular and human labor with relatively little demand for the powers of the human brain, the emerging computerized society is the converse, a brainy, cerebral society with little demand for the functions, physical and muscular attributes, and capabilities of the human body.

For all intents and purposes, computer technology has made the physical body redundant in the production process.

The new factors of production are no longer corporeal but knowledge-based ones such as artificial intelligence, creativity, communications, and decision making. Instead of a society that manipulates physical entities, it is one that manipulates symbols, ideas, icons, intelligence, and knowledge. Instead of a hierarchically organized, people- and paper-mediated society, it is a more horizontal, machines- and systems-mediated society.

Instead of a society with a large laboring class essentially subordinated to a class of managers, it is a managerially oriented society in which people interact through machine-mediated horizontal infrastructures.

A computer-mediated society draws on the highest levels of human intellect, intelligence, and skills. It focuses these on the creation and application of scientific and other kinds of knowledge, information, and intelligence. These products are concentrated in human qualities and expressed in machine-mediated activity and in human communications, reasoning, and analysis.

More than at any time in the past, computer mediation makes success dependent on factors such as innovation, creativity, and originality, as well as on design and perception. The new industrial society demands of its citizens a much greater capability, capacity, and ability to function and manage intelligently. It requires greater emphasis on the scope, speed, and effectiveness of communications, control, and decision making in all environments, whether they be managerial, political, or social. It calls for stronger abstract thinking, more rapid learning, greater capacity to absorb very large quantities of information and knowledge, and the ability to communicate it effectively.

## Computerization and Human Health

Ours is a technologically- and knowledge-intensive society, exacting continuous learning and education to keep up and excel.

In the psychological domain, before the age of computers our society was plagued by physical overexertion, illness, stress, and fatigue, derived from the fact that man himself was one of the most important direct factors in the production process.

Our computer-mediated society is plagued by physical illness as well, but not from overuse or abuse of the physical body in production, rather from abuse or disuse of the body's physical capabilities and capacities.

If our society is to adapt successfully to this new environment, we are going to have to redesign our life styles to overcome the disuse of our bodies through well-planned programs of exercise. But then what do we do about the stresses that are building up as a consequence of the transformation to a computer-mediated society?

In this new society, the most serious diseases are those of the mind, brought on by the extreme demands of an increasingly artificial and cerebral world of work, which makes the most extreme demands on the mind and the brain.

In this new society, the health of mankind is threatened by alienation from the physical world and the excessive demands imposed by an increasingly complex and sophisticated computer-mediated world.

## Toward a Revolution in Educational and Other Societal Institutions

Computer capitalism has made obsolete the traditional base of skills and knowledge of workers, managers, and executives. As a result, people and organizations must invest more time and money keeping up, staying informed, honing talents, improving skills and knowledge, broadening horizons, and updating education to the point where it, too, becomes a continuous process.

We all will use these same computer systems to carve a niche for ourselves in this new society, whether it is by creating more knowledge, initiating more innovations, designing better systems, or improving their value, productivity, and effectiveness. Computers will enable us to learn faster and absorb more, and will prove a valuable means for developing new skills and sources of strength. In these ways, computerization accelerates the rate of change and obsolescence and creates a true hypersociety.

Our educational institutions, in particular, are being strained to their limits to cope, and indeed can no longer keep up. The dilemma this new society poses is described in the *Economist*:

> Two things are certain. One is that over the coming five years, four out of five people in the industrial world will be doing jobs differently from the way they have been done in the previous 50 years. The other is that, outside a tiny group of technocrats, most people are going to have to go back to school, sooner or later, to learn how. . . . The difficulty is that the half-life of people's knowledge is contracting so fast that it now almost equals the time taken to acquire it . . . half the knowledge [an electronics engineer or computer scientist graduating in the summer of 1987] has acquired over the past four years at university will be old hat by 1992. The Engineer will then have to go back for "repotting" if the employer is serious about keeping abreast of competitors. The machinery that has been midwife to this explosion in knowledge—computers, databases, decision-making software, modems, video equipment, CAD terminals, pieces of office automation . . .—is all lumped together under the banner "information technology."

The article concludes:

> All agree that a skilled and flexible workforce is the wealth of nations now, a competitive advantage bringing benefits to the citizenry at large. . . . Four years after the biggest job shakeout in most people's living memory, the training debate has barely begun.[1]

One of the greatest challenges facing the citizens of our computer-mediated global society is therefore to keep abreast of the vast amounts of new knowledge and developments that are added to our base of intelligence capital each year. Indeed, the danger is that the majority of our citizens will not be capable of coping with the demands of this new society and, even if they are, may not have the time, money, or desire to do so. Even the managers, executives, and experts are challenged to keep up as never before. Fundamental changes in our educational system and our institutions of work and pay and the system of taxation may be necessary to enable people to adjust to an advancing computerized society.

As we enter this new era, the number of people opting out, copping out, and burning out will probably increase. We will have created a bimodal society with a wealthy class of people who can handle the demands of the new society, and another class who have given up all hope whatsoever of understanding what is going on or of being able to participate in any meaningful way in the economic and political activities we have taken for granted in the democratic society of the past. This class of people may go the way of the mechanical machinery we have been disposing of in recent years.

Like the old equipment, this class of people may be thrown onto the garbage heap of humanity, with nothing promised them but abject poverty for their lifetime. All this may come to pass if our democratic institutions allow it to happen.

The situation is perhaps not as bad as it might seem, however, for mankind has faced technological and economic changes and challenges of this magnitude in the past and has found ways of dealing effectively with them. It is clear, for example, that the average person will have to develop more proficiency in a greater variety of areas than before if he or she wants to gain meaningful employment, pursue a rewarding career, and progress up the socioeconomic ladder to success. Like the generations of new equipment, some people will be constantly updating their careers.

New fields of expertise will develop in areas no one has ever thought possible or worthwhile pursuing before. The degree of specialization may become so great that individuals will require twenty or more years of education, training, and research to become knowledgeable in their field. In turn, the fields of specialization will become so narrow that only a few individuals in the world will have the ability to understand them or be prepared to make the sacrifices required to acquire and develop them.

At the same time, the computer-mediated society will certainly require people with considerably greater general knowledge and experience to oversee activity and direct the wider scope of social and industrial activity. Managers and executives, the legal and medical professions, teachers, and politicians, for example, will have to develop considerably more breadth and depth of practical and theoretical knowledge than was required in the past. It will become essential for every citizen to develop the same broad general reserve of information for a truly democratic society to evolve.

Meeting these challenges calls for nothing short of revolutions in social and institutional design and engineering. New institutions will be necessary to disseminate education, training, experience, and knowledge to the citizens of this new society so they can play a meaningful role economically, politically, and socially.

Radical as this idea might seem, it actually follows the societal pattern laid out over the centuries.

## Limitations to the Computerization Process

However enormous the power and pervasiveness of computerization, let us not forget that the computer is, after all, only a form of artificial intelligence. Computers do not have feelings and they will never know what it is like to experience love, be a parent, or have a childhood. They will never know sadness, anger, or fear, and they will never be capable of appreciating beauty and kindness.

Computers do not have a spirit and they do not have wisdom or emotions. They do not vote or make decisions on their own behalf. They do not have long-term goals and aspirations as meaningful partners and participants in society. Computers are simply logical, programmable machines that act as servants to humans; humans are not always logical or rational, but that is what makes them more interesting than computers. Irrationality, furthermore, is something with which computers may never be able to cope.

Computers have a distinct "natural" role in this new society, and it is up to us to determine how they are going to be cast and for what purposes. They can help crunch the numbers, relay messages between people, filter and select the appropriate information from vast databanks, report statistics, and simulate sophisticated decision making at the touch of a keyboard. They can also monitor and control activity on the battlefield, in the factory, and the marketplace.

But computers still cannot cope with the highest levels of the decision-making and reasoning processes that man has always performed and that he will always have to perform. It is these abilities and capabilities that set him apart from the new world of computers and the computer-mediated society.

Effective decision making involves not only information retrieval and presentation in graphical form, numerical computation, simulated decision making, and message communication, but also discussion, debate, and one other thing that computers do not and may never have. It is called intuition, that ability to make the right decision even though the statistics say something else. Intuition involves the ability to override the ''rational'' but artificial advice incorporated in the logic, software, and information systems making up the computer-based infrastructures. This uniquely human ability is derived from a lifetime of personal experience and education, profound thought and judgment, and long periods of debate and discussion. It is something that scientists will never be able to understand well enough to emulate on a computer. Intuition is increasingly one of the few things that separates the man on the job from the machines created to serve him.

Ironically, many managers, executives, and politicians do not have the time to allow their intuition to work effectively for them. They are too busy making decisions, communicating, monitoring, just trying to keep up with the flow of information to allow their intuition to intervene. The one-minute manager is a product of this culture, soon to be the one-second manager. The one-minute manager makes a decision just for the sake of making a decision, for the sake of coping with the inflow of information, and for the false sense of security that comes when a decision is made. Like the assembly lines of the past, one-minute management sacrifices quality in the production process.

That quality is essential in a computer-mediated society. The costs of losing it are just too great. The true challenge facing corporate managers, scientists, and technologists is to harness the computer to enable people to better perform those things that people do best.

## People, Power, Politics, and the Computer

Computers have come to play an increasingly important role in politics, particularly in the United States, Canada, and the United Kingdom, and many would agree that they have changed the nature of politics, particularly during election campaigns. They are used as electronic messaging systems to communicate and coordinate activities among politicians and their staff, as a means of managing and using mailing lists strategically, and in electronic polling. In the computer age it has become essential for political parties to maintain up-to-date computer-accessible information on the concerns and voting patterns of major groups in the country.

Parties can maintain computerized records on the voting patterns of opposition politicians. By searching publicly available databanks and cross-referencing them in appropriate ways, a politician can obtain the names, addresses, salaries, and other personalized information on individuals most affected by impending legislation or political issues arising during an election campaign. Computers can identify undecided voters, particular minority groups, and other potential supporters. All this technology and these information resources have become strategic components in the political intelligence and democratic processes of the new society.

In the distant future, the computer may evolve to play a much more critical role in the democratic process by taking charge of the voting and decision-making process entirely.

The new political intelligence systems enable party workers to concentrate their efforts on those groups where the greatest gains in votes are likely, which can make the deciding difference in close elections. Using computers, political parties and campaign organizers can design a much wider variety of minicampaigns, each targeting specific interest groups. With telephone numbers, addresses, and related information from their databanks, teams of party workers can blitz the undecided voters across the country with telephone calls, campaign literature, and personalized letters from influential politicians and business leaders. In ways such as these, computer technology has become indispensable to running and winning elections today.

Computers have become essential to the post-election political process as well. They are used in the offices of the President of the United States and the Prime Ministers of Great Britain and Canada, for example. They are also in Congress and throughout government departments and agencies. In fact, it was a computer that led to the release of confidential information in the "Irangate" scandal in 1986.

An electronic mail system had been installed in the White House for use by the president and his staff. It was obviously considered a highly confidential communication medium because it didn't have the problems of telephones, which could be tapped, or memos, which could be taken out of files, or cameras, which could record events on video tape. White House staff members were unaware, however, that all the electronic messages in the system were stored permanently in computerized archives. When the scandal broke, papers and reports were shredded but the archives were left intact. The Tower Commission, which was appointed by President Reagan to conduct an investigation into the affair, discovered the archives and uncovered sensitive information, which the Commission found invaluable in conducting its investigation.

## Information Power and Democracy

Information and communications technology have also increased the ease and likelihood of abuse by those having privileged access to sensitive and valuable information. The insider trading scandals that rocked Wall Street in 1986 and 1987 were due, in part, to the ability of people such as Dennis Levine and Ivan Boesky to access insider information on corporate takeovers and acquisitions and to use this information to gain the perfect advantage over other stock market traders who did not have the same privileges. They were able to make hundreds of millions of dollars by abusing their special position and authority in this way.

Networks of traders in Zurich, London, and New York can communicate and coordinate their activities to achieve a level of influence, power, and wealth that was never before possible. Technology makes it easy and inexpensive to get to information on impending takeovers, mergers, and acquisitions, just like any other kinds of information, to distribute it around the world, and to coordinate its use to trade anonymously in the stock markets of the world, irrespective of legalities.

In a sense, computer-based infrastructures are neutral to the access, distribution, and use of information, so they are neutral to who benefits and loses. Although they can be used for criminal purposes, they can also help catch the criminal or deter and foil the intended crime. They can, in particular, be designed and operated in the interests of the general public.

In the eighties, governments around the world, together with their various monitoring and regulatory agencies, began to design their computer systems to act as the "policemen" of a computer-mediated society. They programmed their computer systems to monitor, examine, and process the millions of transactions that take place in stock exchanges and trading systems throughout the world. Computers now record detailed information on individual traders and institutions, their clients, and personal relationships that authorities can use in the exercise of their global surveillance responsibilities.

Clearly, the computer is being programmed as the "Sherlock Holmes" of the new society. In this emerging computer-mediated society, Holmes would be hopelessly ineffective without a computer.

It is no longer possible to easily hide anything from our technology, our infrastructures, and our communications media. They work in sometimes mysterious and surprising ways, continually monitoring everything everywhere, and collecting information for distribution throughout the world.

The new media subjects corporate executives and elected politicians to an intense scrutiny, making them much more vulnerable than ever before to their past deeds, beliefs, prejudices, ignorance, and relationships with others. The information derived from this exercise affects the perceptions of the entire world, and it can have devastating consequences. It can destroy careers, or cause a flight of money and capital away from a corporate security, government bond, or national economy. This is the new reality of our culture and our global democratic society.

The power and intensity of the new computer-based media have become so important that politicians must endure constant examination. The media have become so great that they can influence which candidates for political office will survive the first few weeks of a political campaign. In some respects, the new information media is eroding the effectiveness of our political and democratic institutions. It is increasingly unlikely that an elected official or an elected party will survive four years of political office without the continued support and confidence of the majority of the population. The political environment, issues, and public perceptions are changing too quickly, and political leaders are finding it increasingly difficult to cope. At the same time, politicians are being challenged as never before by their inability to understand and explain what is going on around them, much less provide the vision, leadership, and guidance that is expected of them.

Throughout history, information and communications technology have transformed societies worldwide. Two centuries ago, they liberated people and organizations and made it possible for democracies, nation-states, and national governments to emerge. New computer and telecommunications infrastructures are liberating people and nations in a different way by creating infrastructures for a global economy and a global democracy. In the decades ahead, they have the potential to liberate the oppressed peoples and nations of the world from the tyranny of their dictators or their military governments.

In some respects, the nature, scope, and complexity of political issues, and the necessary decisions and the speed at which they have to be managed, have become too great for the old-style political leadership. Politics and political institutions are, therefore, also highly vulnerable in the new computer-mediated society.

The *Wall Street Journal* noted in 1987:

> Ronald Reagan, Mikhail Gorbachev, and Deng Xiao-ping . . . who presume to run countries are being rocked to and fro by a wired world. Communications have become so rapid and so pervasive the leaders can't keep up with events. Reagan can't keep his arms sales to Iran a secret and can't control the flood of revelations and speculations. Gorbachev finds that penning Sakharov up in Gorky doesn't keep him out of the international spotlight. . . . Deng, similarly, needs educated youths, but can't keep them from learning that democracy means choices. . . . The moving force is communications technology. Even the Soviets can't control the telephone. Something published in an obscure newspaper in Lebanon is now instantly known around the world. If an opposition party is allowed in Taiwan, students in Shanghai will soon know. . . . There were fears that a wired world would benefit the demagogues like Hitler and lead to totalitarian societies like Orwell's 1984. So far at least, the effect has been to keep alive the spark of freedom in authoritarian societies and make it harder, not easier, for leaders to manipulate their people. . . . Knowledge has its dangers, but ultimately, it is a liberating force. On the whole, the new communications age is an instrument for human freedom.[2]

## The Future: Our Destiny in Computer-Mediated Economic Systems and Democratic Political Institutions

A recurring theme throughout this book has been that economic and political forces interact to influence the organization of society, its distribution of wealth, and its overall course of evolution. Each force has played a fundamental role in the evolution of democracy and capitalism for the past two or more centuries—a process that continues today.

The computer happens to be the source of the latest and perhaps the greatest social and economic transformation in history.

When a society metamorphoses, as described throughout this book, its underlying technological infrastructure undergoes a radical transformation. The old ways simply do not work anymore. They become obsolete and ineffective, as do the institutions of society.

As the metamorphosis progresses, the society consequently begins to search for new ways of reorganizing itself and to design and build institutions that are founded on the technological, economic and political realities of the new infrastructure.

In the case of the computerization of society, this process of institutional rebirth and redesign is already under way.

With computerization, the rebirth process is somewhat automatic because of the enormous potential advantages that will be bestowed on society. Conversely, the process involves making salient political choices both now and in the future. The new society is being shaped by various autonomous forces that cannot evolve in a fully satisfactory manner for the majority of the people or nations of the world without some degree of guidance and direction. It cannot and will not develop to its full potential by accident.

If it is going to work and work well, it must be designed with the following objectives in mind.

If the past is any lesson, it is important that the new rules and institutions be shaped by a vision of what we want to achieve with this new force in our society. If we can agree on such a vision, then it will simply be a matter of translating it into realities. We can be slaves to this new world or we can be its masters.

Recent events in the global economic community are a sobering reminder that the new world system cannot operate any longer without a new set of rules, regulations, and institutions. Indeed, unless these are devised, everyone will lose—every nation, every corporation, every individual. The enormous interdependence, interconnection, and integration of the world economic system has tolerated enormous volatility and instability in the absence of such rules and regulations, but experience has shown that there are limits to what can be safely managed and endured without risking a breakdown of the entire global economic system and every national economy connected with it.

Without safeguards, the systems cannot be trusted. No one will use them, and more people will call for outlawing them altogether. Instead, we need laws to guide and cushion the world economy from volatility and possible disaster like the ''meltdown'' that took place on October 19, 1987. New guidelines are mandated to assist the efforts of nations such as Brazil and Mexico and all countries of the third world in their attempts to modernize and develop their economies. A new global social contract is essential to ensure that certain privileged minority groups are not going to gain at the expense of the majority solely because of their greed and the institutional advantages they enjoy. Without new rules and regulations, the benefits of a computer-mediated global economic system are simply not going to be realized.

What is needed is a new international spirit of cooperation and a new global convention among nations and peoples everywhere. What is necessary to make this a reality is innovation in international economic and political institutions that may have few precedents in history.

## Toward a Vision of a Programmed Democratic Global Capitalist Society for the Twenty-First Century

The enormous potential of computer mediation is most evident in the financial markets. A vast and rapidly growing reservoir of wealth now exists in global electronic space that is essentially free of the controls of individual nation-states and national governments. This is not necessarily bad, and indeed it is natural to some extent. But as it grows in proportion to the total wealth, it can lead to serious instabilities that can ultimately undermine and jeopardize the operation, growth, and success of the entire global economic system. This reservoir of free-floating wealth has enormous potential benefits for every corporation, every nation, and every person, and the new rules should be designed to realize these benefits.

With the appropriate measures, the global computer-based hyper-structure holds the possibility of generating tremendous synergies and wealth in the global economy. Regional, national, and worldwide markets are already being made more efficient and less costly to operate. The underlying computer-based infrastructure that has made this possible can also provide easy access to information, money, and capital.

Ideally, this hyperstructure can harness and tap the creativity and resourcefulness of all people wherever they are in the world. With adequate safeguards, it can allow every individual to utilize this reservoir of wealth in a responsible manner to create more wealth. It can give every individual an incentive to invest in these markets and to borrow from them to finance the projects and the investments that they deem necessary to grow and prosper.

The enormous potential of the computer and the computer-based global society can be realized if the new computer-mediated corporations, markets, and economic systems can be designed, programmed, and made to operate in ways that facilitate these ends. But this is where the political process comes in. This is the preserve of nation-states, their people, and their elected governments. As in the past, it is up to both economic and political forces to employ these national and global computer-mediated organizations and to originate this new form of capitalism.

Cooperation among governments is a key element of this strategy. In the same way that national governments have traditionally managed their own national economies through fiscal, monetary, and other policies, it is suggested that national governments should undertake cooperative efforts to achieve these same economic goals at the global level.

National governments have traditionally regulated money and securities markets to stabilize their operations and make them work in the interests of the public. They have created institutions fostering innovation, education, employment creation, and investment. The computer-mediated society demands that corporations and national governments manage in a responsible and professional manner, and that they be accountable for their actions and policies. It is vital that they exercise these same professional responsibilities and achieve these same goals at the global level.

The growing budget and trade deficits, for example, were, in part, responsible for the pandemonium on Wall Street in 1987, and the Great Crash had the effect of forcing President Reagan and Congress to negotiate seriously on an agenda to reduce these deficits. But efforts far beyond this may be necessary to bring the full potential of the new global financial marketplace to the citizens of all nations. When democratic rules and regulations are imposed on financial markets so that everyone has confidence in the system and has an incentive to use it, it will work wonders.

It was democratic institutions that led to the Industrial Revolution, and similar institutions will be necessary to realize the benefits of the technological and economic revolution that is taking place at the global level.

The new rules are also going to have to apply to the giant institutions and the computer systems they manage to prevent them from taking advantage of the enormous power, prestige, and privileges they have. The rules, above all, are going to have to be democratic, so that individual investors and shareholders throughout the world will have the confidence to use the new global infrastructures to benefit themselves.

### The Redesign of National Economies to Create a New Form of Capitalism

In some respects, there is cause for optimism. Many of the developments described in this book are fostering and facilitating the evolution of this new global political order. During the eighties, corporations were becoming sensitive to opportunities throughout the world in both highly industrialized and less industrialized countries. Capital was flowing relatively freely into global markets, into those nation-states and economic systems that were receptive to them and where return on investment was attractive. Capital and wealth were spreading throughout the world, from the more advanced industrialized countries to the less industrialized countries, although not all countries were benefiting equally. Global economic wealth was growing rapidly enough to make all but the poorest countries better off in one way or another. These signs may be the early stages of global computer-based capitalism and democracy.

During the eighties, governments in a number of countries began to experiment with an entirely new set of economic and political philosophies and to lead the way in the design of a new society. Some provided incentives for their citizens to invest in the stock markets, thereby broadening the base of individuals owning securities, and others introduced employee stock ownership plans that offered inducements for increased worker ownership and management of the corporations. Several others passed legislation that gave incentives for individuals to save for their retirement by investing in government-administered and private pension plans. Some governments engaged in massive schemes to privatize publicly owned corporations and major segments of nationalized industries, and at the same time made it possible for the general public to purchase shares in these corporations. Were these paving the way for the new form of capitalism?

Taken together, these measures increased the participation of individuals in the stock market and in the ownership of major corporations. By 1986, for example, share ownership in the stock markets by the general public hit record levels in major countries: 26 percent in the United States; 18 percent in Canada; 17 percent in the United Kingdom; 21 percent in Sweden; 35 percent in Hong Kong.

On another front, some respectable international monetary institutions began to accept the idea that securitization of third world debt could offer a solution to one of the most serious problems facing the global economic system. What better way of taking advantage of the new computer-based infrastructures!

Governments were effectively redesigning capitalism and taking advantage of the computerization of the marketplace. They were recognizing the enormous efficiencies that computers gave to all financial markets. They were incorporating the new computerized market infrastructures to channel wealth into national and global markets and to maximize economic growth. In ways such as these, governments were taking the leadership in providing the legal, economic, and political foundations for a new form of capitalism.

Andrew Coyne described the significance of what some have called people's capitalism:

> For in the twilight of the 20th century, a new vision of capitalism is emerging in Western Society. It is a dream of a capitalism of the masses, of a nation of shareholders, each with a stake in the productive means of society. . . . We are witnessing the slow rise of ''people's capitalism''— every citizen a capitalist, every company a coalition of entrepreneurs, the economy a system of competing worker co-operatives. . . . The product of this union is an expanded idea of individualism. Just as democracy puts power into the hands of the individual as voter, just as the market puts power into the hands of the individual as consumer, so broad-based personal ownership of capital gives power to the individual as producer.[3]

## The Scope of Choices, Possibilities, and Potentials Now and in the Future

We have a considerable number of options in how we are going to use the computer and how we are going to design society; indeed, decisions are being made each day that will determine how this new society will evolve and what kind of world our children will live in. The time has come to consider creating, that is, programming, this new computer-mediated society using the appropriate market and political guidance.

The scope of choices is significant but they boil down to two basic ones. As long as we pursue the right one and are consistent, the benefits will be considerable.

Computerized infrastructures and institutions related to them either can be the instruments for new global economic and social development that can raise the standards of living and the level of wealth of the entire world, or they can create greater poverty and inequality. They can facilitate the education of the masses throughout the world, or they can ensure their continued ignorance and backwardness. Institutions in the computer age can also be instruments for world peace, or they can instigate a new costly and dangerous arms race. They can free people, or enslave them and aggravate the ghettos of poverty around the world. They can create sufficient antagonisms, isolation, and alienation to destroy the fabric of society as we know it, or they can create a new society in which all people live in peace and harmony.

We can choose to apply the new technology to responsibly manage and preserve our life-giving natural environment, or to continue to deplete and ultimately destroy it together with ourselves and our children. We have a choice whether we design and program this new society to bring out the creativity in everyone, or to magnify society's mediocrity and backwardness.

## A Matter of Choice

There is no doubt about which of these two futures we should choose to follow. We know that we must follow as closely as possible the one that has always led to democratic progress, and stay as far away from the other as possible.

We must continue to build democratic institutions, but this time, the new institutions must reflect the realities of the new computer-mediated global society.

Whatever we do, one thing is abundantly clear. Capitalism now incorporates the computer, and it will play a pervasive role in our future. Capitalism and the computer will continue to transform our society economically, politically, and culturally. They will continue to affect the way wealth is acquired, accumulated, and managed. In true Schumpeterian style, capitalism is continuing to innovate, adapt, and change itself.

Capitalism is expanding into a new dimension beyond three-dimensional space—into the silent, invisible *hyperspace* of wealth expressed in electronic bits and bytes that are processed, communicated, invested, and controlled by people mediated by computers. It is up to all the citizens of this global human society to ensure that programmed capitalism expands and evolves into the dimensions of a programmed democratic society.

## Notes

1. *Economist*, "Training for Work," pp. 93–101.
2. *Wall Street Journal*, "Nowhere to Hide," p. 16.
3. Coyne, "Changing Vision of Shareholding," p. 43.

# Bibliography

Beniger, James R. *The Control Revolution: Technological and Economic Origins of the Information Society*. Cambridge, Mass.: Harvard University Press, 1986.

Braudel, Fernand. *Civilization and Capitalism*, vols. 1–3. London: Williams Collins & Sons, Co. Ltd., 1984.

*Business Week*. "American Express Expands Its Supermarket." 25 July 1983, p. 72.

*Business Week*. "American Express: Something for Everyone in Money Management." 10 September 1984, pp. 114–116.

*Business Week*. "Computer Revolution at Dun & Bradstreet." 27 August 1979, pp. 72–78.

*Business Week*. "Detroit Barrels Down a Back Road to Banking." 25 August 1986, pp. 77–78.

*Business Week*. "Dow Jones Digs Deeper into Financial Data." 22 July 1985, p. 69.

*Business Week*. "The Golden Plan of American Express: Now the Company Has to Make Its Financial Empire Work." 30 April 1984, pp. 118–122.

*Business Week*. "The Information Business." 25 August 1986, pp. 82–90.

*Business Week*. "Instant Relic: The New Exchange Floor." 12 January 1987.

*Business Week*. "Mighty Sears Tests Its Clout in Credit Cards." 2 September 1986.

*Business Week*. "Nationwide Banking: A Welcome Mat—Not a Slammed Door." 24 June 1985.

*Business Week*. "The Peril in Financial Services." 20 August 1984, pp. 52–57.

*Business Week*. "Playing with Fire." 18 September 1985.

*Business Week*. "Publishers Go Electronic: An Industry Races to Relearn the Information Business." 11 June 1984, p.84.

*Business Week*. "The Synergy Begins to Work for Sears' Financial Supermarket." 13 June 1983.

*Business Week*. "Why the Big Apple Shines in the World's Markets," 23 July 1985.

*Business Week*. "Will Today's Stock Quote Machines Go the Way of the Ticker Tape? The Personal Computer is Fast Becoming the Lynchpin for Quoting Securities." 18 March 1985, p. 144.

*Canadian Business*. "Pillars of the Community: The Scramble for Markets: A Special Report on Banking and Finance in Turmoil." April 1984, pp. 89–91.

Carrington, Tim. *The Year They Sold Wall Street*. New York: Viking-Penguin, 1985.

Chandler, Alfred. *Strategy and Structure: Chapters in the History of the Industrial Enterprise*. Cambridge, Mass.: MIT Press, 1962.

————. *The Visible Hand: The Managerial Revolution in American Business*. Cambridge, Mass.: Belnap Press, Harvard University Press, 1977.

*Christian Science Monitor*. "Stock Trading Follows the Sun." 28 July–3 August 1986, pp. 14–15.

Coyne, Andrew. "The Changing Vision of Shareholding: 'People's Capitalism' the Growing New Force." *Financial Post*. 22 December 1987.

*Data Communications*. "Networking Dollars and Sense: ATMs United Nationwide." October 1987, pp. 85–92.

*Datamation*. "Citi's Techno Boss?" 1 August 1984.

David, Stanley M. *Future Perfect*. New York: Addison-Wesley, 1987.

*Economist*. "Dilemmas for 24-Hour Futures." 7 February 1987, p. 78.

*Economist*. "Messrs Glass and Steagall Turn in Their Graves." 7 February 1987, pp. 73–74.

*Economist*. "On the Move: Global Investment Management: A Survey." 8 November 1986, pp. 1–30.

*Economist*. "The Other Dimension: Technology and the City of London, A Survey." 6 July 1985.

*Economist*. "A Survey of International Banking: The Consumer Is Sovereign." 22 March 1986, pp. 1–68.

*Economist*. "Training for Work: In Search of Missing Skills." 20 December 1986.

*Economist*. "Will American Shares Be Sold As a Loss Leader?" 12 May 1984, pp. 91–92.

*Economist*. "The World Is Their Oyster: International Investment Banking: A Survey." 16 March 1985, pp. 1–84.

Eichner, Alfred. *The Megacorp and Oligopoly: The Micro Foundations of Macro Dynamics*. Cambridge, Mass.: Cambridge University Press, 1976.

*Encyclopedia of Banking and Finance*, 8th ed. Boston: Bankers, 1983, p. 696.

Ferris, Paul. "Gentlemen of Fortune: The World's Merchant and Investment Bankers." London: Weidenfeld and Nicolson, 1985.

*Financial Post*. "Shared Money Machines Will Change Our Buying Habits." 17 May 1986.

*Financial Times*. "Japan's Genie Is Out of the Bottle." 3 December 1986.

*Fortune*. "The Big News at Reuters is its Money Machine." 8 August 1983, pp. 91–97.

*Fortune*. "Citicorp After Wriston." 9 July 1984.

*Fortune*. "Citicorp: What the New Boss Is Up To." 17 February 1986, pp. 40–44.

*Fortune*. "The Stock Market of the Future—Now." 29 October 1984, pp.105–110.

*Fortune*. "Unleashing Banks on Wall Street." 29 September 1986, pp. 99–101.

*Fortune*. "Would You Buy Stocks Where You Buy Socks?" 9 July 1984, pp. 130–133.

Galbraith, John Kenneth. *The New Industrial State*. New York: Signet Books, 1967.

Garsson, Robert. "Easy Money." *Datamation*. June 1984.

*Globe and Mail*. "Banks Win Unrestricted Entry into Securities Field: 'Little Bang' Becomes a Big Explosion." 5 December 1986.

*Globe and Mail*. "Computerized Trading Poses Threat to TSE, Bunting Warns." 31 July 1985.

*Globe and Mail*. "Computers Have a Chap Working Like a Yank." 18 November 1986.

*Globe and Mail*. "London Exchange Set for 24-Hour Trading." 17 September 1986.

*Globe and Mail*. "The Man Who Rocked the Money World." 20 January 1986.

*Globe and Mail*. "Putting Investors into the Loan Business Is Soaring." 2 February 1987, p. B14.

*Globe and Mail*. "Selling Money for Profit." 18 January 1986, p. A10.

*Globe and Mail*. "Traders Love New York, But It's Not as Big an Apple as They Thought." 21 August 1986.

*Globe and Mail*. "Trends Signal End of Trading Floors." 17 June 1985.

Goldenberg, Susan. *Trading: Inside the World's Leading Stock Exchanges*. New York: Harcourt Brace Jovanovich, 1986.

Hamilton, Adrian. *The Financial Revolution*. New York: Free Press, 1986.

Heilbroner, Robert. *The Worldly Philosophers: The Lives, Times and Ideas of Great Economic Thinkers*, 5th ed. New York: Simon & Schuster, Touchstone Books, 1980.

Innis, Harold A. *Empire and Communications*. London, Toronto: Oxford University Press, 1950.

Kuhn, Thomas. *The Structure of Scientific Revolutions*, 2d ed. Chicago: University of Chicago Press, 1970.

Miller, Morris. *Coping is Not Enough*. Homewood, Ill.: Dow Jones—Irwin, 1986.

Munkirs, John R. *The Transformation of American Capitalism*. Armonk, N.Y.: M. E. Sharpe, 1985.

*New York Times*. "Can Wall Street Afford Its Specialist?" 9 November 1986.

*New York Times*. "Turning McGraw-Hill Upside Down." 2 February 1986, p. 1F.

Piore, Michael J. and Charles F. Sabel, *The Second Industrial Divide*. New York: Basic Books, 1984.

Polanyi, Karl. *The Great Transformation: The Political and Economic Origins of Our Time*, 9th ed. Boston: Beacon Press, 1968.

Schumpeter, Joseph. *Capitalism, Socialism and Democracy*, 3d ed. New York: Harper Torchbooks, 1950.

Shamoon, Sherrie. "The Sharing of ATMs: Proprietary Systems are Becoming Obsolete—No One Can Compete with a Shared Network." *Datamation*. 15 March 1986.

Sobel, Robert. *Inside Wall Street*. New York and London: W. W. Norton, 1977.

Thompson, Donald. "Big Bang: The City Revolution Begins." *Business Quarterly*. November 1986, pp. 79–83.

Watchel, Howard. *The Money Mandarins: The Making of a Supranational Economic Order*. New York: Pantheon, 1986.

*Wall Street Journal*. "Electronic Market–Data Delivery Expands Beyond Simple Stock-Quote Terminals." 19 June 1985, p. 33.

*Wall Street Journal*. "Limited Service Banks Appear Doomed by Appeals Court Ruling." 23 May 1985, p. 8.

*Wall Street Journal*. "Nowhere to Hide." 30 December 1986.

Williams, Monci Jo. "The Great Plastic Card Fight Begins." *Fortune*. 4 February 1985, pp. 18–23.

# Index

A. C. Nielsen, 54
Allstate Insurance, 124
American Express, 55, 64, 65, 68, 69, 121–124, 141, 153; Travel Related Services Company, 121–122
American Stock Exchange, 96
American Telephone and Telegraph, 45, 50, 78, 79, 81, 116
Amsterdam Exchange, 102, 158
Arbitrage, 11–12, 107, 167
Artificial intelligence, 4, 94, 108, 114, 175, 179
Automated clearinghouse, 70, 72, 74
Automated teller machines, 10–11, 59–75, 114, 136, 137
Automatic Data Processing Inc., 50, 51, 68, 79

Bache Securities, 130
Bank cards, 59–75
Bankers Trust, 146
Bank Holding Company Act, 144, 148
Banking, 37, 58–76, 115–132, 133–149; limited service, 144; nationwide, 119, 137, 143–144; regional, 144. *See also* Glass-Steagall Act; McFadden Act
Bank of America, 116, 117, 120, 143
Big Bang: in Britain 104, 106, 151–153, 159; in Canada, 154–155; in Europe, 159; in Japan, 153–154
Black Monday, 11–12, 110–112. *See also* October 19, 1987

Brady Commission Report, 166–168
Bretton Woods Agreement, 31, 85–86, 170, 171
Brokerage, 49, 77–85, 89–91, 92–112, 114–117, 120, 122–132, 133–149
Brussels Stock Exchange, 158
Bunker Ramo, 50

Canada, 104, 112, 154–155, 163, 193
Capitalism (Capital), 14–16, 21–34, 87, 92–93, 190–193
Carte Blanche, 65, 69, 119
Cash management account, 127–128, 138, 139, 145
Certificate of deposit, 138–139
Charles Schwab, 143
Chase Manhattan, 70, 143, 153, 155
Chicago Board of Trade, 98, 160, 168
Chicago Board Options Exchange, 96–97
Chicago Mercantile Exchange, 87, 110, 160, 167
Chicago Midwest Exchange, 103
CHIPS. *See* Clearinghouse Interbank Payments System
Choice card, 65, 69, 119
Chrysler Corporation, 131
Cincinnati Stock Exchange, 99
Cirrus, 68, 75
Citicorp, 46, 68, 69, 75, 78, 79, 81, 90, 117–121, 144, 153, 155
Clearinghouse Interbank Payments System, 74

Coldwell Banker and Co., 124
Commercial banks. *See* Banking
Commercial paper, 138–139, 145, 147
Commodity Exchange, 97
Communications, 8, 36; revolution in, 176–177, 188. *See also* Gutenberg Revolution, Telecommunications
Compact disc, 46–47
Competitive Equality Banking Act, 148
Compustat, 56
Computer: nature of the, 3–5, 183–184; simulation, 6–7, 178. *See also* Computer mediation, Artificial intelligence
Computer-aided: design, 6, 178; instruction, 8–9; learning, 8–9; manufacturing, 6
Computer Assisted Trading System, 157, 158
Computer axial tomography, 9
Computer-mediated: economic system, 156–181; society, 9, 12–13, 21, 175–195; trading, 77–91
Computer mediation, 18
Control, 18–29, 39–40, 168–170, 172. *See also* Capital; Information; Money
Copernican Revolution, 13–14, 35
Creative destruction, 15, 105
Credit card, 64–65, 69–71, 73–75, 136. *See also* Bank card; Debit card; Magnetic strip card
Currency trading, 87–89, 159–161

Dai-Ichi Kangyo Bank, 164
Daiwa Securities, 164
Databank (Database), 8, 11, 39–44, 53, 54, 90, 114, 177, 181
Datastream PLC, 54
Data Resources, 55
Dean Witter Reynolds, 124, 125, 164
Debit card, 11, 73, 114, 137. *See also* Credit card; Smart card; Magnetic strip card
Defense, 6–7
Depository Institutions Deregulation and Monetary Control Act, 139
Deregulation, 81; of banking 133–134, 139–140; in Britain, 151–153; of brokerage, 95, 140–141; of securities underwriting, 141–142
Derivative instruments, 107–109
Designated order turnaround, 99
Dialogue Information Service, 43–44
Diners Club card, 65, 69, 119
Discount brokerage, 141, 142
Discover card, 70, 126
Disintermediation, 147, 150
Dow Jones, 50–51, 80, 81, 89, 90
Dun & Bradstreet, 50, 51, 53–54

Economic cooperation (coordination), 111–112, 170–174, 190
Economic democracy, 21–23
Economic intelligence system, 28–29, 33–36, 165–166
Economic synchronization, 29–30, 107
Economic transformations, four great, 30–33
Education, 8–9, 181–183
E. F. Hutton, 50, 79, 124, 168
Electronic Data Systems, 132
Electronic trading. *See* Computer-mediated trading
Entree, 75
Euromarket, 151, 163

Factories, 5–6, 175–176
Federal Reserve Board, 28, 29, 74–75, 146, 148
Fedwire, 74–75
Financial community, four pillars of, 36–37, 133
Financial services sector, 10–11. *See also* Automated teller machines; Banking; Brokerage
Financial supermarket, 113–132, 133
Fireman's Fund, 122
First Boston, 146
Fiscal and monetary policy, 28–29, 168–171, 191
Fixed commissions, 140–141, 151–152
Flexible manufacturing systems, 6
Floating exchange rates, 85–86
Ford Motor Company, 131

Fuji Bank, 164
Futures: financial, 11, 98–99; commodity, 97–98

Garn-St. Germain Depository Institutions Deregulation Act, 140
General Electric Corporation, 130
General Motors, 131–132
General Motors Acceptance Corporation, 131–132, 147, 148
Glass-Steagall Act, 134, 135–136, 146–147, 148, 149
Global economic order, 170–174
Global Electronic Markets Company, 120
Global financial centers, 103, 150–151, 155–156
Goldman Sachs, 164
Gold Standard, 85–86
Group of Seven, 171–172
Gutenberg Revolution, 13–14

Health care, 9
Hong Kong Stock Exchange, 111, 168
Honor card, 67
Household Finance, 130
Hutton, E. F., 50, 79, 124, 168
Hypercorporation, 132, 168
Hypermarket, 112, 132
Hypersociety, 181
Hyperstructure, 3–4, 90–91, 132, 151, 166, 168, 190–191

IMNET, 50, 128
Industrial Revolution, 5, 14, 32–33, 38, 192
Inflation, 27, 87–88, 112, 135, 138
Information, 22, 25–26, 29–30, 38–57, 172, 178–179, 184. See also Control
Information infrastructure, 38–57
Infrastructure, 4, 16, 76, 77, 79, 90–91, 133
Insider trading, 186
Instinet, 53, 84–85, 89, 103, 155
Insurance industry, 36, 116, 122–123, 129–130, 136. See also Financial community, four pillars of; Financial supermarkets

Intelligence system, 25–26, 35–36, 39–40
Intelligent economy, 33–37, 112
Intelligent machines, 3, 12–13. See also Artificial intelligence
Interactive Data Corporation, 54
Interbank market, 88, 90, 99
Interest rate futures contracts, 98
Intermarket trading system, 99–100
International Business Machines (IBM), 45, 78
International Monetary Fund, 85, 86
International Money Market, 87–88, 98–99
International Securities Regulatory Organization, 159
International Stock Exchange, 159
Interstate banking. See Banking; McFadden Act
Investment banking, 130, 135–136, 144–147, 149
Investors Diversified Services, 122–123
I. P. Sharp, 50, 51, 53, 79, 89

Japan, 149, 153–154, 161, 162, 163–164, 171
J. C. Penney, 70, 130
J. P. Morgan, 146

K-Mart, 129–130, 131
Kemper Corporation, 130
Keynesianism, 28–29
Knight-Ridder, 49–50, 78

Lehman Brothers Kuhn Loeb, 123
LEXIS, 43
London Financial Futures Exchange, 159
London Stock Exchange, 102, 103, 104, 151–153, 155, 157–158

Magnetic strip card, 60–61, 63–65, 137. See also Debit card; Smart card
Management, 18–19, 58, 89–90, 113–132, 179–180
Manufacturing, 148, 176. See also Factories
Marketplace, 20–21, 77

Marx, Karl, 14
MasterCard, 64, 65, 67, 68, 75, 119
May Day, 140–141, 164
McFadden Act, 134–135
McGraw-Hill, 47, 49, 51, 54–56, 120
Mead Corporation, 43, 51
Medicine, 9
Merrill Lynch, 50, 71, 79–80, 81, 84, 90, 111, 124, 126–129, 139
Metamorphosis, 16, 117, 189
Mitsubishi Bank, 164
Monchik-Weber, 55
Monetarism, 28–29
Monetary policy. See Fiscal and monetary policy
Money, 26–29, 58–76. See also Capitalism
Money market funds, 138, 139, 142, 145
Monitor Service, 52, 88–89
Montreal Exchange, 103, 156
Mpact, 67–68
Mutual Funds, 162

National Association of Securities Dealers, 51, 82–85
National Association of Securities Dealers Automated Quotation System (NASDAQ), 82–85, 90, 100, 102–103, 155–156, 157
National CSS, 54
National sovereignty. See Sovereignty
Nationet, 68, 75
Nationwide banking. See Banking
Natural resource industries, 10
New York Stock Exchange, 90, 93, 99, 100–101, 102–103, 107, 110–112, 141, 157–158, 164, 167–168
NEXIS, 43
Nielsen, A. C., 54
Nikko Securities, 164
Nippon Life, 124
Nomura Securities, 105, 153, 164
NYCE, 69
NYNEX, 120

Obsolescence, 133, 175–179, 181
October 19, 1987, 11–12, 110–112, 166–168, 190

Offices, 5
Oil companies, 70
Open Automatic Reporting System, 100
Optima card, 69
Options, 96–97
Over-the-Counter Market, 82–84, 167

Paris Bourse, 158
Pension funds, 162
People's capitalism, 193
Personal computer, 41–42, 46, 79, 101, 114
Phibro Corporation, 130
Philadelphia Stock Exchange, 159–160
Physical economy, 4
Plaza agreement, 171
Plus, 68, 75
Point-of-sale systems, 11, 61, 63, 67, 70, 72, 74, 75
Politics, 38–39, 185–186
Portfolio insurance, 11, 108–109, 167
Primerica, 130
Programmed capitalism, 3, 195
Program trading, 94, 107–108
Prudential, 122, 130, 141, 164
Psychological economy, 33–36, 112
Psychological system, 34
Psychology, 33, 35, 180–181
Publishing industry, 8, 47–51
Publix, 70
Pulse, 67–68, 69

Quotron, 50, 80, 81, 89, 90, 103, 121

RCA, 120
Reader's Digest, 49
Real economy, 33–36, 112
Regional banking. See Banking
Regulation Q, 134, 135, 138–139
Retail services industry, 36, 59, 61, 64–65, 68–73, 114–132. See also Financial; Financial supermarkets
Reuters, 50, 51–53, 80, 81, 84–85, 88–89, 90, 155, 160
Robots, 10, 71
Round-the-clock trading, 105–106, 159–160. See also Twenty-four-hour trading

Rule 415, 141–142
Rule 390, 100–101, 157, 158

S&P 500 Index, 99, 107, 110
Salomon Brothers, 130, 146, 161, 164
Sanwa Bank, 164
Schumpeter, Joseph, 14–15, 49
Sears: Roebuck, 45, 69–70, 71, 78, 116, 124–126, 141, 148; Savings Bank, 70, 124
Securities industry, 36, 105–109, 116, 122, 123, 128, 130, 135–136, 137–142, 144–148, 159–160. *See also* Brokerage
Securitization, 147–148, 150
Security Pacific National Bank, 130, 143
Shearson: Lehman, 153, 164, 168; Loeb Rhoades, 122
Singapore International Monetary Exchange, 159, 160
Smart card, 11, 72–73, 75. *See also* Debit card; Magnetic strip card
Smith, Adam, 14
Society, 21, 175–195
Society for Worldwide Interbank Financial Telecommunications, 75
Software, 53, 177–178; publishing of, 47
Sovereignty, 21, 29, 31, 168–170, 172–174. *See also* Control
Specialist system, 94, 101–102, 111, 157, 167
Speculation, 91, 107–109, 166, 167–168
Standard & Poor's, 55
Star Wars. *See* Strategic Defense Initiative
Stock Exchange, 92–112; International, 159. *See also* Individual exchange listings
Stock Exchange Automated Quotations

System, 157–158
Strategic Defense Initiative, 3, 6–7
Stress, 106, 180–181
Sumitomo Bank, 155, 164
Sydney Futures Exchange, 159
Sydney Stock Exchange, 111
Synergy, 89, 113–114, 123–124, 133, 190

Telecommunications, 7
Telenet, 51
Teleport Communications Inc., 129
Telerate, 50–51, 89, 90
Television, 8, 26, 39, 45
Thrift institutions. *See* Banking
Tokyo Stock Exchange, 102, 111, 153, 159, 160
Toronto Stock Exchange, 102, 103, 156, 168
Trade Development Bank, 123–124
Transportation, 8–9
Treasury bills, 138
TRW, 50, 51
Twenty-four-hour trading, 11, 158–159. *See also* Round-the-clock trading

Underwriting of securities, 128, 135–136, 140–142, 146–148

Visa card, 64, 65, 68, 75, 119
Volatility, market, 108, 165–166, 173

Western Union, 121, 129
West Germany, 112, 155, 171
Workplace, 16–18

Xerox Corporation, 130–131

Yamaichi Securities, 164

# About the Author

Maurice F. Estabrooks, a senior economist with the Federal Government of Canada, has held positions as a systems analyst, engineer, planner, and manager. He studied at Mount Allison University, the University of Alberta, and Carleton University, and holds degrees in physics, applied mathematics, and economics.